Christian de Lisle, MA, worked for many years in the City of London and as a commercial consultant. Since his official retirement he has acted as a consultant to Hewlett-Packard (UK) Ltd and their clients on financial calculations and related computer programs. He has also been retained as a consultant by many firms and trade associations, including the Association of International Bond Dealers. As a result of his work he has become aware of the many types of calculation which were required but for which no formulae or programs were readily available, and this work provided the incentive to writing this book.

Other relevant publications by the author are:

The Sinclair Book of Management Calculations (1973 out of print)

The Martin Book of Management Calculations (1979)
 Woodhead-Faulkner (Publishers) Ltd,
 Fitzwilliam House,
 32 Trumpington Street,
 Cambridge CB2 1QY

A "software" pamphlet, related to the HP-12C,
"Calculation of Fixed Interest Loans" (1984)
 Hewlett-Packard Ltd,
 Nine Mile Ride,
 Easthampton, Wokingham,
 Berkshire RG11 3LL

Business Interest Calculations

CHRISTIAN de LISLE, MA

WATERLOW PUBLISHERS LIMITED

First edition 1985
© C. de Lisle 1985

Waterlow Publishers Limited
Maxwell House
74 Worship Street
London EC2A 2EN
A member of the British Printing & Communication Corporation PLC

ISBN 0 08 039231 8

British Library Cataloguing in Publication Data

de Lisle, Christian
    Business interest calculations.—Waterlow's
    practitioner's library
    1. Interest
    I. Title
    332.8'2   HG1621

Typeset by Allset Composition, London.
Printed and bound in Great Britain by
A. Wheaton & Co. Ltd., Exeter

Acknowledgments

In a way Hewlett-Packard Ltd can be partly blamed for the appearance of this book; for since the advent of their first "business calculator", over ten years ago, I have been able occasionally to proffer advice regarding financial and business calculations. The answering of many of their client queries, over the years, has provided the most detailed knowledge of a host of "user problems" and the types of financial calculations that many require. Many of such queries and problems have therefore been included, inter alia, in the pages following.

Indeed, I am greatly indebted to Hewlett-Packard for the use of a variety of their computers and calculators, in particular their latest business calculator, the HP-12C, on whicn nearly all the calculations herein can be "worked"; and grateful too for their many kindnesses and the friendships which I have made, too numerous to mention individually.

Save perhaps for one senior HP specialist who for years has been in charge, in the UK, of their calculator and "small computer" Division — under a variety of changing titles! Tony Collinson, known to many an HP user as a fount of invaluable technical advice, never ceased to give help and encouragement in the production of instructional user handbooks, software and one-off programs written exclusively for HP and their users. To him therefore, although this book is not an HP production, my thanks are due for his continuing encouragement and help — and his friendship which I much value.

Also for their advice and help, on so many occasions, my most grateful thanks to both LVM, a well known actuary now happily retired in Devon, and PE of Ackroyd and Smithers; advice which, over many years, has been quite invaluable.

Lastly, my very sincere thanks to my Publishers for their expert assistance and to all those others who, in one way or another, have helped in the calculations following.

C. de L.

Contents

Introduction

Given data and a scientific formula it would not be unreasonable to assume that the answer would be the same the world over. Unhappily such an assumption, if applied to financial calculations, would be both optimistic and totally unrealistic. To take one example, a simple home loan mortgage calculation: given precisely the same loan parameters, the monthly payments required will be different depending on whether the borrower lives in the USA or Canada. And different again in the UK, this time dependent on whether the loan is made by a bank, a local government authority or a building society.

To understand why financial markets appear to have their own structure, practices and methods of calculation it is necessary to go back to the early days of barter and exchange. In those days there were few aids to calculation and because of this all such calculations were kept as simple as possible. Later, a few centuries ago, with the advent of logarithms, calculations did become slightly more sophisticated − although the accuracy of 4 figure log tables still leaves much to be desired. Nevertheless, whereas compound interest could now be calculated, simple interest, being more easily understood, still reflected the usual method of quoting a loan rate.

With the advent of microchip computers and calculators the most complicated calculations can be achieved to a very high degree of accuracy and with extreme rapidity: but the old habits die hard and even now, in some parts of the States for instance, for loans where the "true rate" is always compounded, the simple interest quotations are still enshrined in regional and local legislation. Other markets, more "with it", have changed to a more sophisticated scenario and so, now, there are various ways of calculating the same thing − each market usually being quite convinced that "their" way is the correct one.

Financial statisticians tend to be parochial in their thinking and expertise; ask a High Street banker to calculate or explain a banker's loan or certificate of deposit and the answer will quickly be forthcoming. Mention a building society loan or a Bond-yield-to-maturity calculation and often a reference to a building society or stockbroker will be suggested. Ask a broker how to calculate a CD and he may refer you to a bank, ask a High Street building society manager how to calculate a bond yield and he will probably profess total ignorance − and yet he will be able to calculate the value of an ex gratia payment to a year-end reconciliation both rapidly and accurately while his banking and broker counterparts look on bewildered.

1

"Business Interest Calculations" aims to pull all these different types of interest/rate calculations together, showing how they relate to one another and how usefully the knowledge of one type of calculation assists in the understanding of another.

As will be seen from the contents, "Business Interest Calculations" is divided into two parts, Part I dealing with interest problems in general relevant to business, Part II relating exclusively to fixed interest loans and consequent calculations.

The problem besetting any author writing on technical matters is that of for whom he is writing. If he assumes that the reader knows little of the subject, and starts his explanations at the lowest level, inevitably the expert statistician will soon become bored. Alternatively, writing solely for the expert, creating a book purely for reference purposes, would mean that an inexperienced beginner would soon become well out of his depth and completely lost in a welter of actuarial signs and in-market technicalities. Within reason "Business Interest Calculations" caters for the less experienced, on the assumption that the "expert" bored to tears by the simplicity of some explanations can skip those passages and simply draw the book off the shelf for reference purposes.

Nevertheless, even the expert may find some pages worth pursuing for, when considering the calculation of interest, even the most sophisticated and knowledgeable can occasionally find themselves astonished! I related, once, a little fable to an expert and elegant statistician: two friends were walking home from work when one of them asked the other for a loan of £25 to pay-day, two days hence. The lender hesitated but agreed in the end on the promise of a couple of drinks, totalling £1.50, when the loan was repaid. While the lender had no intention of charging interest, as the arrangements stood, the £1.50 was in fact the interest charged — at over 4 million per cent! Anticipating the gasps of disbelief, let us consider the mathematics. Repaying £26.50 on a loan of £25 is a rate of 6% — this for TWO days, thus the ANNUAL interest, the nominal rate, is $6 \times 365/2 = 1095\%$ p.a. and consequently the EFFECTIVE rate is 4,152,502.98%.

Often, too, by a clever juxtaposition of figures an expensive loan can be made, at first glance, to seem unexceptional. A High Street hire purchase agreement, for instance, with (say) an outstanding amount of £240 to be paid over the next 24 months, with monthly payments of £24, might be accepted without quibble — until one finds that the effective interest rate charged is 170%.

Readers will appreciate that any mathematical treatise is more prone than other less technical books to drafting errors; a misplaced bracket or transposed sign can have a disastrous effect on any question and is the bane of any professional computer programmer, leading invariably to GIGO, an irreverent term denoting "Garbage in — Garbage out"!

Notwithstanding the efforts made, therefore, to eliminate errors there is always the ever-present possibility that some ill-disposed Gremlin will somehow infiltrate one or other of the following pages; if so I beg the reader's indulgence and request any information as to the target area so that, in due course, other readers can be spared the same annoyance. Incidentally, financial markets are never static and should any reader discover that, since publication, any market has altered or updated its present rules or conventions the information would be most gratefully received.

C. de L.

Part I

CHAPTER 1

Some Simple Reminders

Calculations

As readers will doubtless be following the explanations, calculations and examples throughout this book on their own calculators or computers it might be useful at this stage to mention a few characteristics regarding calculations in general and those below in particular.

All the calculations herein are calculated to an accuracy of 10 significant figures (rounded up/down, NOT cut off). Readers using their own equipment may thus experience minor differences from the text if using a simple calculator with only a six or eight figure display or a computer working (say) to an accuracy of 15 sig.fig.

Be careful, also, if glancing through an example and then deciding to follow the calculation halfway through on your own calculator. For although the presentation will normally be to two decimal places, the underlying calculation will always be to 10 sig. fig. For $81.03567899 \times 2 = 162.07$; whereas, shown as only 81.04 and multiplied by 2 the value equals 162.08.

Furthermore, in a long calculation there are often various methods of laying out an equation, and, depending on the accuracy of the calculator or computer and the order or method employed, the answers may vary fractionally. For example:

$$1.50^{50} = 637,621,500.20$$

whereas $\qquad (1/1.50)^{-50} = 637,621,498.60$

$$5^{.5} \times 6^{.5} \times 10^7 \qquad\qquad = 54,772,255.74$$

$$(5 \times 6)^{.5} \times 10^7 \qquad\qquad = 54,772,255.75$$

$$\sqrt{5} \times \sqrt{5} \qquad\qquad = 4.999999998$$

with configurations of only 8 sig.fig. $\quad = \quad 5.00000000$

Logarithms

Whenever calculations require the use of LOGs, "logs natural" will be employed herein, not "logs ten".

Currencies

Financial values in the examples below will usually be stated in either sterling (£) or dollars ($) but often the currency prefix will be omitted. In any event such values, being decimal currencies, can always be related by the reader, from a calculation viewpoint, to his own currency, if required, without any adjustments. Appreciating, of course, that an example of (say) 50,000 for a "home loan" might be considered reasonable in the UK or USA but might just purchase a rabbit hutch in Italy!

Simple Interest

At the risk of losing the sympathy of the reader, by explaining high school mathematics to those who have purchased this book with the avowed intention of dealing with more complex problems, in interest calculations it is usually sensible to "start at the beginning" — even just for record purposes.

£100.00 lent at an interest rate of 10% at the end of 1 year will provide an interest amount of £100.00 $\times$ 10/100 = £10.00; or £100.00 $\times$ (1 + 10/100) = £110.00 (capital + annual interest).

If however the loan was for a lesser period, say 60 days, then the interest will reduce: 100 $\times$ 10/100 $\times$ 60/365 = 1.643835616; normal rounding = 1.64, or upward = 1.65.

In interest calculations it is always wise to discover exactly how the "accrued interest" (the a/i) is to be considered: either as the "actual" amount (using the full precision of the computer/calculator — say 10 significant figures) or brought to 2 decimal places, cut off, rounded up normally or always rounded upward. Compare the £1.65 above. This is not just a matter of presentation but one which can affect the calculation significantly.

Working, as we did above, from the conventional "actual" calendar, the capital and interest for the 60 actual days is:

$$100 \times (1 + (10/100 \times 60/365)) = 101.65$$

Later it will be seen that for financial matters often the 30/360 "financial calendar" (see below) is employed, in which case:

$$100 \times (1 + (10/100 \times 60/360)) = 101.67$$

Percentages

Remember, as if you didn't know, that there are two different methods of deducting or discounting with percentages — a trap sometimes for even the most sophisticated — and for political parties!

Many years ago, at a General Election, all the party manifestos pointed out that by voting for them inflation would be reduced. However, two of the major parties categorically stated that if inflation continued unchecked at 20% per year, the pound sterling would be worth only 80 pence the year following − calculating $[100 − (100 \times 20/100) = 80]$ − when, of course, you and I know that the correct value must be:

$$\frac{100}{1 + (20/100)} = 83.33 \text{ pence.}$$

and: $100 + 10\% = 110$

but $110 − 10\% = 99$

$110/1.10 = 100$

£246 + VAT at 15% = 246 + 36.90 = £282.90
$$282.90/1.15 = £246.00$$

Incidentally, given the VAT percentage, to determine the VAT amount, from a price which includes the tax:

$$\frac{\text{Price (incl: VAT)}}{1 + (\text{VAT}/100)} \times \frac{\text{VAT\%}}{100} = \text{VAT amount.}$$

$$£\frac{282.90}{1.15} \qquad \times .15 \qquad = £36.90 \text{ VAT.}$$

A useful factor, as a denominator, is:

$$1.15/.15 = 7.6666667 \text{ and } 282.90/7.666667 = £36.90$$

If VAT was 10% the useful factor would be 11.

Compound Interest

A £100 loan with annual interest at 12% will require £12 to be repaid each year with the capital to be repaid at the end of the term of the loan, the above being at "simple interest".

If, however, the interest is "rolled up" so that both the interest and the capital sum are repaid together at the end of a ten year term, the interest would be "compounded"; for as the interest is held over and not paid annually the lender is, in effect, relending the annual interest each year and consequently he charges interest on each portion − at the original rate. In other words a series of small loans on top of the main loan: which when not referred to as compound interest is sometimes called "interest on interest", producing a quite unwarranted derogatory image! In this example then the amount payable at the end of a term of 10 years will be:

$$£100 \times 1.12^{10} = £310.58$$

The (1 + i) and the "n"

Percentage interest rates throughout the text *in formulae* are expressed as a DECIMAL, namely by the symbol "i". 12% therefore for calculation purposes will be .12 = i — which saves dividing the rate by 100 each time it is used. "n" is employed to denote the number of years in the term of the loan — hence in the example above:

$$100(1 + i)^n = 100(1.12)^{10} = £310.58.$$

Period (p) Compounding

Should the lender prefer £1 to be paid each month (instead of £12 each year) i.e., monthly compounding, or, to use an alternative description, payments with monthly "rests", then "p" is used to denote the number of compounding *periods* in any ONE year. 12% with MONTHLY rests would become an interest RATE of 12/12 = 1.00% monthly, and the i/p (here 12/1200 = .01) is so treated in all formulae below. (1 + i/p) in this example is therefore 1.01 and over a term of 10 years (120 months) would be expressed as:

$$(1 + i/p)^{np} \qquad\qquad = (1 + 12/1200)^{10 \times 12}$$

$$1.01^{120} \qquad\qquad\qquad = 3.300387$$

In other words:

Present Value (PV) $\times (1 + 12/1200)^{10\times12}$ = **Future Value (FV)**

$$(PV)\ 100 \times 1.010^{120} \qquad = 330.0386895$$

$$£100 \times 3.300386895 = £330.04 \qquad (FV)$$

Discounting

Discounting is simply the converse of compounding: instead of compounding the present value (PV) to the future value (FV), discounting converts the future value back to the present time. In the above example where the future value was £330.04 (true 330.0386895) the present value is £100 at a rate of 12% nominal, with monthly rests. Above £100 was multiplied by (1 + i/p) to the power of 120. To discount simply divide the future value of £330.04 by the (1 + i/p) namely 1.01 to the power of 120. But alternatively, on many occasions as we shall see below, we can, most usefully, MULTIPLY the FV, the £330.04, by (1 + i/p) to the power of MINUS 120.

compounding

$$PV \times (1 + i/p)^{np} = FV$$

discounting

$$FV \times (1 + i/p)^{-np} = PV$$

$$330.04 \times \quad 1.01^{-120} = 100.00$$

To find the Interest Rate %

$$100 \times ((FV/PV)^{1/np} - 1) = \text{Interest Rate}$$

$$100 \times ((330.04/100)^{1/120} - 1) = 1.00\% \text{ monthly}$$

and $\qquad\qquad 1.00 \times 12 = 12.00\%$ nominal

As we shall see in Chapter 4 (et seq.) the *nominal* rate is often referred to as the IRR, the Internal Rate of Return.

Remember, although the values above are shown rounded to 2 places of decimals, for convenience, the calculations are made to the full precision of the calculator/computer (here 10 sig.fig).

To find the term

$$\frac{\text{LOG} \quad FV/PV}{\text{LOG} \quad (1 + i/p)} = \text{Term (np)}.$$

$$\frac{\text{LOG} \quad 330.0386895/100}{\text{LOG} \quad 1.01} = \frac{1.194039709}{0.009950331} = 120 \text{ (months)}.$$

Either "logs natural" or "logs ten" are applicable. Above Ln (logs natural) were employed.

The Effective Rate

It will be appreciated that with periodic compounding, above, the rests were monthly, and the lender received a slightly greater return than he would if interest were paid annually, at the borrower's expense. Unfortunately except when the rate of interest is 12%, which is simple to divide mentally by 12, we all tend to speak of interest in terms of "annually" or p.a., or the "nominal" rate, and then, almost perhaps as an afterthought, if necessary mention that the rests are semi-annual, quarterly or monthly.

To save interminable calculations, comparing different loans with different characteristics, the most sensible method is to think in terms of the "effective" rate which the structure of the loan represents and in that case each loan, whatever its compounding characteristics are, will always be comparable.

If p = the number of period interest payments in any one year i.e., the rests, then:

$$100 \times \left(\left(1 + \frac{NOM}{p \times 100}\right)^{p} - 1\right) = \text{EFFECTIVE}$$

$$100p \times \left(\left(1 + \frac{EFF}{100}\right)^{1/p} - 1\right) = \text{NOMINAL}$$

Above the 12% nominal rate, with 12 rests per year, converts to an effective rate of:

$$100\left(\left(1 + \frac{12}{1200}\right)^{12} - 1\right) = 12.68250300\% \text{ Eff.}$$

If we now take this *effective* rate and calculate the future value from a present value of £100 over a term of 10 years we will see that the FV is precisely the same as if we had calculated by a monthly rate over 120 months.

$$£100 \times 1.12682503^{10} = £330.04 \text{ (see above)}$$

Thus the effective rate employed annually is the same as the periodic rate calculated over the period term. As this method can be used for all periodic rests, semi-annual, quarterly, monthly, weekly or even daily, it will be appreciated that the effective rate can thus be used as the yardstick of the true value of the interest rate of any loan (see Chapter 6).

To return to the Introduction, 1095%, being the nominal rate for a two day loan of £25, namely a day's calculation over half a year, requires an effective rate of:

$$100\left(\left(1 + \frac{1095}{100 \times 182.5}\right)^{182.5} - 1\right) = 4,152,502.98\% \text{ (effective)}$$

Some comparisons

Assume a loan of 100 at an interest rate of 10% pa:

	Effective rate	*Rests*
$100 \times (1 + (10/100)^{1})$	= 110.00	Annual
$100 \times (1 + (10/200)^{2})$	= 110.25	Semi-Annual
$100 \times (1 + (10/400)^{4})$	= 110.38	Quarterly
$100 \times (1 + (10/1200)^{12})$	= 110.47	Monthly
$100 \times (1 + (10/5200)^{52})$	= 110.51	Weekly
$100 \times (1 + (10/36500)^{365})$	= 110.52	Daily
(more precisely)	= 110.515594	

Daily compounding naturally provides the highest return to the lender from all the options above.

Continuous Growth

An even greater value, although not substantially greater, is obtained when compounding is "from moment to moment" or, as it is more usually called, "continuous compounding".

To calculate this continuous compounding we must use the exponential factor (symbol e), namely 2.71828182818 or, more conveniently, 2.718282.

If the reader has a calculator which has LOGS NATURAL (Ln) facilities, by the input of 1 and pressing the (e^x) exponent key (or on some calculators the "anti-log" key), 2.718281828 will display.

To find the compound value raise this value by the required "i" value:

$$2.718281828^{.10} \quad = \quad 1.105170918$$

and $100(1.105170918 - 1) = 10.5170918\%$ Continuous.

With a calculator, with the above facilities, an even simpler way is to input the "i" value and press the e^x key (or anti-log key) outlined above:

$$e^{.10} = 1.105170918 \text{ (displayed)}$$

which, when multiplied by the principal (here £100 loan), will provide the capital plus the interest at continuous compounding.

So if you saw $100e^{.1}$ you would realise that 100×1.105170918 equals £100 at 10% continuous interest over a period of ONE year, which is £110.52:

$$£100e^{.1} = £100 \times 1.105170918 = £110.517092 \ (£110.52)$$

Compare this to the £100 at DAILY interest per year:

$$£100 \times \left(\left(1 + \frac{10}{100 \times 365}\right)^{365} - 1 \right) = £110.51559420$$

fractionally less than that at 10% continuous interest above.

The "effective" rate of return of continuous interest

It is obvious that continuous compounding, from moment to moment, must be the ultimate in compound interest and therefore this interest rate must be regarded as the EFFECTIVE rate. This is important because later we shall be calculating loan repayments, for example, where the compound interest periods are different to the payment periods required. And should the interest be "continuous growth" but the payment periods be (say) monthly then some adjustment is necessary. In fact the method is to divide the "i" factor by the periodic payment factor (p) before employing that factor to become the exponent of the "e" factor — and if that sounds complicated the following example will doubtless clarify:

Instead of using $e^i(2.718282^i)$ we must use $e^{i/p}(2.718282^{i/p})$ and thus taking a rate of 10% continuous compounding with monthly payments the calculation would be:

$$e^{.1/12} = e^{.0083333} = 1.008368152$$

which is the $(1 + i/p)$ for the particular calculation concerned. We shall return to this calculation, and other variations, later.

If the effective interest rate is continuous, from moment to moment, the "ultimate" in rate interest, then surely there can be no greater interest rate related to any particular nominal rate — or can there?

An American calculation

Well, not really, but because the Americans often employ the "financial calendar" in many of their rate interest requirements, possibly a spurious rate could be spawned. Employing "actual/360", meaning in this context the "actual" number of days are employed but with a base of 360, instead of 365, for calculations in the financial year, an unlikely, but not impossible, situation could arise where:

$$\$100 \times (1 + (10/36000)^{365}) = \$110.6691452$$

which, glancing back, you will see is fractionally GREATER than the interest due from continuous compounding! And although this value must be fractionally spurious it is mathematically acceptable in the USA for some of their calculations.

"Discrete"

Technically, all compound interest, if not at continuous compounding, is said to be discrete interest.

This term is rarely employed in financial circles in the UK but it is sometimes met in American financial and computer treatises to differentiate between conventional periodic compounding (10% discrete = 10% nominal) and continuous growth (10% = 10.517092%). And seldom do the pamphlets concerned provide any explanation!

The Gross Equivalent

Above we considered £100 at 10% interest, nominal, for one year, the interest being £10. If this amount was subject to income tax at a basic rate of (say) 30%, the NET amount would become $10 \times (1 - 30/100) = £7.00$, in other words $10\% \times .7 = 7\%$ NET.

Many U.K. institutions which borrow from the public are required by the Revenue authorities to pay tax on the interest due to the lender direct to the authorities. The lender, the public, thus receives the interest "net after tax". As sometimes institutional tax is a variable, and as there is always competition between different institutions, it is often felt necessary to draw the public's attention to the "equivalent gross rate" of interest, that is what the true interest would be if it was not subject to the basic rate of tax. If the net rate was 7% then the "gross equivalent" — at basic 30% tax rates — would be advertised as 10%. Sensible, informative and perfectly understandable.

A digression

Some years ago, to everyone's surprise, this conventional and familiar method of comparing the gross and net rates of interest was challenged in a well orchestrated campaign.

In the past, the argument ran, we had all been wrong in grossing up the net **RATE** for this, it was argued, related only to ONE year's perspective. For a ten year loan:

$£100 \times 1.07^{10} = £196.72$ capital and rolled up interest.

Given this return and assuming a basic tax rate of 30%, the reader would quite rightly find the net rate and gross it up as below:

$$\left[\left(\left(\frac{196.72}{100}\right)^{1/10} - 1\right) \times 100\right]/.7 = 10.00\% \text{ gross}$$

But what we should be doing, said the protagonists of this revolutionary method, is to gross up the net **AMOUNT** — not the rate.

Instead of the above 7% net of tax being grossed up to find a "grossed up net" of 10%, the calculation, they suggest, should be:

$$\frac{(196.72 - 100)}{.7} = 138.16 \text{ gross amount}$$

and $\left(\left(\frac{100 + 138.16}{100}\right)^{1/10} - 1\right) \times 100 = 9.07\%$ gross

This after 10 years. If the term had been for (say) 5 years their gross equivalent, found by the same method of calculation above, would be 9.511%. But for ONE year, it will be found, by this method, that the gross equivalent is 10% — proving, from their point of view, that the conventional method is only applicable for ONE year.

At the time the Treasury was responsible, inter alia, for advertising National Savings Certificates and normally quoted the net rate, grossed up by conventional means, related to the basic current tax rate. Suddenly all the advertising related to the "gross equivalent" ceased and some wondered, therefore, if perhaps there might not be some substance to the suggestion and that we had all been wrong in the past. The more sophisticated and indeed the institutions, presumably advised by their actuaries, however continued unperturbed, calculating and advertising in the old, familiar and conventional manner.

A few years later, an incoming Treasury official queried the caveat on the grossed up net advertising for such money instruments as they were responsible for and was, presumably, appraised of the reason. Sending for the file, after a moment's study, he succinctly pronounced it a "nonsense" – or words to that effect! For, he said, (that which we all knew anyway) in law all tax must be paid ANNUALLY and tax amounts cannot be accumulated – and paid in "years to come".

Paying tax on monies lent

Lenders to building societies always have their interest paid net after tax, the societies having paid the tax due (in a "composite rate" form) to the Revenue, whereas interest on deposits made to banks was, prior to April 1985, paid to the lender in gross form, no tax having been deducted at source.

Years ago when the Government first instructed building societies to remit to the Revenue each year the tax value of all the interest due to their depositors, the building societies argued that this was an unfair and unrealistic demand – for, they pointed out, many of their investors were non-taxpayers; and so in the event it was agreed that a "composite rate of tax" (CRT) need only be remitted. This CRT (adjusted each year if necessary) stands now, and has so stood for some years, at 25.25% – related to the basic rate of tax at 30%.

As a result of the difference between banking and building society practice and the advent of CRT, over the years there has been a bewildering plethora of rates provided by various institutions, building societies and others, in advertisements aimed at inducing the public to make deposits with them.

To give a simple example of the confusion that can occur: assume that an institution proposes to borrow at a NET rate, that is to provide interest to the lender AFTER tax has been paid to the Revenue. Assume too that the particular institution proposes to calculate the interest monthly, instead of annually.

If the borrowing NET rate quoted is 7.00% and basic tax rate 30%, what is the overall effective rate? In other words, what would be the advertised grossed-up rate, taking into account that the interest is calculated monthly?

Some institutions ignore the effective rate aspect, others don't but have different views on the methods of calculation!

(1)   7.00% net, converted to its effective rate (based on a monthly com-
       pounding) becomes 7.229008% which grossed up from a "basic" tax
       rate of 30%

       = 7.229008/.7 =   10.33% the grossed up effective.

(2)   7.00 grossed up becomes 7.00/.7 = 10.000000% which when converted
       becomes

                                                10.47% effective grossed up.

(3)   Alternatively (and quite incorrectly − see below), working on the
       assumption that only 25.25% of the gross has been remitted to the
       Revenue (see above), recalculating the above we get:

       7.229008/.7475 =   9.67% the grossed up effective.

(4)   7.00% grossed up becomes 7/.7475 = 9.364548%, which when con-
       verted becomes

                                                9.78% effective grossed up.

The correct method is first to convert the quoted net rate to its effective
rate, and then "gross up" that value accordingly − here by basic rate of tax −
see (1) above, giving an effective rate of 10.33%.

April 1985

Age-old banking practice changed on 6 April 1985, in that thereafter the
Government ruled that banks would no longer be allowed to provide their
lenders with gross interest, free of tax, and insisted that all banks fell into line
with building societies' methods. This change of practice was considered a
good opportunity by the building societies and other institutions, including
banks under their new instructions, to regularise their advertising procedures
and to have an agreed policy on such matters.

   Incidentally, although in the future banks will also be permitted to remit
the composite rate of tax (CRT) to the Revenue, in the same manner as
building societies, prior to providing interest to the lender, as far as the lender
is concerned he or she can and must assume, on receipt of the net interest,
that the *basic rate* of tax has been deducted − the value of the CRT being an
internal bank/building society/Revenue matter and not one to concern the
individual lender.

   After April 1985, according to the new regulations and conventions
applying to loans made by the public to institutions:

− *The gross rate* denotes a rate of interest, untaxed at source, which may be
   liable to tax (at whatever rate the investor may, in due course, be assessed),

— *The net rate* denotes the rate of interest paid to the UK investor after tax has been remitted to the Revenue, and for basic tax rate payers that there is no further tax to be paid.

Interest, however, continues to be paid gross to corporate bodies, charities, clubs, societies, trusts and other specifically designated organisations. Also gross payments are permitted to an investor not ordinarily resident in the UK, providing the appropriate declaration form has been signed.

Non-taxpayers. Those lenders who are not liable for any annual tax unfortunately cannot recover or reclaim from the Revenue any tax previously deducted by either banks or building societies. So non-taxpayers who previously tended to lend to banks (receiving interest gross) instead of societies (receiving interest net) now have this bank haven closed to them. Bank managers are however always able to advise such investors as to their best course of action, such as saving with National Savings Certificates etc.

— *The gross equivalent rate* is a net rate of interest "grossed up"; in effect becoming a rate which assumes that tax has not, as yet, been paid: 7% net divided by .7 = 10% gross.

Higher-rate taxpayers will be assessed on the difference between the basic tax rate paid to the Revenue and their particular tax bracket. If for example the basic tax rate is 30% and the investor's tax rate is 50% in due course the Revenue will demand a further 20% tax on the interest received.

— *The compound annual rate (CAR)* is simply the effective rate of any periodic interest which we have discussed earlier.

Unlike building societies, who have always thought in terms of net rates, many accustomed to gross philosophies continued to think in gross terms. And because, too, at the time of the changeover the CRT suddenly became a matter of consideration and discussion, many basic-rate taxpayers, having been assured by the banks that there was no more tax to pay, assumed wrongly that they would be better off — in that only 25.25% had been deducted from their gross interest due. And indeed hopefully, and again wrongly, that if they were in (say) a 50% tax bracket the difference required by the Revenue would only be 20% (+ 25.25%), costing them in effect only 45.25% instead of the full 50%.

However, the CRT, (as already mentioned, a matter entirely between the borrowing institutions and the Revenue) can, and sometimes does, provide one advantage to the lender in that because the borrower, banks or building societies, have to remit (at present) only 25.25% to the Revenue they can afford to offer slightly higher NET rates of interest than they would if they had to remit the full basic tax rate (30%). For example, if a bank's GROSS lending rate to (say) a charity (not liable for the withholding basic tax) is

13%, the net rate, if the basic tax was 30%, would be $13.00 \times .7 = 9.10\%$. But because the banks have to remit only 25.25% (instead of 30%) to the Revenue, they can afford to offer lenders a slightly higher NET rate of $13.00 \times 0.7475 = 9.71750\%$ which, in effect, would probably be rounded to (say) 9.75%. A 12.25% GROSS rate to a charity might well be rounded and offered NET as 9.00% (calculated by $12.25 \times .7475 = 9.156875$) — providing in effect a gross equivalent, to basic tax payers, of $9.00/.7 = 12.85\%$.

Borrowing money

It must be appreciated that the above rate structures and abbreviations relate to the public *lending to* an institution — not borrowing from. Later we shall see terms such as MIRAS and the APR constantly used when the public *borrows from* banks and building societies — and while it may seem, at first thought, rather absurd to have yet another term such as the "CAR" above to represent, with a lending philosophy, what all of us know is the effective rate, it will certainly help to avoid confusion with the "APR" (annual percentage rate of charge) which, in a borrowing environment, represents the effective rate — truncated to one place of decimals (see later — Chapter 6).

Actuaries

The dictionary definition of an actuary is one who makes calculations for insurance companies. Indeed, the main expertise of actuaries is to evaluate various intricate calculations related to annuities and savings of the clients of their individual companies and the expectation of life of those clients. To get it wrong is costly, to get it right the actuary is worth his weight in gold! Actuaries are thus steeped in all kinds of interest rate calculations, and such related matters, and sometimes use a sort of actuaries' "shorthand" to denote certain calculations. These actuarial signs, or some of them, will be found to be extremely useful in shortening the form of long equations and in disentangling complicated formulae: they are also valuable for computer programmers who are always faced with the necessity of getting a host of brackets in the right place — and in the right order!

At this stage don't worry about what the precise calculations represent, for this will be explained in detail later.

$a_{\overline{np}|} = (1 - (1 + i/p)^{-np})/(i/p)$ annuities ORDinary

$\ddot{a}_{\overline{np}|} = [(1 - (1 + i/p)^{-np})/(i/p)] \times (1 + i/p)$ annuities DUE

$s_{\overline{np}|} = ((1 + i/p)^{np} - 1)/(i/p)$ savings ORDinary

$\ddot{s}_{\overline{np}|} = [((1 + i/p)^{np} - 1)/(i/p)] \times (1 + i/p)$ savings DUE

The calendars

Invariably many interest calculations depend on the number of "days" the interest is due and one of the difficulties encountered, when using the actual calendar inevitably arises when trying to divide 365 exactly into two! To avoid this problem the "financial calendar" was evolved, whereby a year is assumed to have only 360 days, each month comprising of 30 days — irrespective of the "actual" number of days to which we are normally accustomed. This calendar is often referred to as 30/360 to differentiate it from the "actual" 365 normal calendar; and often data related to interest problems denotes either "actual/actual", or "30/360" or, "actual/360". The latter denotes that the 360 base will be used for all calculations but that the "actual" number of days, between two dates, will always be used for accrued interest and other related interest factors. Chapter 18 and Appendix D also refer.

Days charts (actual)

Although many readers will have calculators or computer programs to determine the actual days between two dates, for interest purposes, some may not; and if lacking such facilities the table directly below or the "days" chart at Appendix E may be found useful.

January	(31)	31	July	(31)	212
February	(28)	59	August	(31)	243
March	(31)	90	September	(30)	273
April	(30)	120	October	(31)	304
May	(31)	151	November	(30)	334
June	(30)	181	December	(31)	365

(add 1 day from March onward if a leap day intervenes)

(see 2 year days chart Appendix E)

Leap days

In some types of interest bearing obligations by convention leap days are ignored. As computer/calculator programs seldom provide the number of "days between" two dates *less* leap days there is often a good deal of time wasting finger-counting which can sometimes lead to inaccuracy. Below is a quick and sure way of determining the number of leap days between any two dates, between the years 1901–2099 inclusive. (Appendix D also refers.)

$$\left(\text{INT} \frac{\text{Year 1}}{4} \right) - \left(\text{INT} \frac{\text{Year 2}}{4} \right) = - \text{Leap days.}$$

(INT = Integer. Ignore any fractions of a year.)

When the actual date falls between 1 January and 29 February (both inclusive) subtract 1 from year.

The number of leap days (if necessary to be deducted from any "days between") between 1 January 1980 and 1 June 2000 are shown below.

$$\text{INT} \frac{1980 - 1}{4} - \text{INT} \frac{2000}{4} =$$

$$\text{INT } 494.75 \quad - \text{ INT } 500.00 =$$
$$494 \quad - \quad 500 \quad = -6 \text{ leap days.}$$

(1980, 1984, 1988, 1992, 1996, 2000)

There are 7,457 "actual" days between the two above dates, hence (7,457 − 6) = 7,451 days between, excluding leap days.

To find a day of the week

In some types of interest calculations the interest received is assumed in the calculation to be immediately reinvested and if the day on which the interest, or capital redemption value, is due happens to fall on a non-banking day, some statisticians consider that the resulting yield should be adjusted fractionally to accommodate the loss of one or two days' interest – which can be considerable if dealing in millions of pounds or dollars in the case of fixed interest loans etc. So sometimes it is necessary to be able to find, and check, the day of the week of a future (or past) date.

Providing the number of "days between" and the day of the week of one of the dates is known the other date/day can easily be found.

Let 1 = Monday, 6 = Saturday and 7 or 0 = SUNDAY

$$(\text{Known day/week}) + \left(\left(\text{FRAC } \frac{\text{Days Between}}{7} \right) \times 7 \right) = \text{Day of week.}$$

(FRAC = Fraction. Ignore the integer part of the number.)

If, for example, the day of week of January 3rd 1983 is a Monday, what is the day of the week of Christmas Day the same year?

There are 356 (actual) "days between" the dates in question. Let Monday = 1.

$$1 + ((\text{FRAC}(356/7)) \times 7) =$$
$$1 + ((\text{FRAC } 50.85714 \times 7) =$$
$$1 + (.85714 \quad \times 7) =$$
$$1 + \quad\quad 6 \quad\quad = 7 = \text{SUNDAY.}$$

If the sum is greater than 7 subtract 7.

If the dates above related to 1980, 3 January would be a Thursday (4) and the days between (because of the leap day) would be 357:

$$4 + ((\text{FRAC}(357/7)) \times 7) =$$
$$4 + \quad\quad 0 \quad\quad = 4 = \text{THURSDAY.}$$

CHAPTER 2

Repayment Loans

The methods of calculating repayment loans (mortgages, home loans etc.) form the basis of a number of other important loan amortisation calculations, such as those for bonds, notes, debenture loans etc., and are therefore worthy of careful examination.

The concept is that even   repayments consisting of varying portions of capital and interest are made throughout the term of the loan so that at termination, or "maturity", the loan is fully repaid. Even accepting the apparent clarity of that statement, confusion and misunderstanding still seem to arise.

Some years ago a matter of civil litigation came before the Courts. The case related to a house cum business premises mortgage which was not fully paid by the time that the firm concerned went into liquidation. The whole case turned, if over simplification is permissable, on the two interest rates, the quoted simple interest rate and the rate of interest actually charged, to provide the "balance outstanding"; both of which apparently serviced the loan. The borrower argued that he was only liable for the interest resulting from the quoted simple interest rate. In the event the court did not agree and the case stood as a precedent until the Consumer Credit Act was enacted in 1974, which finally established the method on which the true rate of interest for repayment loans is based and laid down that, in certain circumstances, the borrower must be informed of the effective rate of interest required.

In an endeavour to assist the Court the author submitted, inter alia, the following parable:

Assume that you lend a friend £1000 and you ask him for 10% simple interest per year. Thus you would expect to receive £100 each year and the £1000 returned when either you or he wished to conclude the arrangement. But you rightly consider that open-ended loans, those without a term, are unsatisfactory and so you suggest a term of 10 years. Your friend agrees and thus you will receive £100 each year (10% simple interest) and the £1000 back at the end of the 10 years. But you have yet another thought. Suppose your friend at the end of ten years is not in a position to repay the loan in due time? Taking him to Court or waiting until he does pay will be expensive and so you suggest to your friend that he repays each year part of the capital amount. As £1000 neatly divides into £100 each year it would mean that your friend will be repaying you £200 at the end of each year for the next ten years, £100 in interest, at 10% simple interest, and £100 in capital. Your friend agrees and the arrangements are concluded and at the end of the ten years all the interest and the capital amount will have been repaid. After some time your friend tells you that he is having second thoughts! For he says that in the last year he will be paying you £100 in interest (10% on £1000) but by that time he will have repaid some £900 of the capital. And so it looks to him as if you will be charging him 100% in the last year, 50% in the penultimate year and so on backwards.

And he is perfectly correct if one considers only the *simple* interest perspective. But when a repayment loan is contracted, the periodic payments (which include both interest and capital) are not averaged but are even throughout the term. During the course of the loan as the capital "still outstanding" diminishes so does the interest − the capital slice in the payments increasing as the interest decreases. So the interest, in effect, is discounted − at compound interest.

In this example, whatever it is, the *true* rate is considerably in excess of 10%. In fact it is 15.098414%.

Repayment loan calculations

To demonstrate the concept of repayment loan calculations let us take a short-term loan of 100, over a term of 3 years only, at 10% nominal interest. In this case the annual repayments required will be 40.21148036 and whereas this 10 sig.fig. value will be used in the calculations below it will be shown for simplicity, as £40.21. At this stage don't worry how this value was determined.

Incidentally, for this repayment loan example, what the British call the SIMPLE interest (S.I.) rate, and what the Americans call the "ADD-ON rate", is $((40.21 \times 3) - 100)/3 = 6.88\%$. The true rate cost for repayment loans, which the British call the "nominal" rate and which the Americans call the "APR" (annual percentage rate), is (in the above example) 10%. The British "APR" (annual percentage rate of charge), as we shall see later, has a somewhat different meaning, namely the effective rate (truncated to one place of decimals) when there are extra charges to be included in the cost.

In rate interest matters when one is not entirely certain of the exact calculation, or to see if a given formula is valid, it is not a bad idea to consider "what happens to the money" and, if necessary, to visualise the concept by making out a schedule, and tracing it through with a simple example to see what happens.

Capital	× Int (Cap + int)	− Pmts	= Residual loan	Year-end
(100.00 × 1.10) as	110.00	− 40.21	= 69.79	1.
(69.79 × 1.10) as	76.77	− 40.21	= 36.56	2.
(36.56 × 1.10) as	40.21	− 40.21	= 0.00 (at maturity)	3.

It will be seen above that the repayments are made (deducted) AFTER the interest each year has been calculated, in other words the payments are "in arrears" and this is called, actuarially, an "annuities ORDinary" calculation — as opposed to when payments are made "in advance" (as for example in a leasing contract), when the calculations are then called "annuities DUE".

Discounted cash flow (DCF) methods of calculation

Investment (loan value)	-100.00
40.21×1.10^{-1}	$=\ 36.56$
40.21×1.10^{-2}	$=\ 33.23$
40.21×1.10^{-3}	$=\ 30.21$
	$=\ 100.00\ -100.00$
Net Present Value (NPV)	$=\ \ \ \ 0.00$

Because the NPV = 0.00 the Internal Rate of Return (IRR) is exactly 10% (DCF calculations are fully examined in Chapter 4).

An alternative method of discounting

40.21	$\times\ 1.10^{-1}$	$=$	36.56 at maturity
$(36.56 + 40.21) \times 1.10^{-1}$		$=$	69.79
$(69.79 + 40.21) \times 1.10^{-1}$		$=$	100.00 at commencement

The concept is that any interest engendered is always "reinvested" immediately at the same interest rate as the original quoted (nominal) rate per cent. Schedules, of course, are unnecessary for the same answer can be found by formulae.

Formula for repayment loans with payments in arrears (annuities ordinary)

$$\text{LOAN} \div \frac{1 - (1 + i)^{-n}}{i} = \text{ANNUAL payments}$$

$$\text{LOAN} \div \frac{1 - (1 + i/p)^{-np}}{i/p} = \text{PERIODIC payments}$$

$$\text{PAYMENTS} \times \frac{1 - (1 + i/p)^{-np}}{i/p} = \text{LOAN}$$

$$100 \div \frac{1 - 1.10^{-3}}{.10} = 40.21 \text{ ANNUAL pmts}$$

$$40.21 \times 2.486852 = 100.00$$

Referring to the actuaries section in the previous chapter we saw some formulae represented by actuarial symbols. Thus if an actuary saw 40.21 $a_{\overline{3}|}$ at 10% "nominal" he would immediately realise that the loan value would be Pmts $\times$ actuarial factor, namely here, 40.21 $\times$ 2.486852 = £100.00.

There are various equations possible which can provide the actuarial factor — in this example 2.486851991 to 10 sig.fig.

Here, we must refer back to the above DCF schedule and employ a geometrical progression calculation: where the sum (Σ) equals the last term (1) multiplied by the ratio (r), the constant multiplier, less the first term (f) with the whole of the above divided by the ratio minus 1.

$$\Sigma = \frac{rl - f}{r - 1} \text{ (geometrical progression)}$$

as exampled above by:

$$\frac{(1.10^{-1} \times 1.10^{-3}) - 1.10^{-1}}{1.10^{-1} - 1} \quad = a_{\overline{n}|} \text{ factor}$$

$$\frac{(.909090 \times .751315) - .909090}{-.0909090} \quad = a_{\overline{n}|} \text{ factor}$$

$$\frac{-.226077454}{-.090909} \quad = 2.486851991$$

Thus at 10%

$$\frac{100.00}{a_{\overline{3}|}} = \frac{100.00}{2.486852} \quad = 40.21 \text{ Pmts.}$$

By a series of algebraic transpositions the geometrical progression, working periodically instead of annually,

$$\frac{((1 + i/p)^{-1} \times (1 + i/p)^{-np}) - (1 + i/p)^{-1}}{(1 + i/p)^{-1} - 1}$$

becomes the $a_{\overline{np}|}$ factor

$$\frac{1 - (1 + i/p)^{-np}}{i/p}$$

There are various other transpositions, derived from the geometrical progression formula above, often seen to produce the actuarial factor $a_{\overline{n}|}$:

(a) $\dfrac{1}{i} - \left(\dfrac{1}{i} \times (1 + i^{-n}) \right) \quad = a_{\overline{n}|}$

$\dfrac{1}{.10} - \dfrac{1}{.10} \times 1.10^{-3} \quad = 2.486850$

(b) $\dfrac{1}{i/p + \dfrac{i/p}{(1 + i/p^n) - 1}}$ $= a_{\overline{np}|}$

$\dfrac{1}{.10 + \dfrac{.10}{1.10^3 - 1}}$ $= 2.486850$

(c) $\dfrac{1 + i/p^{np} - 1}{1 + i/p^{np} \times i/p}$ $= a_{\overline{np}|}$

$\dfrac{1.10^3 - 1}{1.10^3 \times .10}$ $= 2.486850$

To find the term (annuities ordinary)

$$\dfrac{LOG \dfrac{pmts}{i/p} \div \left(\dfrac{pmts}{i/p} - Loan\right)}{LOG \quad 1 + i/p} = np$$

$$\dfrac{LOG \dfrac{40.21}{.10} \div \left(\dfrac{40.21}{.10} - 100\right)}{LOG \quad 1.10} = 3 \text{ Years.}$$

It is usual always to set out the periodic formula realising that when calculations are annual there is no "p" factor.

"Mission Impossible"

Occasionally when finding a term of a loan on a computer or calculator "ERROR" (or some such term), to your surprise, will display. This may not be, as you may at first think, an input error but it could be the result of an "impossible" combination of data values.

Some readers may be aware from personal experience that when the interest rates of their home loans are increased the monthly payments will rise accordingly. Sometimes building societies will permit those of their borrowers who would find difficulty in meeting the increased payments to lengthen the term of their loan instead of lifting the monthly payments to the new required structure.

BUT, building societies are somewhat reluctant to lengthen any term to over 35 years, very occasionally stretching a point to 40 years, because when the term of a loan stands at this length of time the result is that the periodic repayments only just cover the INTEREST engendered in each period – and thus no capital is ever repaid, the result being, in practice, an everlasting loan — until the current debit balance is redeemed by a capital payment.

Assume a loan balance outstanding of £6,950 with 22 years to run to termination. The payments up to now have been £850 per year but with current rate changes to 13% nominal, under the arrangements agreed when the loan was constructed, the lender is entitled to payments of £970 annually to repay the loan and interest:

$$\frac{6,950.00}{a_{\overline{22}|}} \text{ at } 13\% = 969.38 = (\text{say}) \text{ £970.00 Pmts}$$

The borrower, already in some difficulty, finds the latest lift in payments more than he can manage and so the lender agrees to keep the payments the same as before, namely £850, and increase the length of the term — to what?

At least that was the idea, until the lender came up against a snag as soon as he commenced to calculate in order to determine the lengthened term. For these parameters are "impossible" because mathematically logs must be POSITIVE and . . .

$$\frac{\text{LOG } \dfrac{850}{.13} \div \left(\dfrac{850}{.13} - 6,950\right)}{\text{LOG } \quad 1.13} = \frac{\text{LOG } -15.89}{= \text{LOG } \quad 1.13}$$

Therefore the lender must now find the "nearest to the impossible", namely some value fractionally greater than LOG Zero. £6950 × .13 = £903.50 and working through the numerator of the above equation it will be seen that it reaches LOG 0. And while mathematically Zero cannot be logged it can be assumed that any payments GREATER than £903.50 are legitimate — although the loan may take the borrower's entire life to redeem!

Providing rates remain at 13% nominal, payments of £903.51 annually will require a term of 94 years to maturity — payments of £904 some 62 years. And so the lender, rightly deciding that normally a term longer than 35-40 years is bordering on the anti-social, decides, in this instance, on annual payments of £910 for a term of 40 years (plus a few odd months).

To find the interest rate % — Solve for "i"

Now for the bad news!

By transposition of the above formula we have found the payments, the loan amount and the term, BUT the interest rate cannot be so found; for no one yet has discovered a method of isolating all the "i" factors to one or other side of the equation. So the only method of finding "i" is to guess a rate, work it through the formula, and hope that the guess will "fit" the parameters required. If not, guess and guess again!

Not a very rewarding labour even with clever interpolation. But since the advent of computers and programmable calculators there is no problem: for the programmer merely instructs the computer to guess and go on "looping", as it is called, until the right interest rate is thrown up consistent with all the parameters required. (The reader's attention is directed to Appendix B so that if he wishes he can have some idea of exactly how a computer program interpolates and "loops" to provide finally the required rate.)

Showing the interest in "Business Interest Calculations"

In view of this problem of finding "i", various interest rates will sometimes be categorically stated without continual references to derivation by looping, interpolation, etc.

In the first example, at the beginning of the chapter, we had a loan of £1000 at 10% simple interest over 10 years: and we mentioned in passing that the true nominal rate was 15.098414%.

We can "prove" that the rate is correct by outlining the full formula/ equation with the "full" i/p factor:

$$£1000 \times \frac{1}{(1 - 1.1509841448^{-10})/.1509841448} = £200 \text{ pmts}$$

Assuming the precise nominal rate of interest *is* 15.09841448%, with payments "in arrears" of £200, − just to show there is no sleight of hand − by schedule, annuities ORDinary:

Loan PV	Rate	Pmts	Balance	Year-end
1000.00 ×	[1 + (15.0984/100)]	− 200	= 950.98	1.
950.98 ×	"	"	= 894.57	2.
894.57 ×	"	"	= 829.63	3.
829.63 ×	"	"	= 754.89	4.
754.89 ×	"	"	= 668.87	5.
668.87 ×	"	"	= 569.86	6.
569.86 ×	"	"	= 455.90	7.
455.90 ×	"	"	= 324.73	8.
324.73 ×	"	"	= 173.76	9.
173.76 ×	"	"	= 0.00	10.

(Schedules for annuities DUE are at the chapter-end)

If rate proof was unnecessary, the rate being given for example merely to highlight other factors, then instead of the full proving formula, the short actuarial equation would be set out:

$$£200 \frac{£1000}{a_{\overline{10}|}} \text{ at } 15.10\%$$

"Balloon payments"

Consider, if instead of the above parameters a borrower preferred to make a £100.00 capital payment (a "balloon payment") *at the end of the term* so that his periodic payments were consequently reduced. How are we to find the new payments? This balloon amount will reduce his present loan amount — but certainly not by £100 — for the £100 is to be paid in ten years' time, a future value. So we must discount this amount back to its present value by taking the same rate of interest, namely 15.098414% in this example:

$$(FV)\ 100 \times 1.1510^{-10} = 24.51\ (PV)$$

If we deduct this from £1000 we get £975.49, so the reader will find that

$$\frac{Loan - (Bal/(1 + i/p)^{np})}{pmts\ a_{\overline{np}|}}\ at\ Rate\ \%$$

$$\frac{1000 - 24.51}{pmts\ a_{\overline{10}|}}\ at\ 15.10\%$$

$$\frac{975.49}{(1 - 1.1510^{-10})/.1510} = 195.10\ pmts$$

To find the term with a balloon

$$\frac{LOG\left(\frac{pmts}{i/p} - BAL\right)/\left(\frac{pmts}{i/p} - loan\right)}{LOG\ \ \ \ \ 1 + i/p} = np$$

$$\frac{LOG\left(\frac{195.10}{.151} - 100\right)/\left(\frac{195.10}{.151} - 1000\right)}{LOG\ \ \ \ \ 1.150984145} = 10\ (years)$$

Loans with "Emissions"

Some years ago there was a plethora of what some called "Arab loans", although all such loans by no means originated from the Middle East. In short, those who made vast commissions, possibly from the then oil boom, needed somewhere to "park" their (sometimes) ill gotten gains, at interest, but immediately realisable, in case some coup d'état occured in their own country. Therefore they desired to "lend" their funds, often running to several million dollars, usually at a most attractive rate to the borrower, with a "bank guarantee", which if disaster struck they could then "sell" at a going rate. Rarely were such loans ever consummated for few banks were prepared to "give guarantees" unless the principal was well known to them, and in nearly all cases the principals wished to remain anonymous!

In order to pay the many agents, which quickly arrived on the scene, all demanding commission, fees etc, the lender demanded an "emission" – providing (say) a $100 loan for which the borrower would only receive (say) $97 but would still be required to repay $100 at the end of the term – a 3% "emission" lender's fee.

What the borrower required to know, from his agents, was the precise "true cost" in terms of the rate of interest.

Present value *to the borrower* $97, interest in arrears of (say) 10% p.a., with a repayment of $100 at the end of 10 years.

The true computed rate = 10.498745% = 10.50% emission rate and employing this rate in the equation below we will find $10 interest per year.

$$\frac{\$97 - (100 \times 1.10498745^{-10})}{a_{\overline{10}|}} \quad \text{at } 10.498745\%$$
$$= \$10 \text{ interest pmts per year}$$

or $60.15/(10 \times 6.015)$ $= 1.00$

or $60.15 - (10 \times a_{\overline{10}|})$ $= 0.00$ (at 10.498745%)

Pro-rata values

Loans, of the type as seen above, are "pro rata" in relation to repayment and loan values:

$$£200 \frac{£1000}{a_{\overline{10}|}} \text{ is as equally true as } \$20 \frac{\$100}{a_{\overline{10}|}} \text{ both at } 15.10\%$$

Let us assume that for the $100 loan above, the lender suddenly decided that a condition of the loan would be that the *total* capital value of the loan, namely $100, would have to be repaid at the end of the term and that each year he would *still* expect to receive $20. In that event, as the total capital amount of $100 is to be repaid at the end of the term of the loan, the $20 annual payments *must* represent *interest only*, and NOT, as in normal repayment loans, partly interest and capital. What, therefore, would be the new interest rate – for that is the only factor which is now unknown? Taking 20%:

$$\frac{100 - (100/((1 + i/p)^{10})}{20\, a_{\overline{10}|}} \quad \text{at } 20\%$$

$$\frac{100 - (100 \times 1.20^{-10})}{(1 - 1.20^{-10})/.20} = \$20$$

The 20% here represents the "yield to maturity" for this set of parameters, becoming a "fixed interest" loan, issued over a ten year period. The 20% interest rate will provide $20 (interest only) payments each year on each $100 lent, the loan ($100) amount being repaid (redeemed) at 100% at the conclusion (maturity) of the loan. We shall return to this "fixed interest" type of calculation, where loans are repaid in full at maturity, in Part II, when examining bond yields to maturity and certificates of deposit.

Mortgage repayment loans based on the financial calendar

In practice loans employing 30/360 are unusual; nevertheless, if required, adjust the RATE %, *not* the payments or term.

We know that:

$$\frac{\$1000.00}{a_{\overline{300}|}} \text{ at } (11/12)\% = \$9.80 \text{ monthly payments}$$

As above with $(11/12)\% \times 365/360$ the monthly payments become \$9.91.

Annuities DUE

"Annuities due" (where payments are made "in advance") will be examined in great detail later.

If $\quad a_{\overline{n}|} = $ "annuities ordinary" (payments in arrears)

then $\ddot{a}_{\overline{n}|} = $ "annuities due" (payments in advance)

and $\quad a_{\overline{n}|} \times (1 + i/p) \quad = \ddot{a}_{\overline{n}|}$

whereas

$$\frac{100.00}{a_{\overline{3}|}} \text{ at } 10\% \quad = 40.21 \text{ pmts in arrears}$$

as $\quad 100/2.486852 \quad = 40.21$

but $\quad \dfrac{100.00}{\ddot{a}_{\overline{3}|}} \text{ at } 10\% \quad = 36.56 \text{ pmts in advance}$

$\quad 100/(2.486850 \times 1.10) \quad =$

$\quad 100/2.735537 \quad = 36.56$

or, of course, $40.21/1.10 \quad = 36.56$ pmts at BEGINNING
of the compounding period

PAYMENTS IN ADVANCE

Capital − Pmts	Int (Cap + int) = Residual loan	Year-end
$(100.00 - 36.56) \times 1.10$ as 69.79	= 69.79	1.
$(\ 69.79 - 36.56) \times 1.10$ as 36.56	= 36.56	2.
$(\ 36.56 - 36.56)$	= 0.00 (at maturity)	3.

(where, in this instance, 36.56 above represents 36.55589124)

Compare the above annuities due payments in advance schedule, to that at the beginning of the chapter for annuities ordinary, payments in arrears.

CHAPTER 3
Annuities Ordinary and Balances

General

In the last chapter we have seen how to calculate a mortgage-type loan, the loan or payments per period, the term and, if the reader was interested in Appendix B, the interest rate.

But there are many other essential requirements apart from those basic values, possibly the most important being the loan outstanding (LOS), or the "balance", at any particular period within the term of the loan.

Balances

Before examining balances etc it must be stressed that the calculations in this chapter are based on normal banking practice and NOT on those of the (UK) Building Societies Association — for BSA calculations, as will be seen in a later chapter, are arranged differently in that the reconciliation of loan balances is made annually even though the payments required are monthly — so don't try and calculate the balance of your own building society home loan by the methods of calculation as set out below — for they will be fractionally different!

Formula

$$[(\text{Loan} \times (1 + i/p)^{np})] - \left(\text{Pmts} \times \frac{(1 + i/p)^{np} - 1}{i/p}\right) = \text{LOS(np)}$$

Before continuing with the above calculations consider the factor above, which we noted fleetingly in Chapter 1:

$$s_{\overline{np}|} = \frac{(1 + i/p)^{np} - 1}{i/p} = \text{actuarial savings factor}$$

for this term is much used in interest rate matters and the simplicity of this symbol is useful in shortening some formulae. Savings, ordinary and due, will be discussed in later chapters: for the moment, suffice it to recognise the term $s_{\overline{n}|}$ or $s_{\overline{np}|}$.

It will be seen, therefore, that the above balance formula could be written as follows:

$$\text{Loan} \times (1 + i/p)^{np} - \text{Pmts } s_{\overline{np}|} \text{ at } i/p\% = \text{LOS(np)}$$

Assume a loan of £1000.00 over a term of 25 years with annual payments of £118.74 at a nominal interest rate of 11%:

$$118.74 \quad \frac{1000.00}{a_{\overline{25}|}} \quad \text{at } 11\% \text{ nominal.}$$

What would the balance of the loan be at the end of 20 years (with a further 5 years to run)?

It is shown as follows:

$$(100(1 + i)^{20}) - 118.74 \; s_{\overline{20}|} \text{ at } 11\% = \text{LOS (20)}$$

and calculated thus:

$$(1000 \times 1.11^{20}) - \left(118.74 \times \frac{1.11^{20} - 1}{.11}\right) = £438.87 \text{ LOS(20)}$$

I use the term LOS, loan outstanding, and not "balance" to avoid conflict with "balloon payments" for in fact the LOS of £438.87 could also be considered as the balloon for the above parameters. And often in formulae both balance and balloon are shortened to BAL. For, from a different perspective, assume that the above £1000 loan was for a term of 20 years and that a balloon payment of £438.87 was being paid at the end of the loan period; the annual payments, for the next 20 years, therefore, employing the methods in Chapter 2 to find payments with a balloon must be:

$$\frac{1000 - (438.87 \times 1.11^{-20}) \text{ at } 11\%}{a_{\overline{20}|}} = £118.74 \text{ annual pmts.}$$

Last Payments

Supposing a £1000 loan was constructed so as to require monthly payments, over a term of 5 years, at 11% nominal — the 60 monthly payments would be:

$$\frac{1000.00}{a_{\overline{60}|}} \text{ at } (11/12)\% \text{ (monthly)} = £21.74 \text{ monthly pmts.}$$

When you work out the true payments it will be found that the figure is 21.74242307 which a bank would round to £21.74 monthly.

If the loan ran its full term of 60 months what will be the last payment? Obviously if the precise amounts paid are fractionally less each month than the "true" (calculated) payments, then at the end of the loan term there must be a few pence outstanding to the credit of the lender, a debit balance against the borrower.

$$\left(1000 \times \left(1 + \frac{11}{1200}\right)^{60}\right) - \left(21.74 \times \frac{1.0091667^{60} - 1}{.0091667}\right) = \text{LOS}$$

End of term balance $= £0.1927$

Last Pmt $(21.74 + .19) = £21.93$

Alternatively if the monthly payments had been rounded UP to £21.75 then the last payment would be $(21.75 - .60) = £21.15$.

An alternative method of obtaining the correct LOS is as follows:

$$(\text{Loan} - \text{Pmts } a_{\overline{n}|}) \times (1 + i/p)^n = \text{LOS}(n)$$

and taking the example above:

$$[1000 - (21.74 \times (1 - 1.009167^{-60})/.009167)] \times 1.009167^{60} = \text{LOS}$$

$$[1000 - (21.74 \times 45.99303341)] \times 1.009167^{60} = 0.19269400$$

(as above)

The interest and capital portions of the periodic payments

In many cases it is essential to be able to determine the exact amount of interest paid during each payment period or for a calendar year, or indeed for any period between two fixed points in time.

Above, we have seen how the LOS at any period in a loan can be determined, and we also know that the even periodic payment amounts contain portions of capital and interest − the interest portion decreasing as the capital is gradually repaid, resulting in higher capital portions paid in each period.

To find the amount of CAPITAL paid between two points in time

Find the LOS at the beginning and the end of the periods in question and subtract − and the difference must be the capital difference.

To find the INTEREST paid between two points in time

Find the capital difference, as above, and subtract the result from the sum of the payments made between the same period of time.

EXAMPLE.
A £10,000 loan over 25 years, at a nominal rate of 11%, will require monthly repayments of:

$$\frac{10000.00}{a_{\overline{300}|}} \text{ at } (11/12)\% = £98.01 \text{ PMTS monthly}$$

What is the interest paid during the twelve months between the 164th and 176th months?

$$(\text{Pmts} \times 12) - [\text{LOS}(164) - \text{LOS}(176)] = \text{Int. between periods } 164\text{-}176$$

$$(98.01 \times 12) - [(10000 \times (1 + i/p)^{164} - 98.01 s_{\overline{164}|}] - [(10000(1 + i/p)^{176}$$
$$- 98.01 s_{\overline{176}|})]$$

which resolves as:

$$£1176.12 - \left[(10000 \times 1.00917^{164}) - \frac{(98.01 \times 1.00917^{164} - 1)}{.00917}\right]$$

$$- \left[(10000 \times 1.00917^{176}) - \frac{(98.01 \times (1.00917^{176} - 1)}{.00917}\right]$$

$$£1176.12 - (7601.55 - 7243.93)$$

$$£1176.12 - 357.62 = \underline{818.50 \text{ interest portion}}$$

The method of finding the "interest portion" between two periods of time can be useful for finding the tax rebate over a year. For instance, taking the above example, the tax amount, at a basic rate of 30% on the interest amount of £818.50 is $818.50 \times .3 = £245.55$ and as such this could be a remit from the cost of the annual interest paid. See the chapter later in which UK building society home loan calculations are examined and the latest legislation in regard to tax remissions on payments. There is no difference in the above method of LOS calculations for loans constructed with balloon payments.

To find the interest and capital portions by LOS calculations for annuities DUE, however, requires a slight adjustment. In effect the n or np factor, in the above formulae, becomes $(n - 1)$ for annual calculations or $(np - 1)$ for periodic payments.

Taking the annuities DUE example/schedule outlined at the end of the previous chapter, find the interest amount for the first year. If this was related to annuities ORDinary, according to the formulae outlined above, the equation would be:

$$\text{Pmts} - [\text{LOS}(1) - \text{LOS}(2)] = \text{interest for year 1,}$$

whereas for annuities DUE the calculations must be:

$$\text{Pmts} - \left(\frac{\text{LOS}(1)}{1 + i/p} - \frac{\text{LOS}(2)}{1 + i/p}\right) = \text{interest for year 1}$$

$$36.56 - [(63.44 \quad - \quad 33.22) \quad = 6.34 \text{ interest year 1}$$

And checking on the schedule

$(100 - 36.56) \times .10 = 6.34$.

In the annuities ordinary example above, with monthly payments, if this was an annuities DUE requirement the equation would become:

$$(98.01 \times 12) - \left(\frac{LOS(164)}{1 + i/p} - \frac{LOS(176)}{1 + i/p} \right) =$$

$$(98.01 \times 12) - \left(\frac{7261.85}{1.009167} - \frac{6853.58}{1.009167} \right) =$$

$$1176.12 - \quad (7195.89 - 6791.33) \quad = 771.55$$

Int. between periods 164-176.

CHAPTER 4

Discounted Cash Flow Calculations (DCF and DEDCF)

DCF calculations are a most useful method of calculation and as they are often used to check conventional calculations they are examined early in "Business Interest Calculations". They are also often employed to find rates and other peripheral calculations when the loan structure is abnormal – and because of this, such methods are useful to avoid writing yet another one-off computer program!

There are a variety of business-type calculators now on the market, and many computer DCF programs constantly in use, so that many readers will already be fully conversant with both the concept and the working of a DCF calculation. Nevertheless, before examining some slightly more sophisticated DCF and DEDCF and MIRR methods, below are a few notes to bring the less familiar up to date.

Basically DCF calculations consist of an "investment" and a series of actual or projected cash flows (CFs) which, as they are received or disembursed, are then discounted back to the present time by employing a rate of interest, the internal rate of return (IRR).

As with other rate interest calculations, the concept is that as each positive cash flow is received it is immediately reinvested at the current calculation interest rate. Normally it is assumed that all such repayments (CFs) are "in arrears". If it is "in advance", ONE payment, the first, (CF) is subtracted from the "investment" and the term is naturally reduced by one if applicable.

Each cash flow is discounted period by period, either year by year or month by month, even week by week, but no "mix", as such, is permitted. Nevertheless, later in this chapter it will be seen how this limitation can, in some circumstances, be partially circumvented.

The sum of the discounted cash flows subtracted from the investment value results in the "net present value". If the NPV is negative the inference is that the interest percentage chosen, as the IRR, was not sufficient to yield the required return; alternatively if the NPV is positive, then the required yield is exceeded. Thus if the NPV is exactly zero then the IRR exactly fits with the remaining parameters of the data.

Therefore to find the yield, the required IRR or periodic rate of return of any calculation, the method is to guess a rate and then interpolate until the correct rate is found to meet a zero NPV. Computer or calculator programs happily relieve the statistician from such worries.

Let us assume an "investment" of $50,000.00 and a number of cash flows discounted at 11%.

Period	Cash flows		Total CFs	Discounting	(£)
Investment	. . . .				$- 50,000.00$
Year	outgoings	income	CF	$(1 + i/p)^{-np} =$	discounted
1.	10,000	5,000	$-5,000 \times$	1.11^{-1} =	$-4,504.50$
2.	5,000	10,000	$5,000 \times$	1.11^{-2} =	$4,058.11$
3.	5,000	5,000	$0 \times$	1.11^{-3} =	0.00
4.	0	15,000	$15,000 \times$	1.11^{-4} =	$9,880.96$
5.	0	20,000	$20,000 \times$	1.11^{-5} =	$11,869.03$
6. Invest. sold		55,000	$55,000 \times$	1.11^{-6} =	$29,405.25$
				Net Present Value (NPV) =	£708.84

11% was chosen because that was the "return" which the investor required as a yield. As the NPV was positive, the cash flows provide a return greater than 11%. Supposing, however, that instead of 11% above, 12% had been taken as the IRR. The NPV would have been −£1732.30, which demonstrates that the latter return in no way measures up to the yield requirement (of 12%). The IRR which provides a zero NPV for the above schedule is 11.28444454%.

The above type of DCF calculation is used extensively in the property markets, where the cash flows (income, rent, rates, outgoings etc) are known, and in the investment markets, where venture capital is always seeking new projects and, by making +/− cash flow projections, the yield, the annual return on investment capital, can be determined.

In many cases a DCF calculation is the only method of determining the periodic rate of return and often certain fixed interest loans can more easily be resolved by a DCF calculation rather than by a special or "one-off" computer program. Indeed properly used DCF programs can sometimes ensure that some "extra" programs can be discarded − or better still never purchased!

Below are a series of five similar cash flows relating to a simple compound interest loan and which, because there are only 5, are not difficult to input to a computer; but with a series of (say) 300 similar entries time would be wasted and so such entries can be "grouped" together.

A simple example of a loan of £1000 at a 10% rate over a period of 5 years will require some £263.80 annual repayments of capital and interest to service the loan:

$$\frac{1000}{263.80 \ a_{\overline{5}|}} \ \text{at} \ 10\%$$

$$263.80 \times (1 - (1.10^{-5}))/.10 = 1000.009550$$

If the same calculation is made by DCF methods:

£

"Investment" (loan, cost, price) = −1000.00

"Cash Flows"

$$263.80 \times 1.10^{-1} = 239.818182$$
$$'' \quad \times 1.10^{-2} = 218.016529$$
$$'' \quad \times 1.10^{-3} = 198.196845$$
$$'' \quad \times 1.10^{-4} = 180.178950$$
$$'' \quad \times 1.10^{-5} = \underline{163.799045}$$

(positive + value = credit) NPV = $\underline{\quad .009550}$

The future value

The NPV value above is fractionally in excess of Zero because the rounded payments of £263.80 were employed instead of the true value of £263.7974808: the .009550 above is the **Present Value** and to find the FV, the true balance at the end of the loan term:

$$PV \times (1 + i/p)^{np} = FV$$

$.009550 \times 1.10^5 = .015380$ **Future Value** or balance.

Checking by normal methods:

$$(1000 \times 1.10^5) - 263.80s_{\overline{5}|} \text{ at } 10\% = FV$$

$$1610.51 - 263.80((1.10^5 - 1)/.10) =$$

$$1610.51 - 1610.52530 = -0.015380$$

(a CREDIT to borrower due to fractional (rounding) overpayment)

Group discounting by formula

The difference in elapsed time between discounting 5 or 300 similar cash flows would hardly be noticeable in rapid computer working but a statistician using a calculator would find input and discounting some 300 CFs an almost impossible burden and would doubtless find a more profitable pastime!

However, this problem is easily overcome in that the SUM of the groups can be found by employing the annuities DUE factor.

Formula for finding the sum of the DCF groups

$$CF\ddot{a}_{\overline{g}|} \times (1 + i/p)^{-y} = \text{Sum of the DCFs for g periods}$$

Where:

g = the number of groups required
y = the number of the first period in the group

Taking the example above, where there were 5 groups (commencing at period 1):

$$263.80\ddot{a}_{\overline{5}|} \times 1.10^{-1} = \text{Sum of discounts}$$

$$263.80 \times [(1 - 1.10^{-5})/.1] \times 1.10 \times 1.10^{-1} = 1000.00955$$

whereas, taking the last three payments:

$$263.80\ddot{a}_{\overline{3}|} \times 1.10^{-3} \qquad = \text{Sum of discounts}$$

$$= 542.17$$

and (see schedule above):

$$198.20 + 180.18 + 163.80 = 542.18$$

(the minor discrepancy being due to decimal rounding)

The above method incidentally is extremely useful to save time when writing small calculator programs which have limited space and slow retrieval times, for it saves discounting each CF within the "group" separately.

One of the uses of a DCF calculation

We know that for a loan of £1000, over 25 years, the payments annually are £118.74, if the interest rate is 11% nominal.

Given the interest rate and the other parameters from our knowledge of repayment loan calculations, or using a computer/calculator program, it is simple to calculate the payments and balances. From the above we can see that the same calculation can be determined by DCF methods – what, you may say, is so significant about that?

Suppose the borrower missed his payments in the 10th year and failed to make good this omission, paid £200 together with his 15th payment, and then missed completely his 24th payment – what will he owe the lender at the end of the term? I doubt if that particular calculation could comfortably be resolved on a conventional computer/calculator program, but using the DCF method it is simplicity itself – and the answer is £132.05.

***

Remember that $118.74\ddot{a}_{\overline{g}|} \times (1 + i/p)^{-y}$ = group discounting.

Investment	=	−1000.00

***

$118.74 \times ((1 - 1.11^{-9})/.11) \times 1.11 \times 1.11^{-1}$ =	657.47 (rounded)	
10th year 0.00 =	0.00	

***

$118.74 \times ((1 - 1.11^{-4})/.11) \times 1.11 \times 1.11^{-11}$ =	129.74	"
$(118.74 + 200) \times 1.11^{-15}$ =	66.62	"

***

$118.74 \times ((1 - 1.11^{-8})/.11) \times 1.11 \times 1.11^{-16}$ =	127.71	"
24th year 0.00 =	0.00	
118.74×1.11^{-25} =	8.74	
NPV	−9.72	
$9.72 \times 1.11^{25} = 132.05$ FV	£132.05 balance due to lender	

Note

Zeros must always be input to a computer program, and as above they count as one (period) year.

Decimal entry discounted cash flow (DEDCF)

One of the difficulties of conventional DCF calculations is that they are designed to function by discounting period by period, integer 1; whereas many calculations, notably bond calculations, almost always have an "odd days" content. But using the group entry method above and altering the conventional program so that, if required, the FIRST entry (CF) can be a DECIMAL fraction, then each subsequent discounting will be by the addition of 1 to the decimal value.

Below is a loan example which figures extensively in Part II, the term being 665 days divided by 182.5 = 3.643835616, that is to say 3 discounting periods and 117.5 odd days which account for the remaining 0.643836 (.0643836 × 182.5 = 117.5); with an investment of 97.166952 and cash flows of 2.75 with 100 being added to the last payment. As the first input period is the odd days decimal I have named this method the **DEDCF** calculation, the "**DE**" being for Decimal Entry and not, I hurriedly add, for the **de** Lisle DCF method as I believe it has sometimes been called.

"Investment" $= -97.166952$

"Cash Flows" (coupon)

2.75 $\times 1.03888750^{-.643835616}$ $=$ 2.683276

$2.75 \times \ddot{a}_{\overline{2}|} \times 1.03888750^{-1.643835616}$ $=$ 5.068991

102.75 $\times 1.03888750^{-3.643835616}$ $=$ 89.414686

$\qquad\qquad\qquad\qquad\qquad$ NPV $=$ 0.00

"Investment" $= -97.166952$

"Cash Flows" (coupon)

$2.75 \times 1.03888750^{-.643835616}$ $=$ 2.683276

$2.75 \times \dfrac{(1 - 1.03889^{-2})/.03889 \times 1.03889}{1.03889^{1.643836}} =$ 5.068991

$102.75 \times 1.03889^{-3.643836}$ $=$ 89.415686

$\qquad\qquad\qquad\qquad\qquad$ NPV $=$ 0.00

Note

(1)   In a *Decimal Entry* Discounted Cash Flow calculation the decimal fraction must naturally be added to the y factor.

(2)   Dividing $\ddot{a}_{\overline{2}|}$ by $1.0389^{+1.643836}$ is the same as

multiplying $\ddot{a}_{\overline{2}|}$ by $1.03889^{-1.643836}$

Usually the division format is found to be more convenient.

Annuities Due

In the event that a DCF annuities due calculation is required, the only difference to the above annuities ordinary method is that the "investment", the loan, must be reduced by ONE periodic payment, which means that the periods are also reduced by one.

$\qquad$ 106.97 $\ddot{a}_{\overline{25}|}$ at 11% nominal for a loan of £1000 (annuities DUE)

The investment, consequently, becomes $106.97 - 1000 = -893.03$

$\qquad 106.97 \times ((1 - 1.11^{-24})/.11) \times 1.11 \times 1.11^{-1}$ $=$ 893.03

Discounted cash flows with a differing periodic base

It has always been appreciated that one of the limitations of normal DCF formulae is that the discounting descenders must be integers and as such these integers must refer to the same periodic discounting throughout the whole calculation, in other words the cash flows must be either annual, semi-annual, quarterly, monthly, or even weekly but must NOT be mixed. And this limitation also obtains with the decimal entry of the first cash flow (DEDCF).

What happens then when a mix is a must? What happens if the income (+CF) of an investment is (say) £135 for 120 months and there is (say) an outgoing tax bill (−CF) of £150 every quarter? If the interest rate of return was required to be 10% nominal, what is the cost of the investment — and equally important, how can we employ a DCF calculation, which is the obvious method to use here, where there is a "mix" in the periodic base?

Naturally a long way round is:

$$135 \times 1.008333^{-1}$$

$$135 \times 1.008333^{-2}$$

$$(135 - 150) \times 1.008333^{-3}$$

$$135 \times 1.008333^{-4}$$

and so on until 120 periods are completed.

But the simplest alternative is to convert the quarterly payment rate to equate with the monthly rate, here $(10/12)\%$.

$$1.008333^{12/4} = 1.025209$$

$$135 \times \frac{(1 - 1.008333^{-120})/.008333 \times 1.008333}{1.008333} = £10,215.61$$

and:

$$150 \times \frac{(1 - 1.025209^{-40})/.025209 \times 1.025209}{1.025209} = £\ 3,752.20$$

and then

$$£10,215.61 - 3,752.20 = £6,463.40 \text{ NPV Investment Cost.}$$

The above example was outlined entirely to demonstrate the possibility of changing the integer base on occasions; but readers will probably have already realised that this particular example could just as easily, indeed probably more easily, have been calculated thus:

$$135a_{\overline{120|}} \quad - \quad 150a_{\overline{40|}} \quad = £6,463.40$$

$$\text{at } (10/12)\% \qquad \text{at } 2.520891\%$$

Some drawbacks to the DCF concept and method of calculation

Unhappily, one of the drawbacks when using the traditional DCF calculation to find a IRR is that just occasionally there may be more than one mathematically correct answer. This should not mean that statisticians should lose confidence in the concept, for such abnormalities occur extremely rarely and only when cash flows are abnormal and, sometimes perhaps, unreasonable and unrealistic.

For example, an investment of £3,000.00 with monthly cash flows of:

    £1,700 for 5 months
    −£1,700 for 5 months
        0 for 9 months and
    £3,400 for the 20th and final month.

$$£$$

Investment . . . .   −3000.00

CF.

$$1700 \times \frac{(1 - (1 + i/p)^{-5})/i/p) \times (1 + i/p)}{(1 + i/p)} = \quad ?$$

$$-1700 \times \frac{(1 - (1 + i/p)^{-5})/i/p) \times (1 + i/p)}{(1 + i/p)^6} = \quad ?$$

0.00 X for 9 months   = 0.00

$$3400 \times (1 + i/p)^{-20} \qquad\qquad = \underline{\quad ?\quad}$$

NPV = 0.00

Some DCF computer/calculator programs may be unable to compete with these somewhat unrealistic values but in fact there are THREE different interest rates, all of which will meet the CF inputs:

    Rate A.   2.416119% monthly, converted to nominal   28.99%
    Rate B. 11.875488%   "   "   "   "   147.50%
    Rate C. 32.255473%   "   "   "   "   387.17%

Superimpose the above rates into the formula schedule set out above and in all three cases the NPV will be zero!

In these circumstances the temptation must be resisted to opt for one or other of the rates which "seems sensible"; for instance the periodic rate of return of 2.42% monthly − for if the cash flows had been annual then doubtless the statistician would have chosen 11.88% as being the most likely IRR!

If there is a series of alternative rates, derived from abnormal CFs, or a series of negative CFs, then one must reject the whole thing and think again. In the Chapter following, alternative methods, the Modified Internal Rates of Return (MIRR) and the Financial Management Rates of Return (FMRR), both designed to overcome such problems, will be examined. But before considering an alternative technical and mathematical assessment of the cash flows, and before turning to an MIRR calculation, because clearly the conventional DCF method, here, has failed, should one not consider if there is no simple method of getting a ROUGH rate?

In effect the business, for an outlay of £3000 over 10 months, made nil profits, and therefore the £3000 was "unproductive". The business, however, or probably the property, was then sold after 9 months for £3400, a total "profit" of £400 over 20 months.

$$1200((3400/3000)^{1/20} - 1) = 7.53\% \text{ yield over the 20 month period.}$$

Rough and ready, but if nothing more it provides confirmation that the previous DCFs were all totally invalid (see next chapter).

It is certainly not the intention to decry the DCF method of calculation: for in general terms it is a first-class discipline, capable of unscrambling rate interest values in circumstances that no other method of calculation could achieve so quickly and simply; and the method only runs out of steam when the CFs themselves are of doubtful practical value. Furthermore, DCF disciplines are not the only interest rate calculations in which anomalies sometimes occur — with apparently no logical explanation!

A loan of $490 was made to be repaid by $200 six months in advance with $300 to be paid six months after the loan was made. At a semi-annual 20% rate we find $490 - (200 \times 1.20) = $250 and $250 \times 1.20 = the last required repayment of $300. A semi-annual rate of 25% (nominal 50%) will also service this loan precisely!

A family decided to go on holiday, the total cost being £2,270. This cost was paid for in the following manner, £200 six months in advance of the start of the holiday, £480 three months in advance of the start of the holiday and then three months after the end of the holiday the final payment of £1,650. What is the interest rate on which these figures were calculated? The answer is simply EITHER 10% or 50% per quarter!

$$2270 - [((200 \times 1.10) + 480) \times 1.10] = 1500$$
$$1500 \times 1.10 = 1650$$
$$\text{Final repayment} = 1650$$

Now do the whole thing again with 50%!

This anomaly became a matter of litigation and I understand that the Government Actuary's Department, a very valuable but low profile branch of Government, ruled that the lesser rate could be assumed as correct.

Series Compounding

Although it has nothing to do with discounted cash flow calculations, it might be of interest as how series *compounding* can be calculated, in the same fashion as series discounting above.

Consider:

$$10 \times 1.10^6 = 17.72$$
$$10 \times 1.10^7 = 19.49$$
$$10 \times 1.10^8 = 21.44$$
$$10 \times 1.10^9 = \underline{23.58}$$
$$= \underline{\underline{82.22}} \text{ Total}$$

By the series compounding formula:

$$\text{pmts } s_{\overline{g}|} \times (1 + i/p)^y$$

Where: g = the number of groups required.

       y = the number of first period in the group.

In the above example g = 4 as there are four group periods.

                     y = 6 as the group commences with the 6th period.

$$10s_{\overline{4}|} \times 1.10^6 = 82.22$$

$$10 \times (1.10^4 - 1)/.1 \times 1.10^6 = 82.22$$

CHAPTER 5

Financial Management Rates of Return (FMRR and MIRR)

In the last chapter it appeared that sometimes employing DCF calculations there is an occasional possibility of inaccurate or multiple answers. To avoid such inaccuracies a "Modified Internal Rates of Return" (MIRR) calculation may have to be employed. The use of the "Financial Management Rates of Return" (FMRR) method of calculation, which was also mentioned in the preceeding chapter, stems from a slightly different, although in some cases related, problem.

Whereas conventional DCF calculations, as outlined in the last chapter, will be used extensively throughout this book, the MIRR and FMRR methods are individual calculations to be used only as required.

With DCF calculations, like many other interest rate calculations, the accrued interest is conceptually reinvested immediately on receipt. While this is perfectly valid and acceptable for (say) repayment loans, it is open to grave question when DCF calculations are related to (say) real estate management. For in property management most of the cash flows can usually be fairly accurately projected, as most of the values (rentals, rates, repairs, rent increase, wages, taxes, heating etc) are well known; and if DCF calculations are employed to determine whether a proposition is viable or not, difficulties immediately present themselves. If rental income is reinvested at the IRR, and if the calculated IRR is (say) 20%, the whole structure of the calculation must be open to question if the current market investment rate is (say) only 10%. In other words if the income is "actually" going to be reinvested (unlike repayment loans which are merely notionally reinvested to accommodate the practical calculations), then to base future projections, rates of return, etc on a false premise is absurd.

When employing the DCF calculation, for short or long-term repayment loans, nominal rates of up to (say) 40% to 50%, while being perhaps socially undesirable, are not unrealistic. But in the real estate world the general feeling is that unless the IRR falls within the compass of 5%–20%, the assumptions become less valid as a measure of investment.

Before examining methods of overcoming this "reinvestment" problem, two examples may be of interest, designed as they are to stress the difficulty of combining notional reinvestment rates of interest with practical "current market rates".

Investment A	Years	Investment B
£		£
Inv. −5,000.00		Inv. −5,000.00
CFs 0.00	1.	5,500.00
0.00	2.	0.00
0.00	3.	0.00
0.00	4.	0.00
8,811.71	5.	437.25

By DCF, or as below, calculation, the IRRs will be found respectively as:

A: $100((8811.71/5000)^{1/5} - 1) = IRR = 12\%$

B: $100((10056.78/5000)^{1/5} - 1) = IRR = 15\%$ (see below for the FV)

The investments appear similar for they both require the same investment amount and are both for a term of 5 years. Because of its higher IRR, at first glance, of the two Investment B would appear the better investment. But the 15% IRR was determined ONLY because the calculation assumed that the £5,500 received in the first year would be immediately reinvested — at 15%:

Investment A	Investment B
$£5,000 \times 1.12^5 = £8,811.71$	$£5,500 \times 1.15^4 = £\ 9,619.53$
	437.25
	£10,056.78

Indeed as £10,056 is greater than £8,812, Investment B appears the more profitable investment — *while based on that notional structure.* But when the reinvestment rate falls in line with the practical current market value of (say) 10%, then the perspective changes:

$$£5,500 \times 1.10^4 = £\ 8,052.55$$
$$437.25$$
$$£\ 8,489.80$$

which is now LESS than investment A.

So unless Investment B can be serviced by a rate of 5% more than the going market rate (which is unlikely), Investment A is, in practice, in the real world, the better bet.

Again consider two further investments, £5,000 Investment A, and £7,500 Investment B. At the end of 5 years, with no further income, Investment A is valued at £12,441.60 (on £5,000) whereas Investment B shows £17,158.18 (on £7,500).

Investment A: $100((12,441.60/5000)^{1/5} - 1) = 20\%$ Yield IRR

Investment B: $100((17,158.18/7500)^{1/5} - 1) = 18\%$ Yield IRR

At first glance, again because of the higher yield, Investment A looks the more attractive, but consider; the initial investment for Investment A was £2,500 less than Investment B and to put both investments "on all fours", for comparison purposes, this amount must be invested by Investor A. But with a current market rate of only 10% this would produce only (£2,500 $\times$ 1.10^5) namely £4,126.28, which, when added to the £12,441.60, is LESS than Investor B's total. So, in this case, because of the market rate limitation, Investment B is the more profitable.

$$100((12,441.60 + 4,126.28)/7500)^{1/5} - 1) = 17.18\% - \text{less than } 18\%$$

Financial management of the rate of interest

The FMRR method of calculation is to employ TWO rates, the "safe" rate (usually slightly below the market going rates) and the "risk" rate (usually the sort of rate the entrepreneur would like as a return on his venture capital).

Below is the method employed to harness these two conflicting rates to provide an NPV or an IRR nearer, it is thought, to reality in real estate projections.

A projected development – adjusted by FMRR

	£
Initial Investment	−12,000.00
Projected Cash Flows:	
Year 1. (setting up costs)	−25,000.00
2. (setting up costs)	−25,000.00
3. (profits commencing)	15,000.00
4. (losses + more investment)	−10,000.00
5. (profitability returns)	15,000.00
6. (project sold)	125,000.00

A *conventionally* calculated IRR will be found to be slightly in excess of 20% nominal but, as the current market investment rate is (say) in the region of 12%, management considers that, for DCF calculations, the SAFE rate should be 10% and the RISK rate 15% and, taking these two rates as their guide, require to know what the projected rate is likely to be. If, by these methods, the FMRR *is less than 18.5%*, management will *not* proceed with the project.

The Method

First, discount all the NEGATIVE CFs at the SAFE rate, and add to the original investment.

Secondly, tidy up any anticipated periodic deficit by investing in the previous year (period) to that extent — again at the SAFE rate.

Thirdly, having eliminated any negative cash flow, AT THE RISK RATE find the Future Value. Lastly, find the FMRR.

In short, admittedly a slight over-simplification, *discount the negative CFs* at the *safe rate* and *compound the positive CFs* at the *risk rate*.

Taking the example above:

Discounting the negative CFs by 10%

£12,000 + (25,000/1.10) + (25,000/1.10^2) = £55,388.43 PV.

In the fourth year there is a deficit of −£10,000.00. If, however, £10000/1.10 = £9,090.91 is invested, at the "safe rate" of 10%, in the previous (third) year, it will be worth £10,000 in the fourth year so that in that (fourth) year there will be a ZERO income/outgoing.

But in the THIRD year, before the above (£9,090.91) investment, there was an income of £15,000 so the true CF for that year is now £15,000 − 9,090.91 = £5,909.09.

To obtain the FV:

$$125,000 + (15,000 \times 1.15^1) + (0.00 \times 1.15^2) + (5909.09 \times 1.15^3)$$

$$= £151,236,99 \text{ FV}$$

$$100\left(\left(\frac{\text{Future Value}}{\text{Present Value}}\right)^{1/n} - 1\right) \qquad = \text{FMRR}\%$$

$$100\left(\left(\frac{151,236.99}{55,388.43}\right)^{1/6} - 1\right) \qquad = 18.22\% \text{ FMRR}$$
Not management-viable

The modified internal rate of return (MIRR)

Whereas the FMRR calculation overcomes the problem of the reinvestment market rate, the modified IRR calculation is designed to overcome the original problem we faced earlier, in Chapter 4, when there sometimes appeared to be two or more answers to the same problem.

In fact the MIRR method also calculates with the "two-rate" concept, discounting (not compounding) the positive cash flows by the risk rate. And as this is similar to, but somewhat easier than, the FMRR method, many use the MIRR instead of the FMRR. For instance, in the last example the MIRR method would find an IRR of 17.66% (c.f. FMRR 18.22% above) or (see later) the "alternative MIRR" would present it as 17.92%.

Taking the example in the previous chapter which provided the statistician with three separate answers from a conventional DCF calculation, the investment was £3,000, with £1,700 income for 5 months, a £1700 deficit for the next 5 months — and then 20 months after the original investment was made the property was sold for £3,400.

Applying the modified IRR calculation:

Negative CFs discount 10/12%

£

Investment -3000.00

Months 1–5 positive – ignore

$-1700 \times \ddot{a}_{\overline{5}|} \times 1.0083333^{-6}$ $= -7954.55$ (months 6–10)

No more negative CFs

$$\text{Present Value} = -10{,}954.55$$

Positive CFs discount 15/12%

$1700 \times \ddot{a}_{\overline{5}|} \times 1.01250^{-1}$ $= 8190.32$ (months 1–5)

Months 6–10 negative – ignore
Months 11–19 nil   – ignore

3400×1.0125^{-20} $= 2652.03$ (month 20)

$$\textbf{Present Value} = 10{,}842.35$$

and $10{,}842.35 \times 1.0125^{20}$ $= \textbf{Future Value £13,900.24}$

The MIRR % is therefore:

$$100p\,[(FV/PV)^{1/np} - 1] = 1200\left[\left(\frac{13{,}900.24}{10{,}954.55}\right)^{1/20} - 1\right] = 14.37\%$$
$$\text{MIRR}$$

It will be recalled, some pages back, that as a rough calculation the approximate IRR was found as 7.53% nominal.

An alternative MIRR

There is yet another and somewhat simpler alternative method, a modification of the above MIRR, and one which may well commend itself to those who use a DCF/IRR calculator; this is to treat the negative PV, found by the latest method, as the "investment".

Taking the last example with the PV = £10,954.55 (see above) and employing .01104899340 as the i/p:

$$
\begin{array}{lr}
 & \text{£} \\
\text{Investment} \ldots\ldots\ldots\ldots\ldots\ldots\ldots\ldots\ldots = - & 10{,}954.55 \\[2mm]
1700 \times \dfrac{(1 - 1.011049^{-5})/.011049 \times 1.011049}{1.011049} = & 8{,}225.35 \\[2mm]
3400 \times 1.011049^{-20} \qquad\qquad = & 2729.20 \\[1mm]
\text{NPV} = & 0.00
\end{array}
$$

and consequent on the NPV equalling Zero the i/p is verified as being correct and therefore:

$$\underline{\text{MIRR} = 1.104899340 \times 12 = 13.26\%}$$

Note

For any reader interested in gaining a deeper insight to FMRR and MIRR calculations the Realtor's National Marketing Institute of Chicago, in their series on Marketing Investment in Real Estate, include an excellent pamphlet "Finance Taxation Techniques", one of the authors being Stephen D. Messner who, amongst others, furthered the technique and the development of the FMRR concept.

CHAPTER 6

The (UK) Consumer Credit Act 1974 and the Disclosure Regulations

In the 1960s successive governments had been considering seriously how the general public could be protected from excessive lending rates, how they could compare one loan with another, and how to clarify once and for all the fact that the effective rate of a repayment loan is roughly double the simple interest (SI) quotation rate – for at that time the great preponderance of "High Street" loans (hire purchase and small money lender loans) were SI quoted.

To this end the Crowther Report made various recommendations, most of which were finally incorporated in the Consumer Credit Act 1974; and in playing a very minor role in its production has been a matter of no little satisfaction to your author.

In the Introduction we have seen two examples of excessive lending rates and while it was clear that no one can stop the unwise from borrowing foolishly, at least they can be shown how foolish they are. By making it illegal to lend without first telling the borrower the precise cost in terms of interest rates was thought to be one way of mitigating the swingeing rates of interest which the Money Lenders Act of 1925 was designed to stop but didn't.

Disclosing the effective rate for any loan would not only, it was hoped, stop excessive asking rates, often clothed in verbal respectability, but would also be a method whereby the untutored could compare the merits of one loan against another without the necessity of calculation. For who could tell, at a glance, which is the cheaper loan, one rated at 3% quarterly or another at 11.90% with monthly payments? Comparing the effectives (12.55% and 12.57% respectively), the choice is simplified. To quote the effective rate for a repayment loan it is necessary first to calculate the precise periodic internal rate of return, then the nominal rate, and thus the effective rate – and if all this is necessary there would seem less point in quoting a simple interest rate to any borrower!

Advertisements and quotations

After some years in operation, few in the UK who are connected in any way with lending or rate interest matters are likely to be ignorant of the Regulations. Nevertheless, for the record, the essentials are summarised below.

The vital statistics

From May 1985, for any loan under £15,000, or of any amount if the loan is secured on land (e.g., a home mortgage loan), the term, the total charge for credit, (the total interest and extras payable) and the annual percentage rate of charge (the APR) MUST be disclosed in all advertisements and quotations.

(a) *The term*
The term of the loan may sound obvious and need no further explanation, but, as we shall see in the next chapter, all loan parameters are inter-related and cannot be considered in isolation.

(b) *The total charge for credit*
The charge is the total amount of interest to be paid PLUS any extras such as commitment fees, search fees, valuations, legal fees, insurance fees and ANY other charge made against the borrower connected with the loan in question.

(c) *The Annual Percentage Rate of Charge*
This somewhat pretentious term is simply the effective rate TRUNCATED to ONE decimal place. Unhappily this term has been almost universally shortened to the mnemonic APR (as the author knew it would); unfortunately, for, as we have seen previously, "APR" in the USA represents the *nominal* rate, not the effective, and all recommendations to avoid the use of "APR" in the UK fell on deaf ears!

Low cost credit exemption

Subject to other provisions the APR need not be disclosed unless it exceeds 13% or unless it exceeds the (highest of) the clearing banks' base rates plus 1% − should this be higher than 13%. However, nowadays many institutions, either for reasons of social conscience or merely to be on the safe side, always advertise the APR irrespective of whether exempt or not.

Note
Throughout the following pages the APR will often be calculated and provided − at less than 13%. In all cases such a calculation must be made to determine whether the rate is exempt or not. So the text provision of an APR is not intended to imply that it must necessarily be disclosed.

Truncation

Why did the Regulations require the effective rate to be *truncated* to one place of decimals, and not simply rounded to two places? In a repayment loan the calculated payments are almost invariably rounded to 2 decimal places (pounds and pence) and in that case there is a +/− balance at the end of the term. In that event the original periodic interest rate and quoted nominal (from which the effective rate stems − and hence the APR) will require adjustment − for rarely does such a tailor-made quotation include the adjusted "last payment". This would mean that once the precise payments were agreed, fractionally + or − the calculated payments, any lender would need to recalculate the new true rate in order to provide the correct APR − for there would be no guarantee that the rounding up/down of the payments would be sufficiently small as not to affect the effective rate. But by truncating to one place of decimals the problem of recalculating for fractional changes is rather neatly overcome.

A (property collateral) loan of £1000 at 11% nominal over 300 months will require an advertised APR of:

$$100((1.009166667^{12}) - 1) = 11.57188410 \% \text{ Effective}$$

$$= 11.5 \qquad \% \text{ APR}$$

but such a loan would be serviced by *calculated* payments of £9.8001130769 which will be tailor-made (rounded) to actual payments of £9.81 and in this event the *corrected* nominal and effective rates are:

$$\frac{1000.00}{9.81 \ a_{\overline{300}|}} = 0.917688851 \% \text{ Monthly}$$

$$= 11.01226621 \% \text{ Nominal}$$

$$= 11.585446400 \% \text{ Effective}$$

$$= 11.5 \qquad \% \text{ APR}$$

It will be seen therefore that whereas the effective rate increases fractionally the APR remains unaltered, because the tolerance provided by the need to show ONE place of decimals ONLY obviates the necessity to recalculate the effective rate for merely fractional "round-up/down" changes. Of course if the payments were rounded upward by a more substantial amount, or extra charges were suddenly levied, then a recalculation for a new APR would be necessary.

Sometimes, of course, the avaricious lender can turn this truncating to his advantage. A loan of £10,000 over a term of 10 years with a nominal rate of 10.49% will require £134.88 of monthly payments, the APR being 11.0%. But the APR will also be 11.0% if the nominal rate is calculated by:

$$1200[(1 + (11.099999999/100))^{1/12} - 1] = 10.57\%$$

− and the resulting monthly payments will be £135.34!

Last Payments

There is no reason why, when rounding payments (up or down) the "last payment" cannot be stated, instead of assuming that all payments are "even" throughout the term. For example a loan of £1000 at 10% nominal (effective 10.4713%) over a term of 300 months requires payments of £9.087007455. Rounding UP to exactly £9.09 results in an overpayment of £3.97 at the end of the term. Instead of calculating a new effective rate the lender could state that the "last payment" required is £5.12 (£9.09 − £3.97). Alternatively if the monthly payments are rounded down to £9.08, the last payment will be £18.38.

Calculations and the UK lending law

Below some examples related to the Consumer Credit Act are provided, but this chapter neither pretends, nor attempts, to cover all the legal niceties of the Act and its Regulations. For those, however, who need to examine in greater detail the ramifications of the Consumer Credit Act, and its updated regulations (May 1985), with all the latest legal requirements and the possible difficulties arising therefrom, a practical guide to "truth in lending" can be found in "Consumer Credit Agreements: A working Handbook to Truth in Lending" by Karpinski and Fielding, published by Waterlows. It should prove invaluable in preventing any institution, or private lender, straying unknowingly outside the confines of the law.

The charge for credit for a repayment loan with a balloon payment

A £10,000 loan with a £2,000 balloon payment at the end of twelve months, at a monthly rate of 1% requires monthly payments of £730.79. In this case the "charge for credit" is:

((Pmts   × np) + Balloon) − Loan   = Charge
((730.79 × 12) + 2000)   − 10,000 = £769.48

The above somewhat obvious calculation was set out simply because I have occasionally heard argument as to the exact charge for a loan with a "residual balance" (or balloon payment). The argument is that different payments can equally well be found if the balloon payment is discounted back to the present time and subtracted from the PV, namely:

$$\frac{£10000 - (2000 \times 1.01^{-12})}{a_{\overline{12|}}} = \frac{£8225.10}{a_{\overline{12|}}} \text{ at } 1\% = £730.79$$

and in that case, so the argument runs, the "charge" is surely:

(730.79 × 12) − 8225.10 = £544.38 *not* £769.48

In both cases the charges are correct — but for different loans, one for £10,000 with a final balloon payment of £2000 and the other for £8225.10 with no balloon payment. The only reason why £8225.10 came into the argument was because, in order to determine the correct monthly payments, the balloon payment had to be discounted back to the present time, and consequently subtracted from the PV.

Commitment fees and "extras"

As outlined above, all extras must be included in the charge for credit, and therefore included in calculating the APR. Commitment fees et al. are, unless otherwise stated, usually "front-end" fees, paid when the loan is advanced.

Mathematically in order to calculate the correct interest rate the front-end fees must be subtracted from the loan amount but naturally added to the total interest. Taking the first example in this chapter and assuming a £15 commitment fee, the comparisons are below:

No commitment fee			*Commitment fee of £15*	
$\dfrac{£1000}{9.81a_{\overline{300}|}}$	at 0.91769%	(monthly)	$\dfrac{£1000-15}{9.81a_{\overline{300}|}}$	at 0.93486%
	11.01227%	(nominal)		11.21835%
	11.5%	(APR)		11.8%
£(9.81 × 300) − 1000		(charge for	£1943 + £15	
= £1943		credit)	= £1958	

The rules, however, permit some flexibility where necessary. The (UK) Office of Fair Trading pamphlet "Credit Charges, Part II, Advertisements and Quotations", provides an interesting example. A £50 loan with an interest charge of £10, has 12 payments of £4.62 and a final (13th) payment of £4.56.

Determined thus:

$$
\begin{aligned}
50 + 10 &= 60 && \text{(Loan + interest)} \\
60/13 &= 4.615385 \\
&= 4.62 && \text{(rounded)} \\
&= 4.62 && \text{(12 payments)} \\
60 - (4.62 \times 12) &= 4.56 && \text{(final payment of)}
\end{aligned}
$$

The OFT pamphlet requirement is to find the APR, which is given as 38.1%. This value is derived from a normal calculation taking *thirteen* payments of £4.62:

$$\frac{50}{4.62a_{\overline{13}|}}$$

	at	2.727766 %	Monthly
	"	32.733186 %	Nominal
	"	38.119214 %	Effective
	"	38.1	% APR

But if a DCF calculation is employed, the monthly rate will be found to be a precise 2.714636%, the nominal as 32.575628%, the effective as 37.907524% and thus the *true* APR as 37.9%:

		£
Investment		−50.00
Cash flows	$4.62a_{\overline{12}\rceil}$	46.78
	$4.56 \times 1.027146^{-13}$	3.22
	NPV =	0.00

To verify:

$$(50 \times 1.027146^{13}) - 4.62\,[(1.027146^{13} - 1)/.027146] = -0.06$$

which means an over-payment of .06 and thus the "last payment" becomes $4.62 - .06 = 4.56$.

Tolerances

The reason why the OFT provided the APR as 38.1% instead of the correct 37.9% was because of the "tolerances" permitted in such cases.

The Regulations provide tolerances of +1% or −0.1% above or below the advertised APR, *or* (as in this example) when all payments but one are equal the difference in the one odd payment may be ignored providing it is no greater than 1 penny per period. The example had 13 periods and therefore 13 pence tolerance was permissable: in fact the difference was well inside the required tolerances, being $4.62 - 4.56 = 6$ pence only.

An APR of 30% could therefore be advertised as:

$$30 \times (1 + (1/100)) = 30.3\%$$

or $30 / (1 + (.1/100)) = 29.9\%$

It must be remembered that these rules and regulations and all the calculations for "disclosure" were all worked out in the mid 1970s and were designed originally to be used with the "Tables" provided by the OFT, on the assumption that small traders had no other means of calculating. But since then calculators and other aids have progressed considerably. And whereas nowadays tables are less necessary, the tolerances etc. that the tables required remain.

Early redemption for loans

Let there be no mistake, the early redemption of a loan can be costly to a lender, both administratively and by upsetting the cash flows of a carefully prepared lending policy. A penalty, therefore, for such disruption is legitimate. Previously, there were no rules as to the amount which a lender might exact as a penalty for early repayment; from May 1985, such penalties will be legally recognised. But amounts greater than those calculated by the formulae below will contravene the latest Consumer Credit Act Regulations.

The deferment factor (d). Irrespective of how payments are structured, for a loan of longer than 5 years, for calculation purposes, it is assumed that the lender can be charged a penalty of ONE month's interest — for a loan of less than 5 years TWO months' interest — sometimes necessarily worked on a days basis.

Where n = total sumber of repayments in the life of the loan
       m = number of payments NOT paid due to early redemption
       d = deferment periods, one or two months (or in days)

calculate as follows for a *repayment* loan:

$$\frac{(m-d) \times ((m-d)+1)}{n(n+1)} \times \text{total charge for credit} = \text{rebate}$$

$$(m \times \text{pmts}) - \text{rebate} = \text{total amount repayable.}$$

Assume a £1000.00 loan over 36 months with monthly payments of £38.00 (payments in arrears). What is the final repayment amount if the borrower wishes to redeem after the 29th repayment had been made, in other words he wishes to redeem the loan at the end of the 30th month? There are 30 repayments so far made and because the life of the loan is under 5 years, a two months' penalty is permitted. Hence n = 36, m = (36 − 30) = 6, d = 2:

$$\frac{4(4+1)}{36(36+1)} \times ((36 \times 38) - 1000) = \text{rebate}$$

$$\frac{20}{1332} \times 368 \qquad\qquad = £ \quad 5.53$$

and the balance due is

$$(6 \times 28) - 5.53 \qquad\qquad = £162.47$$

Calculate as follows for a single *lump sum* loan:

$$\frac{(n-d-m)}{n} \times \text{total interest} = \text{rebate}$$

Total interest due less rebate = final payment (calculated on a days basis at simple interest).

A lump sum loan of £180 over a period of 260 days at 19.50% (simple interest) requires a final repayment of:

$$£180 \times (1 + (19.50/100 \times 260/365)) = £205.00,$$

namely a repayment of the original loan (£180) plus £25 interest.

If the borrower wished to repay early, after 150 days, the final payment required, which will include 2 months' penalty (here 61 days' interest), will be:

$$\frac{260 - 61 - 150}{260} \times 25 \quad = \text{£4.71 rebate}$$

$$\text{£205} - 4.71 \qquad\qquad = 200.29 \text{ final balance.}$$

Compare more conventional calculations:

$$\text{PV £180} \times (1 + (19.50/100 \times 260/365)) \quad = \text{£205.00 FV}$$
$$\text{FV} - \text{PV} = \text{total interest due} = \text{£205} - 180 \quad = \text{£ 25.00 interest}$$

and

$$\text{PV £180} \times (1 + (19.50/100 \times (150 + 61)/365)) = \text{£200.29 FV}$$
$$\text{£205.00} - 200.29 \qquad\qquad\qquad = \text{£   4.71 rebate.}$$

An aside

A quick yardstick, or benchmark, rule to relate (roughly) a simple interest (SI) rate to a true *effective* rate for a repayment loan is to "double the SI".

Take the illegally expensive High Street HP example in the Introduction, namely an outstanding amount of £240 to be repaid by 24 monthly payments of £24. Here the SI rate is 70%, which if "doubled" suggests an effective of 140% — when in fact it is 170%. But with more conventional levels of simple interest the rule is reasonably accurate.

If the SI quoted for the above loan was 10% the required payments would be £12. $(240 \times (1 + (.10 \times 2)))/24 = \text{£12}$ — and calculating:

$$\frac{240}{12a_{\overline{24}|}} \text{ at } 1.5130844\% \text{ monthly} = 18.16\% \text{ nominal} = 19.75\% \text{ Effective.}$$

for: $100(1.015130844^{12} - 1) = 19.74690140\%$ Effective.

By the same methods of calculation, a quoted SI of 15% requires monthly payments of £13 — and an effective rate of 30.01% and, to continue the example further, a quoted SI of 20% will need servicing by monthly payments of £14, which, if calculated as above, will provide an effective rate of 40.72%.

CHAPTER 7

UK Building Societies and Home Loans in General

General

Because so large a part of the community in the UK borrow from building societies it is hardly surprising that the societies in general are sometimes the object of some criticism; often from those who tend to forget the help which the societies invariably give to those borrowers who, through no fault of their own, have temporary difficulty in meeting the monthly repayments on their mortgages.

Some of this criticism may well soon be a thing of the past: at the time of writing the whole building society world is in a state of flux. For not only have many members of the Building Societies Association (BSA) decided to go their own way, but in July 1984 the Government announced its intention to introduce new legislation which would permit the societies to engage in general banking business. The announcement, although very much in line with BSA pronouncements, does however raise certain difficulties and problems which remain to be resolved.

First a review of the existing methods used by most of the BSA members, then some thoughts on what they may do in the future.

One criticism has undoubtedly been of the somewhat old fashioned (some would say archaic) method of interest calculation which, despite this age of the computer, the building societies have insisted on maintaining – and may well continue to do in the future.

Unlike banking loans, where the quarterly or monthly payments are either "balanced" after each payment is made, or where the amount outstanding (and therefore the interest) is calculated on a daily basis, building society loans, although invariably requiring monthly payments, are based on the assumption that annual repayments of principal and interest are all made in one lump sum on the last day of the society's financial year.

The reason for this quill-pen method adopted, and unhappily maintained to this day, by the BSA is that in the days before computers and electronic calculators all amortisation had to be carried out either by the use of amortisation tables or by four-figure log tables, with guess-and-guess-again interpolation. Annual calculations with annual reconciliation were naturally a good deal less burdensome than conventional monthly calculations.

UK building society methods of calculating home loans

As outlined above, building societies calculate, initially, their payments ANNUALLY, divide by 12 and round up unless the value is an integer. These values are usually found from the BSA Mortgage Repayment Tables brochure, which bases all calculations on £1000 per rate/term. Thus a 7.90% quoted rate, over a term of 20 years will show a monthly payment of £8.43 — for £1,000:

$$\frac{1000}{a_{\overline{20}|}} \text{ at } 7.90\% = £101.095441 \text{ ANNUALLY,}$$

which when divided by 12 = 8.424620 and this value, when rounded up to the next whole penny (.01), provides £8.43 payments monthly — precisely as provided in the scale-payment tables mentioned above. BUT unhappily BS loans, unlike conventional repayment loans, are NOT pro rata per £1,000. For a loan of £4650.00, over 20 years at 7.90% nominal, the payments are NOT, as one might sensibly assume, £8.43 × 4650/1000 = £39.20.

The Building Societies Mortgage Repayment Tables provide the following example:

$$
\begin{array}{llll}
4000/1000 \times 8.43 & = 33.720000 & = & 33.72 \\
600/1000 \times \quad '' & = 5.058000 & = & 5.06 \\
50/1000 \times \quad '' & = 0.421500 & = & .43 \\
\end{array}
$$

$$\hspace{6cm} \underline{39.21} \quad \text{BSA monthly pmts}$$

However, as individual building societies recently appear to have decided to quote their own interest rates, and not abide by the long-established method whereby the current rate was decided centrally by the BSA, I suspect that this slightly stylised method is often ignored and the pro rata method adopted. In any case the difference is only fractional.

One obvious criticism is that the building society monthly payments are greater than if calculated conventionally. The BSA riposte is that after a period of time the redemption value will be less with building societies than with banks. True as that may be (for obviously the higher the payments, the lower the outstanding balance), there is no question that the true and effective rate costs are higher with building societies (and with UK local government authorities who also calculate by annual/12 or semi-annual/6 methods) than with lenders, such as banks, who amortise conventionally and reconcile their payments quarterly or monthly.

In the above loan example, the true nominal and effecive rates must be:

$$\frac{4650}{39.21a_{\overline{240}|}} \quad \begin{array}{l} \text{at } 8.11\% \text{ nominal} \\ \text{at } 8.42\% \text{ effective} \end{array}$$

This is against a quoted nominal rate of 7.90%!

Days' interest and annual reconciliation

To take another example, of a £1,000 loan over a term of 25 years, at 11% nominal, BSA scale payments will be £9.90 monthly.

By BSA methods what happens if the loan advanced is made on 16 June? As payments will be "in arrears" the first repayment of £9.90 will normally occur on 16 July and on the 16th day of each month following – that would be 6 payments to the year-end (reconciliation 31 December), namely 9.90 × 6 = £59.40.

Building societies calculate their "days' interest" as days between the required dates plus one day (unlike more conventional means for accrued interest for bonds and other such money instruments); thus the interest due, on a daily basis, from 16 June – 31 December will be for 199 days: 1000 × 199/365 × 11/100 = £59.97, which, added to the loan of £1000 and with the payments already made (£59.40) deducted, provides a balance (due) of £1000.57. But this is, unhappily, not the whole story for it must be appreciated that the BSA monthly scale payments (here £9.90) were calculated on the general assumption that 12 payments would be made each year – when of course most loans commence sometime during the course of a year, with consequently some odd days' interest due between advance and first payment, and a lesser number than 12 payments to the year-end.

The accrued interest due therefore at the first year end is:

$$(\text{Loan} \times i \times \text{days}/365) \quad - (\text{loan} \times i \times \text{pmt months}/12) = a/i$$
$$(1000 \times .11 \times 199/365) - (1000 \times .11 \times 6/12) \qquad =$$
$$59.97 - 55.00 \qquad\qquad\qquad\qquad = £4.97 \ a/i$$

This accrued interest is required, over and above those payments which have already been made up to the 31st Decenber, and it is this amount which will be a charge on the borrower at the end of the first year's reconciliation – NOT the .57 mentioned above. As will be seen later this added complication provides some difficulties if disclosure of the APR etc is required.

This £4.97 may not seem substantial but if the loan was for (say) £50,000 the "extra" outstanding amount would be 50000/1000 × 4.97 = £248.63, and unless the borrower paid this amount prior to December 31st the "extra" amount will remain as part of the loan throughout the loan term, consequently rising to a notional value of nearly £3,500 at the end of the term. We shall return, later, to this matter of the extra amount at the end of the first reconciliation period.

Missed and ex-gratia payments

A missed payment is reflected in the balance at the year-end unless its value is made up before reconciliation date. Mathematically, all payments could be ignored during the course of a year and then paid up, in total, just one day before 31st December. And mathematically the loan would stand fully paid up at the commencement of the new year following. But this method is not recommended, for building societies would hardly approve and the likely outcome would probably be unpleasant!

Ex-gratia payments, as well as the "make-up" of missed payments, are credited by some societies on the date they are received, some wait to the end of the month, others delay credit for 3 months. There is no binding rule, but opinion appears to be veering to immediate credit after receipt (See postscript at end of chapter).

An ex-gratia payment of £100 received with (say) 200 days to run to year-end make up date would show a credit at the year-end reconciliation of (here):

$$£100 \times (1 + (200/365 \times 11/100)) = £106.03$$

Building society options

Pre 1983 the BSA recommended lending rates to all their members who invariably conformed. But during that year several member societies decided to go their own way and what some call the "interest rate cartel" appears to be no longer operative. This "break-away" was given added impetus by the recent legislation regarding the new methods of tax rebates for home loans (see MIRAS below).

Tax rebates

In the UK home loans of £30,000 or less (or the first £30,000 on larger loans) are permitted to receive a tax rebate, at the borrower's basic rate of tax on the INTEREST paid each year. Assuming a basic rate of tax of 30%, for a loan of £1000, at 11% nominal over 25 years, the first tax year's (from April 6th) interest would be $1000 \times 11/100 = £110$ gross and, with 30% tax, the tax rebate would be $110 \times .3 = £33.00$. The following year the tax remit would be $(1110 - 118.80) \times .11 \times 0.3 = 32.71$ and so on. Thus each year as the capital is repaid so the interest element reduces as does the tax remit which is adjusted on the borrower's PAYE or the self employed's tax return the following year.

Mortgage interest relief at source (MIRAS)

In 1983 new legislation permitted the payments to be made NET OF TAX, the method being to treat the nominal quoted rate as net of tax. If the gross rate was (say) 11% then, with a basic tax rate of 30%, the net rate becomes 11 × .7 = 7.70%. ALL calculations thereafter are determined by the net rate, the borrower, for instance, making his B.S. repayments as:

$$\frac{\dfrac{1000}{a_{\overline{25}|}}}{12} \quad \text{at 7.70\% (net of tax at 30\%)} = \text{£7.62 monthly payments} \atop \text{net of tax.}$$

BUT as the Regulations make it quite clear that tax remissions, by way of lower interest rates to produce the net payments, must never be allowed to create the illusion of a reduced effective interest rate, for the disclosure (if required) of the APR *and* the total charge for credit the calculations must always be based on the GROSS perspective, namely the gross payments, NOT the grossed up net payments, here:

$$\frac{1000.00}{9.90a_{\overline{300}|}} \quad \begin{array}{l} \text{at} \quad .928045\% \text{ monthly} \\ \text{at } 11.136539\% \text{ nominal} \\ \text{at } 11.7\% \text{ APR,} \end{array}$$

NOT an APR based on 7.70% namely 7.90%, and the total interest charged is

£(9.90 × 300) − 1000.00 = £1,970.00,

NOT £(7.62 × 300) − 1000.00 = £1,286.00.

Under the "old method", a gross interest rate serviced by gross payments subject to tax remits, the interest element was greater in the earlier years of the loan − and thus so was the tax rebate. Existing or new borrowers opting for the new arrangements, a net interest rate serviced by net payments, will find, when making comparisons, that there will be, initially, a slight increase in net payments. In consequence, of course, the capital value, the balances or loan outstanding at any period of time, will decrease slightly faster than by the "old", conventional, method.

Taking a £10,000.00 loan over 25 years at 11% gross or 7.70% net with monthly payments of £91.67 gross or £76.10 net:

	Conventional method (11%)		
	Year 1		£
Loan			10,000.00
Interest per month	£10,000.00 × .11/12	=	91.67
Tax relief at 30%	£91.67 × .3	=	27.50
Monthly repayments			99.00
Net monthly repayments	£99.00 − 27.50	=	71.50
Balance end Year 1	(10,000 × 1.11) − (99 × 12)	=	9,912.00

Year 2

Loan			9,912.00
Interest per month	£ 9,912.00 X .11/12	=	90.86
Tax relief at 30%	£90.86 X .3	=	27.26
Monthly repayments			99.00
Net monthly repayments	£99.00 − 27.26	=	71.74
Balance end Year 2	(9,912 X 1.11) − (99 X 12)	=	9,814.32

MIRAS method (7.70%)

Year 1			£
Loan			10,000.00
Interest per month	£10,000.00 X .077/12	=	64.17
Monthly payments			76.10
Balance end Year 1 (10,000 X 1.077) − (76.10 X 12)		=	9,856.80

Year 2

Loan			9,856.80
Interest per month	£ 9,856.80 X .077/12	=	63.25
Monthly payments			76.10
Balance end Year 2 (9,856.80 X 1.077) − (76.10 X 12)		=	9,702.57

Which option to select depends on the borrower's individual tax structure; for those with an annual tax liability above the "basic rate", or for those whose "personal residence" is mortgaged above £30,000 the "old method" is necessary − and for those who intend to redeem early, desirable.

The Building Societies Association, 3 Savile Row, London W1 have a variety of useful pamphlets available for those who wish to delve more deeply into MIRAS and related matters.

Mid-term balances

Assume that monthly payments (gross) of £9.90 are correctly made on due date and that, at the first reconciliation, 31 December 1983, the balance was exactly £1000.00. With a nominal rate of 11%, what is the balance on 15 April 1985? (There are 105 days between 31 Dec 84 − 15 Apr 85).

$$1000.00 \times (1 + (11/100)) - (9.90 \times 12) = \ 991.20 \quad \text{Balance end 1984}$$
$$991.20 \times (1 + (11/100 \times 105/365)) \ = 1022.57$$
$$1022.57 - (9.90 \times 3) \qquad\qquad = \ 992.87 \ \text{Balance April 1985}$$

A very different method of calculation than the method outlined in earlier chapters for the conventional "banking" type loans.

Property insurance

Most lenders require total security and as such would require any property mortgaged, the deeds of which comprise collateral for the loan, to be fully insured. Building societies insist on this and, to that end, place the insurance, and pay the annual premiums, on behalf of the borrower. The cost, the insurance charge, is often calculated as 1/12 of the ANNUAL payments which is then divided by 12 and added to the monthly scale payments. In the example above, where the monthly payments (net or gross) were £9.90, the monthly insurance premium would thus be $(118.80/12)/12 = 0.83$ and the new monthly payment will become £10.73. Any such premiums do not enjoy any tax rebates which is why they are added to the net payments.

Penalties for early redemption

Some societies charge for "early redemption", sometimes equivalent to 3 months' payments, sometimes 3 months' interest. The practice varies considerably between individual societies, as does the period for "early redemption", which is usually confined to the first 5–10 years of the loan.

Building societies' and local government authorities' exemption from disclosure

From the previous chapter it will be recalled that the Regulations, made under the Consumer Credit Act, in certain circumstances, require all UK lenders to disclose in quotations and advertisements the term, the Annual Percentage Rate of Charge (the "APR" — the effective rate truncated to one place of decimals) and the total interest charges on the loan, the APR and the "Charge" to include any "extras" such as search, legal and valuation fees etc. The fact that such authorities have previously been *exempt* from disclosure has been the cause of some surprise and criticism.

The reasons for disclosure exemption

The reasons for building societies and local government authorities having been exempted from "disclosure" are often not fully appreciated — hence part of the criticism arising as mentioned above.

Some time before the Regulations of the Consumer Credit Act were due to come into effect, some years ago, it was common knowledge what general course the Regulations related to disclosure were likely to take, and naturally many institutions considered in some detail how best to present their quotations to accord with the type of "disclosure" envisaged. The building societies were no exception, but when they contemplated their future actions they suddenly realised that they, unlike others, had one major problem to overcome — caused by their methods of annual reconciliation.

One of the problems immediately apparent was that of stating the correct term in advertisements etc. We saw above that for the £1000 loan over 25 years at 11% nominal, there was an extra amount of accrued interest of £4.97 to be paid prior to 31 December. It was realised that unless the accrued interest was paid before the year end, the loan balance of £1000 plus £4.97 would stand as the loan over the following 25 years. But if a loan commenced on 1 December, a "worst case scenario", the first payment would not be due until January 1st, AFTER the books had been made up on 31 December. In that case the forward balance would be £1000 **plus** the accrued interest of 1000 X 11/100 X 31/365 = £1009.34 — with no repayment offset.

Remember the building society quotation, above, was "11% over a term of 25 years with monthly payments of £9.90"; the snag which they suddenly faced was that, with the worst-case scenario, the TRUE term was unfortunately NOT 25 years but was:

$$\frac{\text{LOG} \dfrac{(9.90 \times 12)/.11}{[(9.90 \times 12)/.11] - 1009.34}}{\text{LOG} \quad 1.11} = 26.129133 \text{ years}$$

The method proposed at the time to overcome the problem

So what could the Building Societies Association do? At the time the BSA considered that the only way to overcome this erroneous term quotation, in this particular example, was to raise the payments of £9.90 to a level that a quotation of 25 years WOULD be correct. And the method, naturally, employed was to lift the £9.90 monthly payments to:

$$£9.90 \times (1 + (31/365 \times .11)) = £9.992490$$
$$= £9.99 \text{ monthly payments}$$

And to prove that the lifting of the monthly payments, in this particular example, was necessary and indeed correct:

$$\frac{\text{LOG} \dfrac{(9.99 \times 12)/.11}{[(9.99 \times 12)/.11] - 1009.34}}{\text{LOG} \quad 1.11} = \mathbf{24.}969142 \text{ years}$$

And so, some time prior to the regulations being promulgated, new Building Society Mortgage Repayment Tables were prepared which meant a rise in *all* mortgage payments across the board. Not a popular decision – and one which the BSA was most reluctant to pursue. In the event, because this possibility became well known, after the debate in the House of Commons on the Regulations, and on the advice of their professional advisors, the Government decided to exempt from disclosure both building societies and local government authorities.

The new perspective for building societies

But now, once again, the problem resurfaces; for the roles of banks and building societies are likely to become almost interchangable, banks providing home loans and societies cheque books for depositors etc. In general, Government policy appears to be to allow, and to regularise, this equal-footing basis and, to this end, announced in 1984 certain procedures, levels of cash holdings, and a variety of other arcane matters which have no place here – EXCEPT that from September 1985 the exemption from "disclosure" for building societies and local government authorities will no longer apply.

The Options

At the time of writing the members of the Building Societies Association, and indeed other building societies who no longer look to the BSA for guidance, have not decided what action they are going to take when they are forced by the new regulations to disclose the real APR. For obviously something must be done.

There would appear to be three options:
(i)   To change the method of calculation from annual amortisation with annual reconciliation and monthly payments, to the more conventional standards of monthly interest, monthly payments with monthly reconciliation;
(ii) To lift all payments across the board, to avoid providing a spurious "term", as outlined above;
(iii) To invite all borrowers to pay any "excess" should the balance stand above the loan amount borrowed at the end of the "first reconciliation".

My own preference would be option (i), especially as societies are tending towards the banking posture – but old habits die hard and it is doubtful if this sensible solution will be adopted. As obviously no one wants a rise in payments across the board, item (ii), it would appear that item (iii) is a possible outcome. But if item (iii) did become the solution then the APR will have to take account of any accrued interest – and this is bound to cause further problems, such as the correct term to quote and the calculation of the last payment.

To arrive at a correct periodic rate of interest, from which the APR is determined, when the accrued interest is paid is important. With the worst case scenario the borrower would pay his "excess" obviously with his first repayment, in January, and the interest rate difference between paying then or just before the end of year reconciliation would be negligible. But taking the previous example of £1000, over 25 years at 11% nominal where the advance was 199 days prior to the year end, if the accrued interest of £4.97 was paid with the last (December) payment, to find the correct periodic interest payment would require a DCF calculation — and not every small trader has such facilities. However, if this payment was made at the outset, when the loan was advanced (in other words the borrower would receive his loan amount less the accrued interest due for the period between advance and the year end), the difference in the periodic rate would be only fractional — and the APR would be the same owing to the tolerance arising from the "truncation" method of its presentation.

It will be recalled that the year-end balance for this example was £1000.57, so providing the accrued interest was paid before the year end, the present value for calculation purposes would be: £1000.52 − 4.97 = £995.60.

$$\frac{995.60}{9.90a_{\overline{300}|}} \quad \text{requiring} \quad \begin{array}{l} .933069\% \text{ monthly} \\ 11.196824\% \text{ nominal} \\ 11.789684\% \text{ effective} \\ 11.7\% \qquad \text{APR.} \end{array}$$

The term would also be correct, taking the balance at the first year end, namely £995.03 + .57 = £995.60.

$$\frac{\text{LOG } \dfrac{9.90 \times 12}{.11} \Big/ \left[\dfrac{9.90 \times 12}{.11} - 995.60 \right]}{\text{LOG} \qquad\qquad 1.11} = 24.426490 \text{ years.}$$

And add the six months in the first year before first reconciliation:

24.426490 + .5 = 24.926490 years —

fractionally under the required 25 quoted years.

The last payment, in the notional event that the loan ran its full term, would be:

$$995.60 \times 1.11^{24} - 118.80(1.11^{24} - 1)/.11 = £47.015190.$$

The £47 is the balance at the year end at the end of the 24th year. There are 365 − 199 = 166 days to run to maturity so:

47.015190 × (1 + (.11 × 166/365) = £49.37 due in interest.

49.37/9.90 = 4.986869, which means that there are 4 payments of £9.90 due and the LAST payment will be 49.37 − (9.90 × 4) = £9.77.

The Total Amount Paid (TAP) is the total monthly payments PLUS any accrued interest PLUS any fees applicable, here:

$(9.90 \times 300) + 4.97 + \text{nil} = £2,974.97,$

and for a loan of (say) £30,000 cardiac arrest is likely when a first-time borrower is informed, under the disclosure procedure, that his TAP is around £89,250!

One of the problems is how societies are going to quote the term; for the term invariably varies from the reconciliation date onward as to whether the borrower has, or has not, paid the accrued interest due on or before that date. And consequent on which method is employed to determine the term so the APR will vary. A further problem arises over the last payment, again will this affect the APR and the TAP or will it be ignored.

It is obvious that the advertised quoted APR and term will have a general overall perspective, the precise evaluation being made to each individual borrower depending on the exact date of the advance. But if quoted "in general terms" how is the accrued interest to be taken into account? For we have already mentioned that the BSA monthly scale payments assume that they are for a twelve month period, from advance to the end of December. It is possible that a minor adjustment for a general rate/term statement may have to be made to include some element of accrued interest: say half a month's token interest — and this accrued interest could be determined quickly as loan $\times i/24$. $(1000 \times 11/100)/24 = £4.58$ (rounded) which would be deducted from the loan amount before the periodic rate was determined, in order to find the quoted APR.

$$\frac{1000.00 - 4.58}{9.90 a_{\overline{300}|}} \quad \text{requiring} \quad \begin{array}{l} .933275\% \text{ monthly} \\ 11.199300\% \text{ nominal} \\ 11.7\% \quad \text{APR.} \end{array}$$

The final criticism

But until the Societies change their annual reconciliation method and convert to conventional monthly amortising one criticism will inevitably remain, namely " ... the alarming effective rate of building society loans in their latter years ... ", comments seen all too often in newspaper articles and letters from disgruntled borrowers.

Their argument runs as follows: assume a building society 25 year loan of £1000.00, with payments of £9.90 over the term of 300 months, derived from a quoted rate of 11%. Those who make the above criticism calculate as follows:

$$£1000 \times 1.11^{24} - \frac{118.80 \times (1.11^{24} - 1)}{.11} = 100.87 \text{ Balance end 24th year}$$

and then recalculate to find the interest rate for the loan residual amount, £100.87, *over a term of the last 12 months* as follows:

$$\frac{100.87}{9.90a_{\overline{12}|}}$$ which requires a rate of 2.611445% monthly

and this, when multiplied by 12, = 31.34% nominal and 36.25% effective. Against, they point out, a quoted rate of 11.00%!

Apart from the fact that the national average for early redemptions of building society loans is between 6–7 years and that few loans ever run to the quoted termination (these so called "latter years"), I doubt if this criticism is really justified. For ANY annual/monthly converted calculations are bound to find an increasing nominal/effective rate year by year.

At the commencement of this loan the true nominal rate is:

$$\frac{1000.00}{9.90a_{\overline{300}|}} \text{ at } .928045 \times 12 = 11.14\% \text{ nominal}$$
$$= 11.7\% \text{ effective}$$

And, according to the above "final balance" method of calculation, the next year's nominal will be 11.15%, and each year following the rates will rise commensurately, the 22nd year to 15%, 23rd year to 18.21%, the 24th year, as above, to 31.34%.

Those who calculate by this rather esoteric method are somewhat like the unhappy borrower, in Chapter 2, who failed to appreciate that different requirements call for different rates!

Endowment loans

An endowment loan is one which requires the borrower to pay "interest only" monthly payments. The capital value is covered by an endowment insurance policy which repays the loan outstanding at redemption or death of the mortgagor. The additional cost for this facility is usually a quarter of one per cent added to the nominal rate % — for the normal BSA (mortgage) scale payments.

A £8750 loan, UNDER EXISTING B.S. ARRANGEMENTS, at 12% nominal rate, would require 300 monthly payments, EXCLUSIVE of the endowment premium, (here of, say, £160 p.a.) of:

£8750/12 × (12 + .25)/100	= £ 89.33 monthly interest only.	
+ endowment premium payments		
£89.33 + (160/12)	= £102.66	"
Less tax £89.33 × .3	= £–26.80	"
	= £ 75.86 NET cost per month.	

OR applying the net option (MIRAS):

£8750/12 × 12.25 × (.7/100)/12	= £ 62.53 (net) interest only.
£62.53 + (160/12)	= £ 75.86 NET cost per month.

A home annuity scheme

All such schemes, whereby an annuity purchased can equate with the required property mortgage payments, should be referred to tax or financial consultants; for such schemes are not always the most suitable loan arrangements for individual borrowers.

Shared appreciation mortgages (SAM)

The SAM type of loan is quite a recent innovation, dreamed up in the States a few years ago as a result of sudden and substantial mortgage rate increases to a level to which the Americans were unaccustomed and which they resented.

In order to shift a backlog of condominiums, then priced at around $60,000, the estate developer offered purchasers 1/3 off the loan rate providing they agreed to surrender 1/3rd of the sale value, or the valuation price, at the end of 10 years.

The then home loan rate in the States was 15%, usually a fixed rate over a term, and in this arrangement the term would be 10 years so instead, therefore, of repaying $968 monthly for 120 months the purchaser only paid $793, thus making a saving of $175 monthly over ten years.

$$\frac{60,000.00}{968a_{\overline{120}|}} \text{ at 15\% nominal less } \frac{60,000.00}{793a_{\overline{120}|}} \text{ at 10\% nominal}$$

Assuming at the end of 10 years the property neither appreciated nor depreciated, then the rate cost to the purchaser would be:

$$\frac{60,000 - 20,000(1 + i/p)^{-120}}{793a_{\overline{120}|}} \quad \begin{array}{l} \text{1.039922\% monthly} \\ \text{requiring 12.479061\% nominal} \\ \text{13.218140\% effective} \end{array}$$

a saving in rate of around 2.50% p.a. over the 10 years.

The developer, by "losing" £175 per month for 120 months, expects to recoup his loss, 10 years hence, by the capital appreciation related to the 1/3rd surrender value at point of sale or valuation.

Taking a monthly rate of $((15 - 10)/12)\% = .41667\%$, to achieve a break-even figure the surrender value must be:

$$175 \times (1.004167^{120} - 1)/.004167 = \$27,174.00$$

and, in round terms, the property must be sold for, or valued at, $27,000 \times 3$ = $81,000 capital value at end of 10 years — showing a capital appreciation of $100((81,000/60,000) - 1) = 35\%$.

If the developer achieves his object the borrower will have a slightly higher surrender premium, namely $27,000, than for the non-appreciated premium calculated earlier:

$$\frac{60,000 - 27,000(1 + i/p)^{-120}}{793a_{\overline{120}|}} \quad \begin{array}{l} \text{requiring } \text{1.098759\% monthly} \\ \text{13.185110\% nominal} \\ \text{14.011827\% effective} \end{array}$$

But this rate is still lower than if the borrower had opted for the normal 15% home loan rate. According to the above the property cost the owner $60,000 but at the end of 10 years the surrender value is $27,000; nevertheless he saved himself $175 monthly, the difference between monthly payments of $968 and $793.

The shrewd home owner could, of course, have invested $175 monthly at (say) 10% nominal to provide himself with a "nest egg", a future value, of just over $36,000.

These schemes, however, may not always be as financially attractive as they might appear on paper − and of course rest on the assumption that house prices will always rise, admittedly an assumption not altogether without some justification.

Postscript

What follows is only tenuously connected (hence a postscript) with the practice of building societies − and refers to the comment earlier as to when ex-gratia payments should be credited.

We all know that there is a "banker's turn" usually (in very general terms) of around 2% to 3% between the lending and borrowing rates of interest. While we have to borrow at (say) 11% we can only lend at a rate of interest of (say) 8% − in any event, whatever the lending rate, it is substantially less than the borrowing rate!

Now if we, as borrowers, make an ex gratia payment to our friendly building society, what are we doing in practice? By making this ex gratia payment we are not only reducing our overall loan but (from deposit date to the make-up-books year-end) we are also being credited with days' interest − at the same nominal rate of interest which we are paying for our home loan. In effect, therefore, we are obtaining credit at the higher borrowing rate − not the lower lending rate! And whether a large bank or small lender, few care to give credit, at 2% or 3% higher than the "going rate".

How then can this disproportionate ex gratia payment rate be ironed out? A method often employed, which admittedly is not a very scientific one, but which is in practice generally agreed to "work", is to delay the credit − by (say) three months.

Assume an ex gratia payment of £100.00 and a loan interest rate of 11%. The value of this payment at the end of 12 months would be £100 × 1.11 = £111.00, the interest being £11. Obviously if monthly reconciliation was required monthly compounding calculations could be made but working, simply, in annual terms, if the credit was delayed by three months:

$$£100 \times (1 + (.11 \times 9/12)) = £108.25 = £8.25 \text{ year-end interest.}$$

This would provide a "turn" of between 11% and 8.25% which is, in this case, a difference of 2.75%.

Given lending (11%) and borrowing (8.25%) rates above, to find the credit time delay: $12 - (8.25 \times 12/11) = 3$ months.

Assume that the building societies' (gross) mortgage rate (i.e., lending to the public rate) is 13% nominal and that the interest rate to members of the public who deposit their savings with a society (i.e., lent to the society) was 11%. What is the delaying credit time factor?

$12 - (11 \times 12/13) = 1.846154$ months $= 1$ month and 25 days, say a 2 months' delaying credit time factor.

Above was treating the days' interest between deposit date and reconciliation date as simple interest. If, in a context other than Building Societies, it was required to calculate by compound interest:

$$\frac{\text{LOG } 1.11}{\text{LOG } 1.13} = .853887 \text{ years}$$

$$.853887 \times 12 = 10.246641 \text{ months.}$$

$$12 - 10.246641 = 1.753359 \text{ months}$$

and this makes $(1.753359 - 1) \times 30 = 1$ month and 22.6 days

Check:

$$£100 \times 1.13^{10.246641/12} = £111.00$$

CHAPTER 8

Odd Days

There is inevitably a difference between theory and practice, and while the examples in previous chapters are correct and necessary — as examples — practical considerations must also be considered.

In Chapter 7 when the methods of calculation by UK building societies were examined, for their methods differ substantially from the conventional "banking" methods, it was seen that when a loan is advanced it can commence on any date, for the "days interest" are calculated between the advance date and the year-end date, the day when the Societies "make-up" their accounts.

But, with conventional methods, problems can sometimes arise as to when exactly to commence a loan. In the olden days BC (before computers), the usual practice was for lenders, both private and institutional, to require the first payment to be one calendar month (if repayments were monthly) after "closing", the date of the advance, and in that case there was no problem. With the advent of computerised accounting, however, institutions often prefer all their borrowers to make their periodic repayments on one day of th month, say the 1st of each month, or the 30th, sometimes the 15th.

Convenient as this may be for the lender, it raises certain problems if the borrower wishes, as many do, to take out a loan to commence at a date different from the "lender's payment date" for inevitably, in that case, there will be a number of odd days interest to be considered.

The question is how are these odd days to be considered and calculated.

EXAMPLE
Assume a loan of £3000.00 over 24 months at a *simple interest* rate of 6%. The payments required will be $3000 \times (1 + (6/100 \times 2)) = 3360$ and $3360/24 = £140.00$ monthly. The periodic interest rate is .927221972% and the nominal 11.12666367%.

Compound interest method

Supposing that the lender requires all the repayment amounts to be paid on the 1st of each calendar month and that the borrower wishes to receive the loan amount on 15 March, some 15 days prior to 1 April. As a result, because payments are "in arrears", the first instalment will be paid to the lender

1 month + 15 days after the advance is made – 1st May. But not £140, for there are now some 15 days interest to be accounted for.

In effect, therefore, the lender is making two separate loans, £3000.00 for 24 months and £3000.00 for 15 days, joined into one complete loan. Working with a true monthly rate of interest of 0.927221972%, the "new joint loan" (the original loan plus the accrued interest) will be:

$$3000 \times 1.009272220^{15 \times 12/365} = £3013.685721$$

Of course the borrower could pay the lender the £13.69 fifteen days after the advance, and continue with the original loan unaltered; but the normal practice is to recalculate the payments according to the joint loan value, namely:

$$\frac{3013.685721}{a_{\overline{24}|}} \text{ at } .927221972\% \text{ monthly}$$

which provides new monthly payments of £140.64.

Admittedly, the lender could ignore the extra 15 days' interest and permit the borrower to continue to pay, in this example, £140.00 each month for 24 months. In that case the return to lender will be reduced accordingly:

$$\frac{3000.00(1 + i/p)^{15 \times 12/365}}{140.00 a_{\overline{24}|}} \text{ at } X\% \text{ monthly}$$

and this equation provides a computed monthly rate of .890654061% giving a nominal of 10.69% (IRR).

Balances on loans outstanding

From previous chapters we know how to determine loans outstanding (LOS) under normal circumstances; with "odd days" there is little or no difficulty. Let n = the number of periods in the term and k the odd days periodic fraction. In the above example as n = 24 and 15 × 12/365 = .493151 so n + k = 24.493151.

$$PV \times (1 + i/p)^{(n+k)} - PMT \ s_{\overline{n}|} \text{ at } .927222\% = LOS (n)$$

Find the LOS after 6 months:

$$£3000 \times 1.0092722^{6.493151} - 140.64(1.0092722^6 - 1)/.0092722$$
$$= £2321.64$$

To find the number of "odd days" (compound interest method)

Given repayments, the loan, and the rate % it is sometimes necessary to find the number of odd days previously structured.

Taking the above example, calculate the loan amount derived from the rate, payments and the integer "np" factor. (Let Loan″ = the original loan + odd days' interest.)

$$140.64_{\overline{24}|} \text{ at } .927220\% \qquad = 3013.685721 \text{ Loan}''$$

$$\frac{\text{LOG loan}''/\text{loan}}{\text{LOG } (1 + i/p)} \times 365/12 = \text{Days} = \frac{\text{LOG } 3013.685721/3000}{\text{LOG } 1.00927222} \times 365/12$$

$$= 15 \text{ days.}$$

If the basic term (here 24 months) was *not* known, then find the term by the conventional method, outlined in Chapter 2, which in this case will present as:

$$\frac{\text{LOG } (140.64/.0092722)/((140.64/.0092722) - 3013.69)}{\text{LOG } 1.009272220} = 23.999745$$

This must obviously be rounded to 24 months.

The "Disclosure Regulations" issued by the UK Office of Fair Trading provide a relevant example:

A £200 loan is advanced on May 15th with 24 equal monthly payments commencing on July 1st. The total charge for credit is £25.60 which *includes* the interest due for the odd days. The problem, here, is to check the APR which is stated as 11.9%.

As payments are in arrears and as the first required payment is on July 1st, the monthly date prior is June 1st. In that event as the loan was advanced May 15th there are 17 odd interest days. The total interest being £25.60 means that the payments are calculated as £25.60 (charge) + £200 (loan) which when divided by 24 (months) = £9.40 monthly payments.

$$\frac{200 \times (1 + i/p)^{(17 \times 12/365)}}{(1 - (1 + i/p)^{-24})/(i/p)} = 9.40 \text{ Pmts}$$

It will be found that the computed i/p = .00942898929% with a nominal rate of 11.314787% will convert to 11.920405% effective. The APR (UK), therefore, is 11.9%.

Simple interest method

Reverting to the original example, the US statistician would have a somewhat different perspective, working as he would be from a *simple* interest quotation, here of 6%:

$$\$3000.00 \times 6/100 \times 15/365 = \$7.39260274 \text{ accrued interest due.}$$

The US method then is to divide the a/i between each month, namely:

$$\$140 + (7.39260274/24) = \$140.31 \text{ new payments.}$$

If it was necessary to inform the borrower of the (US) APR, the true NOM-INAL rate, it would present as:

$$\frac{\$3000.00 \times (1 + (i/p \times 15 \times 12/365))}{140.31 \ a_{\overline{24}|}} \quad \text{at X\%}$$

Assuming that the i/p = .00908334349 = 10.90% nominal the "odd days" *simple interest method* amortisation is:

$$\frac{\$3000 \times (1 + (.00908334349 \times 15 \times 12/365)}{(1 - 1.00908334349^{-24})/.00908334349} = \$140.31 \text{ pmts}$$

To find LOS (6):

$$((3000 \times (1 + (.0090833 \times 15 \times 12/365)) \times 1.0090833^6)$$

$$- (140.31(1.0090833^6 - 1)/.0090833) = 2320.24 \text{ LOS}(6)$$

To find the number of odd days (simple interest method)

Taking the above example either with the SI interest rate of 6%:

$$\frac{(140.31 - 140) \times 24}{3000 \times .06} \times 365 = 15 \text{ days}$$

or with the i/p as .9080334349:

$$\left(\left(\frac{140.31 a_{\overline{24}|}}{3000.00} - 1\right)/0.009083343\right) \times 365/12 = 15 \text{ days}$$

USA Truth in Lending

Having demonstrated the difference in approach between the European compound interest method and the US simple interest perspective, whereby the accrued interest is split between the original monthly payments, it might be a convenient place to reflect on why such arrangements are made.

There are 51 States in the USA and each state legislature is naturally jealous of its independence — and tends to resist any interference of a Federal nature. Nevertheless in the mid 60s it became imperative that some universal arrangements be made to obtain some standardisation in all the different State lending rates to protect the borrowing public.

So on May 29th 1969 the (Federal) Truth in Lending New Common Standard Public Law (90–321) was duly promulgated. This Act, inter alia, laid down that any borrower subject to the "add-on" (simple interest) quotation must be informed of the APR rate (The "annual percentage rate", the US *nominal* interest rate) — which although useful did not go quite so far down the disclosure road as did the UK some years later.

But although this law was passed there still remain difficulties of individual states' legislation and the extraordinary (to European eyes) number of different categories of lending, each with its own special requirements of max/min rates and methods of calculation.

Some of the categories, all with different rates and methods, are listed below — and there are 51 states!

Small loan lending
Industrial bank and companies lending
Commercial and personal loans
Mutual savings bank and personal loans
Credit loans (credit cards etc.)
Savings and loan associations
Auto-investment sales finance
Finance for "other goods"
Insurance premium finance
Second mortgage lending (wrap around mortgages)
Education loans
Revolving charge accounts
Bank revolving credit

One clause in the above Act stipulates that in any loan accrued interest must NOT be added to the capital balances; and this was the reason why the US statistician calculated, in the example above, by splitting up the total days' interest between the periods and adding the small amount to each of the original payments and did not follow the UK example of creating new payments from the increased capital value.

CHAPTER 9

Short-Term Loans, Rule 78, Constant Payments to Principal, Second (Wrap-Around) Mortgages

Rule 78 method

This method of calculation for repayment loans is based on a simple interest quotation which, being simple to calculate, is often employed for small loans. While it is still employed extensively in the USA, for some State legislation requires its use, in the UK it has become slightly outdated since the advent of the Consumer Credit Act whose regulations require a disclosed APR, which of course requires the calculation, and knowledge, of the true periodic and nominal rates of interest — and if these are known, many lenders now find a simple interest quotation unnecessary. Rule 78 (which is also used in depreciation calculations) is also referred to as the "Sum of the Digits" (SOD) but, doubtless in view of this rather questionable mnemonic, "Sum of the Years Digits" (SOYD) appears recently to have become more fashionable!

Sum of the Digits Schedule

LOAN $3000.00   TERM 24 months   RATE 6%

Months	Interest paid	Capital repaid	Capital balances
			3000.00
1	28.80	111.20	2888.80
2	27.60	112.40	2776.40
3	26.40	113.60	2662.80
4	25.20	114.80	2548.00
5	24.00	116.00	2432.00
6	22.80	117.20	2314.80
7	21.60	118.40	2196.40
8	20.40	119.60	2076.80
9	19.20	120.80	1956.00
10	18.00	122.00	1834.00
11	16.80	123.20	1710.80
12	15.60	124.40	1586.40
13	14.40	125.60	1460.80
14	13.20	126.80	1334.00
15	12.00	128.00	1206.00
16	10.80	129.20	1076.80

17	9.60	130.40	946.40
18	8.40	131.60	814.80
19	7.20	132.80	682.00
20	6.00	134.00	548.00
21	4.80	135.20	412.80
22	3.60	136.40	276.40
23	2.40	137.60	138.80
24	1.20	138.80	0.00
	360.00	3000.00	

The example above, a short term loan of $3000.00 over 2 years with its *simple interest* rate of 6.00%, will require monthly repayments of:

$$(3000 \times (1 + (6/100 \times 2)))/24 = \$140$$

and, if calculated conventionally by the annuities ordinary methods employed in previous chapters, the true nominal rate will present as:

$$\frac{3000.00}{140a_{\overline{24}|}} \text{ at } 0.927222\% \text{ monthly}$$
at 11.126664% nominal

The Rule 78 method

The term "Rule 78" or the sum of the digits arises from the number of digits in the months of any one year, namely, months $1 + 2 + 3 + 4 + \ldots 12$ equals 78, or calculated as $12 \times 13/2 = 78$.

In this example the "charge" is $(140 \times 24) - 3000 = \$360$ and this factor divided by the sum of the digits (in this example TWO years $24 \times 25/2 = 300$): $360/300 = 1.20$ interest factor.

A detailed examination of the schedule above will demonstrate how each succeeding value is determined; for example it will be seen that the interest factor (here 1.20) reduces each monthly interest payment and that the interest subtracted from the monthly payments ($140.00) provides the capital repayment.

The values mostly required by statisticians using this method are the "rebate", (the "unearned interest") and the "remaining principal due".

Below are various calculations with the required formulae; all the examples are based on the schedule example above — so that comparisons can be made to the schedule if necessary.

Legend   (This example)
                                      $
I = The charge   (360)
P = Payments per period   (140)
N = Total number of periods   (24)
T = Number of periods UNpaid.

Note

If any period (p) is required, say the 5th month, the value will be (N − p); above 24 − 5 = T = 19 as there are 19 UNPAID portions.

To find balances:

$$PT - \left(I \times \frac{T(T+1)}{N(N+1)}\right) = \text{Balance (n)}$$

Balance at end of 5th month:

$$140(24-5) - 360\left(\frac{19 \times 20}{24 \times 25}\right) =$$

$$2660 \quad - \quad 228 \quad = \$2432.00$$

To find the total interest paid at the end of the 5 months

$$I \quad - I\left(\frac{T(T+1)}{N(N+1)}\right)$$

$$360 - 228 \qquad\qquad = \$132.00$$

To find the interest paid in the FIRST year

$$I \times \left(1 - \frac{T(T+1)}{N(N+1)}\right)$$

$$360 \times \left(1 - \frac{12 \times 13}{24 \times 25}\right) \qquad = \$266.40$$

To find the interest in the 14th month

$$(T+1) \times \text{int. factor}$$

$$(24-14+1) \times 1.2 \qquad = \$ \ 13.20$$

To find the rebate at the end of the 14th month

$$T \times \frac{I(N-p+1)}{N(N+1)}$$

$$(24-14) \times \frac{360(24-14+1)}{24 \times 25} = \$ \ 66.00 \ \text{rebate}_{14}$$

To find the remaining principal due at the end of the 14th month

$$[(N-p) \quad \times \quad P \ ] - \text{Rebate}$$

$$[(24-14) \times 140] \ - \ 66 \qquad = \$1334.00 \ \text{balance due}_{14}$$

Penalties

In short-term loans early redemption is not popular with lenders and thus
often penalties are imposed. In the past "three months' payments" was often
the custom, but these amounts nowadays are generally considered as somewhat excessive. In this example, for instance, $140 \times 3 = \$420$, which is 14%
of the loan value! (See Chapter 6.)

Comparisons

The values differ only fractionally from the normal conventionally calculated
annuities loan — but it will be realised that to determine outstanding balances
etc, by normal methods, the interest rate must be computer-calculated first;
above, without such a necessity, the calculations are thus considerably
simpler — hence the popularity of this method before the advent of the microchip. And, indeed, this was one of the main reasons why the simple interest
(the add-on) rate was in past days almost the only method of short-term loan
quotations.

Looking back at the answers to the above examples, if such calculations
had been made conventionally, as annuities ordinary, the values would be
respectively:

$2,428.58, $128.58, $252.18, $12.34, $68.83, $1,331.17.

EXAMPLE

Assume a loan of £200 which is to be repaid by one payment of £225 at the
end of 280 days. The borrower wishes to settle at the end of 120 days but the
penalty for early settlement is 2 months' interest. What will be borrower
settle for?

$$(225 - 200) \times [(280 - 120) - (30 + 31)]/280 = \text{ rebate}$$

$$25 \qquad \times \qquad 99/280 \qquad = £\ \ 8.84$$

$$\text{Settlement amount } = £225 - 8.84 \qquad = £216.16$$

This type of Rule 78 method avoids finding the interest rate but which, of
course, could in this example be found and reworked as follows:

$$[(225/200) - 1] \times 365/280 \times 100 \ \ = 16.29464286\%$$

and so:

$$£200 \times 16.29464286/100 \times 99/365 = £8.84 \text{ interest.}$$

or

$$£200 \times [1 + (16.29464286/100 \times (280 - 99)/365)] = £216.16$$

CONSTANT PAYMENT TO PRINCIPAL LOANS

This type of loan is a variation on the conventional annuities ordinary loan, previously outlined, and is structured in such a way that the principal is repaid in equal instalments, the interest on the outstanding balance being paid at the same time i.e., UNeven periodic payments.

Assume a loan of £1000, at 10% asking (quoted) interest, over a term of 10 years, the payments to be annual.

£1000/10 = £100.00 are the annual repayments of principal.

A schedule will demonstrate how the interest is added to this base of £100 and how the periodic payments consequently reduce at each payment.

Year	Interest due	Pmt to Principal	Total Pmt	Balance
1.	100	100	200	900
2.	90	100	190	800
3.	80	100	180	700
4.	70	100	170	600
5.	60	100	160	500
6	50	100	150	400
7.	40	100	140	300
8.	30	100	130	200
9.	20	100	120	100
10.	10	100	110	0
	550	1000	1550	

Formulae

1. *To determine the total charge for credit*

$$\frac{(\text{Loan} \times i/p) + (\text{Pmts to Cap} \times i/p)}{2} \times n = \text{Total interest}$$

$$\frac{(1000 \times .10) + (100 \times .10)}{2} \times 10 = \text{£550 interest}$$

2. *To determine interest per period (p)*

$$(\text{Loan} \times i/p) - (\text{Pmts to Cap} \times i/p \times (p-1)) = \text{interest (p)}$$

$$(1000 \times .10) - (100 \times .10 \times 6) = \text{£40.00 interest period}_7$$

3. *To determine the interest due between periods j and k inclusive*

If j = 4th year and k = 8th year find the interest accruing between years 4 and 8 inclusive:

$$\frac{int(j) + int(k)}{2} \times ((j - k) + 1) = \text{Total interest between j–k incl.}$$

$$\frac{70 + 30}{2} \times ((8 - 4) + 1) \qquad = £250.00 \text{ interest between periods}$$
$$4 \text{ and } 8 \text{ incl.}$$

Assume a loan of £6000.00 over a period of 10 years with monthly payments to principal of £50.00 at a nominal rate of 7.50%. What is the total interest charge?

$$\frac{(6000 \times 7.5/1200) + (50 \times 7.5/1200)}{2} \times 120 \quad = £2268.75$$

Alternatively:

$$\frac{(\text{Loan} + \text{Pmts}) \times i \times n}{2} \qquad = \text{Charges}$$

$$\frac{(6000 + 50) \times .075 \times 10}{2} \qquad = £2268.75$$

And the interest for period 50 is:

$$(6000 \times 7.5/1200) - (50 \times 7.5/1200 \times (50 - 1)) = £22.1875$$

Banker's loans – constant payments to principal

Whereas the above calculations provide the general method of calculation with the required formulae etc, in practice such loans are not quite as simple as those shown above. For when contracting a loan such as this from a bank the usual practice is for interest to be calculated daily and for the payments to be monthly with the compounding quarterly.

This will need a computer program for precise accuracy and for an understanding of how this or that bank calculates the interest due if a payment falls on a Saturday or Sunday (non-banking day). Some banks treat the next interest day as the following Monday and adjust the following month, that is the number of days in each month.

I don't propose to bore the reader with a series of schedules for various types of bank loans but for the record a loan of £4000.00 at 16.50%, *quarterly* compounding, for three years from 28 November 1980 with monthly payments would have monthly payments of 4000/36 = £111.11.

The first thing to note is that £111.11 × 36 = £3999.96, showing that somewhere along the line 4 pence must be added – banks don't like losing even 4p!

In fact the total interest in general terms could be found as:

$$\frac{4000 + (111.11 \times 3) + .04}{2} \times 16.5/400 \times 12 = £1072.51$$

If the payments were monthly AND the interest charged *monthly*:

$$\frac{4000 + 111.11 + .04}{2} \times 16.5/100 \times 3 = £1017.51$$

whereas a bank computer, calculating the number of days in each month, with quarterly instalments, would find the total charge as £1016.56.

(When a month has a "bank holiday" (i.e., a non-banking day) the month is increased by ONE day and the month following is decreased by ONE day — a pre-computer-era practice which has carried over to the present time!)

Constant payments to principal but withheld until maturity

Occasionally the "balloon" method is employed with this type of loan and the schedule below will perhaps explain why such a loan is sometimes referred to as the "upside down serial loan". The formulae above obtain except that formula (2) above, to find the interest per period, now becomes the interest *withheld* per period and is found as follows:

$$(\text{Loan} \times i/p) - (\text{Pmts to Cap} \times i/p \times (np - p)) = \text{interest (p) WITHHELD}$$

Taking the previous schedule loan:

Year	Pmts to principal	Total pmts	Balances		Interest due
1.	100	100	100 × 10/100		10
2.	100	100	200 ×	"	20
3.	100	100	300 ×	"	30
4.	100	100	400 ×	"	40
5.	100	100	500 ×	"	50
6.	100	100	600 ×	"	60
7.	100	100	700 ×	"	70
8.	100	100	800 ×	"	80
9.	100	100	900 ×	"	90
10.	100	100	1000 ×	"	100
	1000	1000			550

Assume a £6000 loan over 120 months at 7.50% nominal, with payments to principal but with the interest due to be withheld to maturity. What is the total interest charge and what is the withheld interest amount for the 6th month?

$$\frac{(6000 \times 7.50/1200) + (6000/120 \times 7.50/1200)}{2} \times 120 = \$2,268.75$$

charge,

and $37.50 - ((50 \times .00625 \times (120 - 6)) = \$1.875$

Interest at end month 6, withheld.

SECOND (OR "WRAP AROUND") MORTGAGES

Unhappily, on many occasions the UK home owner, already mortgaged, wishes to raise further loans and, at the same time, his only real asset is his home. He therefore seeks a "second mortgage". In the UK a second loan usually requires another lender with the borrower supplying appropriate and acceptable collateral. In other words a building society would not provide a "second mortgage" and if a bank was already lending against a property a secondary loan would require further security. In rare cases where a secondary loan is granted against security held for the first mortgage then the secondary lender will have a lien on the property in the event of "failure" by the mortgagor.

But in the United States and Canada a second mortgage or "wrap around" mortgage is normal and is merely a "refinancing" operation. One of the reasons being that such loans are usually somewhat simpler to arrange in those countries where the primary loan is at a fixed rate over a fixed term as opposed to a variable rate (as in the UK, where rates for home loans are usually tied to the current building society and bank lending rates).

In the case of a wrap around mortgage the "secondary" lender, who provides the required secondary funding, in effect "takes over" the responsibility of the first mortgage.

Assume that the borrower of a first mortgage requires a second mortgage and his first home loan has a further 12 years to run (144 months) and the balance at the time of the wrap around arrangement is $20,000.00. His monthly payments are $314, and therefore his present nominal rate is around 16%:

$$\frac{20000.00}{314 \, a_{\overline{144}|}} \quad \text{at} \quad 1.338639\%$$

$(\times 12)\qquad = 16.06\%$ nominal.

Assuming that the secondary lender quotes a rate of 20% and is prepared to lend a *further* $10,000.00 the new payments required by the lender will be:

$$\frac{30000.00}{a_{\overline{144}|}} \quad \text{at} \ (20/12)\% \quad = \$551.00 \ \text{monthly pmts}$$

The yield return to the secondary lender is as follows:

$$\frac{(30000 - 20000)}{(551 - 314) \, a_{\overline{144}|}} \quad \text{at} \quad 2.277433\% \ \text{monthly}$$
$$\text{at} \ 27.329201\% \ \text{nominal}$$
$$\text{at} \ 31.026113\% \ \text{effective.}$$

A secondary mortgage with a residual amount (a balloon end payment) presents no calculation problems providing one keeps to the normal rules where balloon payments are concerned.

A wrap-around loan with differing terms

Wrap-around or "refinancing" mortgages with a variable term can cause difficulties. For example, a client has an existing mortgage with an existing balance of $30,000 over a remaining term of 200 months, the monthly payments being $350.00. He requires a second mortgage for $20,000 over the next 20 years (240 months) and proposes to pay a balloon payment at the end of the term of $15,000. If you accept the "wrap around" required monthly payments of $170.00, what is the lender's rate of return?

Because of the difference in the term parameters, 200 and 240 months, there is no easy method of finding the rate; and so the only method is to employ a discounted cash flow (DCF) calculation, the methods of which were examined in detail in Chapter 4.

In fact the internal rate of return, the yield to the supplier of the secondary mortgage, is 21.731145% nominal, providing an effective rate of 24.032099%.

Taking the i/p as 21.73145/1200 = 0.018109287,

Investment $30,000 − 20,000 $= -10,000.00$

Cash Flows

$$(350 - 170) \times \frac{(1 - 1.01811^{-200})/.01811 \times 1.01811}{1.01811} = 9665.18$$

$$170 \times \ddot{a}_{\overline{39}|} \times 1.01811^{-201} = 130.49$$

$$(170 + 15,000) \times 1.01811^{-240} = 204.33$$

Net present value (NPV) $\quad$ 0.00

Proving, as the NPV = 0.00, that the periodic rate of return of 1.810928736% monthly is precisely the correct rate required to service the two loans. For reasons of space, the rate, 1.811%, was shortened above but the calculation was worked to its full value.

It will be seen from the above that payments for the first 200 months were calculated the same way as for normal second mortgages, using the difference between the first and second mortgage payments. But for the remaining 40 months the full payment for the second mortgage had to be calculated and the balloon had to be added to the last payment.

Days' money

To revert to banking methods of providing interest mentioned a few pages back, a small point perhaps not generally known is that "days' money" is at compound interest during bank working days (weekdays) but at SIMPLE interest over week-ends (Saturdays, Sundays and bank holidays). The end difference between full compound days interest over the full term and that of simple interest at weekends is negligible — around a couple of pounds per million pound deposit, at (say) a nominal rate of 15% over 30 days with 4 weekends intervening. This, of course, also makes the rather doubtful assumption that the daily rate remains constant for 30 days. On both counts therefore I doubt if a formula would be of much practical value, nevertheless where t = total number of days and k = number of weekends intervening:

$$\text{Deposit} \times (1 + (\text{NOM}/36500))^{t-(3\times k)} \times (1 + (3 \times \text{NOM}/36500))^{k} = \text{FV}$$

$$£1,000,000 \times 1.00041096^{30-(3\times 4)} \quad \times 1.00123288^{4} = £1,012,400.47$$

Whereas:

$$£1,000,000 \times 1.00041096^{30} \qquad\qquad = £1,012,402.52$$

CHAPTER 10

Variations in Rate Payment Methods

Conversions

Lenders, whether individuals, banks or institutions, often have variations on how they charge interest on their loans or the method of repayment. For example, mortgages in Canada usually have the interest calculated on a semi-annual basis but payments are still required monthly.

In such cases, where the interest structure differs from the payment structure, the tip for calculation purposes is, FIRST, to convert the INTEREST rate to its EFFECTIVE value and THEN reconvert that effective to the NOMINAL rate based on the PAYMENT structure. And if that sounds a little confusing perhaps an example will help.

Take, for example, the Canadian mortgage discipline mentioned earlier. Assume a nominal rate of 11%, the understanding being that the interest is calculated semi-annually but the payments are to be made monthly.

First bring the investment nominal rate to its semi-annual effective equivalent:

$$\left\{ \left(1 + \frac{11}{200}\right)^2 - 1 \right\} \times 100 = 11.30250\%$$

Then reduce this resulting effective rate to its "nominal rate" based on its periodic structure.

$$\left\{ \left(1 + \frac{11.30250}{100}\right)^{1/12} - 1 \right\} \times 1200 = 10.75607280\% \text{ nominal.}$$

Thus the "working" rate becomes 10.75607280/12 = .89633940%.

In this manner it will be appreciated that, as a result, the *effective* rate of each IRR is the *same* i.e., the effective rate of 11% semi-annual interest charged is 11.3025% and the effective rate of the resulting period payment rate, namely 10.75607%, is also 11.3025%.

The Canadian monthly payments when calculated for a $1000 loan, at 11% nominal over 25 years, are not $9.80, as we have seen in conventional monthly calculations in other chapters, but are:

$$\frac{1000.00}{a_{\overline{300}|}} \text{ at } (10.75607285/12)\%$$

which finds monthly payments of 9.62529176 = $Cdn 9.63 Pmts

"Continuous compounding"

We already know that a £1000 loan conventionally calculated at 11% nominal requires 300 monthly repayments of £9.80 and we also know (Chapter 1) that 11% converted to "continuous compounding" provides a rate of:

$$100(e^{.11} - 1) = 11.6278070\%$$

and so

$$\frac{1000.00}{a_{\overline{300}|}} \text{ at } (11.6278070/12)\% \text{ monthly}$$

will find payments of £10.26 monthly, a value so much greater than £9.80 as to give rise to the suspicion that something is wrong somewhere! And of course it is: for, if you recall, the 11.6278% is the EFFECTIVE rate, the ultimate in rates of interest.

So this rate must be converted to its nominal value for monthly payments as $100[(1 + (11.6278070/100)^{1/12}) - 1] = .92088090\%$, and employing this monthly rate the payments will become more realistic, namely £9.84 monthly. An even quicker way, however, to find the "working rate", namely the $(1 + i/p)$ is:

$$e^{.11/12} = 2.71828^{.11/12} = 1.009208809(1 + i/p)$$

Advance payments

Sometimes both borrower and lender agree that for some reason a repayment loan, the security being property, will be structured with a number of payments being paid in advance — a number of advance payments greater than merely one, for one only, of course, implies an annuities "due" calculation.

Assume a loan of £20,000 at 10% nominal, over a term of 5 years with 60 monthly payments of £425 with the first SIX payments being made in advance. In that case what is the true rate — and the APR (UK) which must be advised to the borrower? Obviously if some payments are made in advance and the original payments are maintained, then the i/p will alter accordingly:

$$\frac{20,000 - (425 \times 6)}{425a_{\overline{(60-6)}|}} \text{ at } x\%$$

and in this case the nominal and APR present as 12.5976% and 13.3% respectively.

But what happens if the interest rate is a fixed requirement and it becomes necessary to find the correct payments, related to a number of advance payments as opposed to just one advance payment?

Some years ago a client company requiring certain borrowers, for certain types of loans, to make 3 payments in advance asked for a short computer/

calculator program. For to find the new payments my client, apparently, was guessing a possible payment structure, checking it against a calculated value, and when found to be incorrect, interpolating and essaying further attempts taking, I gathered, some 20 minutes to provide an answer "to 3 places of decimals". His method of interpolation obviously left much to be desired, for with intelligent interpolation ANY guess, not totally unrealistic, can be made to find the required payments.

For instance, a loan of £20,000, at 12% nominal, over a term of 5 years would require £440 monthly payments — with 3 monthly payments in advance guess £400:

$$400a_{\overline{60-3}|} \text{ at } (12/12)\% = \text{a PV of } £17,314.85$$

As £17,314.85 + (400 × 3) = £18,514.85 is NOT the required £20,000, a quick adjustment provides the correct monthly payments:

$$400 \times 20000/18514.85 = £432.09 \text{ (adjusted for 3 advance pmts).}$$

A junior school calculation provides the correct method of approach:

$$\frac{100 - 3X}{7} = X \qquad 100 - 3X = 7X$$
$$100 = 7X + 3X$$
$$100 = X(7 + 3)$$
$$\frac{100}{7 + 3} = X \qquad\qquad X = 10$$

and an unrealistic but look-alike loan (£100 loan, at 10% with annual payments, over 10 years with 3 advance payments) demonstrates the practical result:

$$\frac{100}{a_{\overline{7}|} + 3} \text{ at } 10\% = \frac{100}{((1 - 1.10^{-7})/.10) + 3}$$

$$\frac{100}{4.868 + 3} = £12.71 \text{ Pmts}$$

Check:

$$\frac{100}{12.71a_{\overline{7}|}} \text{ at } 10\% = £61.87 \text{ Loan}$$

and   £61.87 + (3 × 12.71) = £100 Actual Loan

and above:

$$\frac{20,000}{a_{\overline{57}|} + 3} \text{ at } (12/12)\% = £432.09 \text{ Pmts.}$$

If any loans wth advance payments have *residual balances* (a balloon factor), to be paid with the last payment, then the loan value must be reduced by the discounted amount of the balloon.

$$\frac{Loan - (balloon/(1 + i/p)^{(np-y)}}{a_{\overline{(np-y)}|} + y} = Pmts$$

Where y = the number of advance payments.

Annuities ORD calculations are ALWAYS employed for advance payments unless the advance is only ONE payment (annuities DUE).

Delayed end-of-term payments

A loan of £10,000 over 25 years with a balloon payment of £5,000 at 11% nominal requires servicing by £94.84 monthly payments.

$$\frac{10,000.00 - (5000/(1 + i/p)^{300})}{94.84a_{\overline{300}|}} \quad at\ (11/12)\%\ monthly$$

In this case the "charge" is $((94.84 \times 300) + 5000) - 10,000 = £23,452.00$.

Assume that the negotiated structure of this particular loan is that the balloon payment of £5,000 can be delayed by ONE period (month). The only difference to the conventional structure is that the lender is "out of money" for one period. In this event, either the payments must be fractionally raised to take account of the lengthened balloon payment term, or the lender's yield return will be commensurately reduced.

The new payments will simply be found from:

$$\frac{10,000.00 - (5,000.00 \times (1 + i/p)^{-301})}{a_{\overline{300}|}} \quad at\ (11/12)\%\ monthly$$

$$\frac{10,000 - (5,000 \times 1.00916667^{-301})}{a_{\overline{300}|}} = £94.87\ Pmts$$

Or if the payments remained at £94.84, the fractionally reduced rate will become 10.996426% nominal, found by a DCF calculation.

Low start mortgage repayments

High interest for home loans inevitably causes concern to prospective house purchasers, especially first-time buyers.

Some years ago, in an effort to provide some help to the lower income home purchasers, the British government provided an option scheme whereby, if they wished, borrowers of home loans could opt to pay their monthly payments net of tax instead of recovering the tax rebate later. But recently, now that nearly all mortgage payments can be paid net of tax, if desired, there is no longer need for such a scheme (see MIRAS section earlier).

Perhaps the classic low start mortgage scheme was that sponsored, in the 1970s, by the then National Economic Development Office, in which the first year's monthly payments were "interest only" and subsequent payments rose commensurately thereafter. Unfortunately it required a complex computer program, available only to Local Authorities for a nominal fee, to calculate monthly payments, loan balances etc.

However, institutions are quite capable of producing their own low start loans, several examples of which are outlined below. These schemes vary from a two-tier repayment loan to multi-tier structures, annual constant or percentage lifts and arbitrary payments.

The requirements for any such calculations are, apart from the loan amount and the term, either (a) or (b) or (c) below.

(a) The periodic interest rate and either the first or last payments.
(b) The periodic interest rate and the difference between the various payments.
(c) The various payments, with the periodic interest rate found from a DCF/IRR computer/calculator program.

Two tier repayment loans

Assume a £1000.00 loan, over a term of 25 years, with a nominal rate of 11%.

Traditionally, with a nominal rate of 11%, and a monthly rate of $11/12\%$ the payments each month will be:

$$\frac{1,000.00}{a_{\overline{300}|}} \text{ at } (11/12)\% = \text{£9.80 pmts per month.}$$

If this loan has monthly payments of £7.00 for the first 3 years (36 months), what are te payments for the final 22 years?

Formula

$$\frac{PV \times (1 + i/p)^{np'} - (Pmts')s'_{\overline{np'}|}}{a_{\overline{np - np'}|}} = Pmts''$$

Where: (here)

np	= Total number of periods	(300)
np'	= " " " " 1st Tier Period	(36)
np"	= " " " " 2nd " "	(264)
Pmts'	= 1st Tier Pmts.	(£7.00)
Pmts"	= 2nd " "	(£????)
$s_{\overline{np}|}$	= $[(1 + i/p)^{np} - 1]/(i/p)$	

Applying the above example:

$$\frac{(1000 \times 1.009167^{36}) - 7((1.009169^{36} - 1)/.009167)}{(1 - 1.009167^{-264})/.009167}$$

$$\frac{1091.9167767}{99.282832473} \qquad = \quad 10.99804$$

$$= \text{£}11.00 \text{ Pmts}$$

A DCF calculation will find, with these rounded payments, a monthly rate of 0.916810667%, 11.001728% nominal, 11.5% APR (UK).

Loan		=	−1000.00
(3 yrs pmts)	$7a_{\overline{36}}$	=	213.81
(22 yrs pmts)	$11a_{\overline{264}} \times 1.009168^{-36}$	=	786.19
	NPV	=	0.00

Alternatively, given the original nominal rate of 11% and the FINAL (264 months) payments of £11.00, find the value of the first 36 payments.

$$\frac{1000.00 - [11a_{\overline{264}} \times (1 + i/p)^{-36}]}{a_{\overline{36}}} \qquad = \text{Pmts}'$$

$$\frac{1000 - (1092.11 \times 1.0091681^{-36})}{30.544874} = \frac{213.67}{30.54} = 6.995$$

$$= \text{£}7.00$$

To find the loan outstanding (LOS) at any period

The period of change between the (above) early start payments (£7.00) and the remaining £11.00 payments in the above example after 3 years (36 months) is the "cross-over point".

To find the LOS *before* the cross-over point presents no problem, the conventional methods, outlined previously, being employed. Taking 11% nominal for the above example, with £7.00 low start payments, it will be found that LOS(12) = £1,027.35

eg $[1000 \times (1 + i/p)^{12}] - [7 \times ((1 + i/p)^{12} - 1)/(i/p)]$

Formula for LOS after the cross over point

$$\{[\text{Loan} \times (1 + i/p)^{np'} - \text{Pmts}'s_{\overline{np'}}] \times 1 + i/p)^{(np - np')}\} - \text{Pmts}''s_{\overline{np - np'}}$$
$$= \text{LOS}(np)$$

(where np = required LOS period).

Employing an i/p of .009166667, find LOS (120):

$$[(1000 \times 1.009167^{36} - 7s_{\overline{36}|}) \times 1.009166^{84}] - 11.00s_{\overline{84}|}$$

$$= [1,091.92 \times 2.152204] - 1,382.64$$

$$= £967.38 \text{ LOS}(120) \text{ (X-over value)}.$$

Multi-tier repayment loans (constant lift)

In the case of multi-tier payments there are, as the term implies, a number of differing front-end payments, with constant lifts between years, over the term of the loan.

Assume a £7000.00 loan over a term of 25 years with a monthly rate of 11/12%. The conventional monthly payments are £68.61. Assume the final (240 months) payments are £80.00. Find the other five years' monthly payments.

As we know the interest rate and the "last" payment, we can find the difference between the payments — and thus the various payments concerned.

Formula to find the difference between payments

$$\frac{\text{Pmts}'' \, a_{\overline{np}|} - \text{PV}}{a_{\overline{60}|} + a_{\overline{48}|} + a_{\overline{36}|} + a_{\overline{24}|} + a_{\overline{12}|}} = \text{the difference factor.}$$

$$\frac{(80(1 - 1.009167^{-300})/.009167)) - 7000}{45.99 + 38.69 + 30.54 + 21.46 + 11.31} = \frac{1,162.32}{147.99}$$

$$\text{Difference} = 7.8535630$$

The last 5 years' monthly payments therefore are:

Months				
300 − 60				£80.00
60 − 48	80.00 − 7.8535630		=	£72.15
48 − 36	72.15 −	"	=	£64.30
36 − 24	64.30 −	"	=	£56.45
24 − 12	56.45 −	"	=	£48.60
12 − 0	48.60 −	"	=	£40.75

As the payments were rounded it is necessary to find the precise periodic interest rate by DCF computer/calculator methods which will result in 0.916742115% monthly, 11.00090537% nominal, 11.5% APR (UK).

Employing that i/p, namely .00916742115, the DCF schedule presents as shown on the facing page.

Loan	$=$	-7000.00
$40.75 \times \ddot{a}_{\overline{12}} \times 1.00916742^{-1}$	$=$	461.07
$48.60 \times \ddot{a}_{\overline{12}} \times 1.00916742^{-13}$	$=$	492.85
$56.45 \times \ddot{a}_{\overline{12}} \times 1.00916742^{-25}$	$=$	513.08
$64.30 \times \ddot{a}_{\overline{12}} \times 1.00916742^{-37}$	$=$	523.81
$72.15 \times \ddot{a}_{\overline{12}} \times 1.00916742^{-49}$	$=$	526.79
$80.00 \times \ddot{a}_{\overline{240}} \times 1.00916742^{-61}$	$=$	$\underline{4482.41}$
	NPV $=$	0.01

Suppose that, instead of this rather unwieldy difference, the above loan had payments rising by a constant lift (CL) each year of (say) £5. Take the rate as $(11/12)\%$ monthly.

The method here is to find the *last* series of payments:

$$\frac{PV + [(a_{\overline{60}} + a_{\overline{48}} + a_{\overline{36}} + a_{\overline{24}} + a_{\overline{12}}) \times CL]}{a_{\overline{300}}} = \text{pmt}$$

$$\frac{7000.00 + [(45.99 + 38.69 + 30.54 + 21.46 + 11.31) \times 5)]}{102.0290437} = \text{pmt}$$

$$= [7000 + (147.99 \times 5)]/102.03$$

$$= £75.86 \text{ last pmt}$$

The resulting previous payment becomes: $(£75.86 - 5) = £70.86$, with payments of £65.86, £60.86, £55.85, and £50.86 consecutively.

The monthly rate derived from these rounded payments is .916640446%.

To find the loan outstanding (LOS) at any period of time

This requirement needs some thought — and two formulae, before and after the "cross-over". The formula to find LOS after the cross over point is relatively simple, that before cross-over, unhappily, a good deal more complex.

Formulae

After cross-over point

$$\text{Pmts}'' \, a_{\overline{np - np}} \times (1 + i/p)^{(L - np')} - \text{Pmts}'' \, s_{\overline{L - np}} = LOS(L)$$

Where: (above)

np = Total number of periods   (300)

np' =   "   "   "   "   before cross-over point (60)

L = Period required for LOS.

EXAMPLE
In the most recent example above find the balance of the loan at the end of both the 228th and 32nd months, employing the monthly rate of $(11/12)\%$.

$$75.86a_{\overline{300-60}|} \times (1 + i/p)^{(228-60)} - 75.86s_{\overline{228-60}|} = £3985.48 \text{ LOS}(228)$$

Before cross-over point
In effect it is necessary to find the balance at the end of each 12 months (employing the respective payments for the year concerned). Find LOS(32):

LOS

$$(7000.00 \times 1.00916667^{12}) - 50.86s_{\overline{12}|} = £7167.98 \text{ (after 12 months)}$$
$$(7167.98 \times 1.00916667^{12}) - 55.86s_{\overline{12}|} = £7292.28 \text{ (after 12 months)}$$
$$(7292.28 \times 1.00916667^{8}) - 60.86s_{\overline{8}|} = £7341.73 \text{ (after } \underset{32}{8} \text{ months)},$$

remembering that $s_{\overline{np}|}$ at $(\text{rate}/p)\%$ $\quad = \dfrac{(1 + i/p)^{np} - 1}{i/p}$

Multi-tier repayment loans with NON-constant annual lifts

In this case the lender takes purely arbitrary monthly, or periodic, payments for different years and there is no way of calculating any peripheral requirements without the total payment data and the periodic interest rate.

Assume that with a loan of £10,000.00, over a term of 25 years, the following monthly payments are required:

£ 50 monthly payments for Year 1
£ 80   "   "   "   " 2
£100   "   "   "   " 3
£108   "   "   "   the next 22 years

By DCF calculation i/p = .00917313189% and 11.007758% nominal.

Loan	=	−10,000.00
$50 \times ä_{\overline{12}|} \times 1.00917313^{-1}$	=	565.71
$80 \times ä_{\overline{12}|} \times 1.00917313^{-13}$	=	811.19
$100 \times ä_{\overline{12}|} \times 1.00917313^{-25}$	=	908.75
$108 \times ä_{\overline{264}|} \times 1.00917313^{-37}$	=	7,714.35
NPV	=	0.00

The formula/equation depends on the *differences* between the payments:

$108 - 100 = 8$
$100 - 80 = 20$
$80 - 50 = 30,$

remembering that i/p = .009173132,

$$108a\,\overline{_{300}|} - 8a\,\overline{_{36}|} - 20a\,\overline{_{24}|} - 30a\,\overline{_{12}|} = £10,000.00$$

To find LOS requires exactly the same kind of calculation, as in the last example, where the balance at the end of each year must be found before the LOS (np) can be calculated.

In the above loan, because of the prescribed low start payments, it is to be expected that in the early months (up to 92 here) the balances will be greater than the original loan. Find LOS(16):

$$(10000.00 \times 1.009173^{12}) - 50s\overline{_{12}|} = £10,526.83$$

$$(10526.83 \times 1.009173^{4}) - 80s\overline{_{4}|} \quad = £10,594.00 \text{ LOS(16)}$$

Annual repayments with annual percentage uplifts

Above we have examined a variety of payment structures which commence with a "low start" value and even out over the full term to provide the requisite nominal rate of interest. Sometimes, however, calculations are required whereby there is a percentage lift each year, over the full term, whether payments are annual or periodical.

While payments can be periodic (semi-annual, quarterly or monthly) percentage increases are rarely evaluated other than on an annual basis.

EXAMPLE

A repayment loan of £1000.00 over a term of 10 years at 10% nominal interest would normally have annual repayments of:

$$\frac{1000.00}{a\overline{_{10}|}} \text{ at } 10\% = £162.75 \text{ Pmts}$$

If, however, this loan had payments increased each year by 6%, the relevant formulae are:

Where

$$j = \text{the annual rate of increase}$$
$$\text{"f\%"} = 100\,[((1 + i)/(1 + j)) - 1)]$$
$$= 100\,[(1.10/1.06) - 1] \quad = 3.773585\% \text{ (f\%)}$$

Annuities ORD	Annuities DUE
$\dfrac{PV}{a\overline{_{n}|} \times (1 + j)^{-1}}$ (both at f%)	$\dfrac{PV}{a\overline{_{n}|}}$
$\dfrac{1000.00}{a\overline{_{10}|} \times 1.06^{-1}}$ both at 3.773585%	$\dfrac{1000.00}{a\overline{_{10}|}}$

$$£1000.00/(((1.037736^{-10} - 1)/.037736) \times 1.06^{-1}) = £129.22 \text{ ORD,}$$
$$\text{pmt year 1}$$

$$£1000.00/(((1.037736^{-10} - 1)/.037736) \times 1.037736) = £117.47 \text{ DUE,}$$
$$\text{pmt year 1}$$

$$(\text{or } 129.22/1.10 = £117.47)$$

Check:

Assuming the above repayment loan was only for TWO years the first payment would be found from the above formula as £560.19 and:

$$(1000.00 \times 1.10) - 560.19 = £539.81$$
$$(539.81 \times 1.10) - (560.19 \times 1.06) = -£ \quad 0.01$$

Periodic payments with annual percentage uplifts

Assume, now, that the above 10 year repayment loan required MONTHLY payments (at 10% nominal) and the percentage uplift each year is 6% – how is the first payment found?

Formula

$$\frac{PV}{s_{\overline{p}|} \times (1 + j)^{-1} \times a_{\overline{n}|}}$$
$$\text{(at } i/p\%) \qquad \text{(at } f\%)$$

where

$$f = ((1 + i/p)^p/(1 + j)) - 1$$

In this case

$$(1 + f) = (1.008333^{12})/(1.06) = 1.042182$$

and

$$\frac{1000.00}{(1.008333^{12} - 1)/.008333 \times 1.06^{-1} \times (1 - 1.0421821^{-10})/.042182}$$

$$= 1000/(11.85430949 \times 8.023499742)$$

$$= £10.51 \text{ first Pmt}$$

Check:

Assuming the above repayment loan was for TWO years the second payment would be found from the above formula as:

$$1000/(11.85430949 \times (1.06^{-1}) \times ((1 - 1.042182)^{-2})/.042182) = £47.56$$

Thus the first 12 months' payments will be 47.56/1.06 = £44.87. At the end of the first year the loan outstanding would be £540.90 and, with the payments lifted to 44.87 × 1.06 = £47.56, the final balance at the end of the second year will only show a minor fractional discrepancy of 8 pence, the result of "rounding" the payments.

$$(1000.00 \times 1.00833) - 44.87 \text{ et seq} \dots \text{ for a further 11 months}$$
$$(540.90 \times '') - 47.56 \text{ et seq} \dots '' '' '' '' ''$$

Some practical considerations

In general, for conventional home loans, percentage lifts are more usually applied to the early years of a mortgage rather than throughout the whole term. In that case the simplest method is to take an arbitrary percentage lift and either the first or last payment. Once the periodic interest rate is found by DCF methods other peripheral calculations such as LOS can be found in the same manner as obtained for non-constant payments — for although a given percentage rate is constant, the resulting lifted payments are not. Given a precise nominal interest rate and percentage lift, finding the monthly payments is only possible by calculating, as in previous examples, the value of each year's "block values". And having found the correct payments employ the block method again to find the loan outstanding at any one time. If disclosure is required, after payment rounding, recalculate the new nominal rate.

Assume a £1000.00 loan over a term of 10 years, at 10% nominal with the second through to the fourth years' payments lifted by 6% each year. Find the monthly payments employing (10/12)%.

Formula/Equation (where 1.008 represents 1.00833333):

$$\frac{1{,}000.00}{(((((a_{\overline{84}|} \times 1.008^{-12}) + 1.06^{-1}a_{\overline{12}|}) \times 1.008^{-12}) + 1.06^{-2}a_{\overline{12}|}) \times 1.008^{-12}) + 1.06^{-3}a_{\overline{12}|}}$$

$$54.526981 \quad 65.257649 \quad 59.072035 \quad 69.195308 \quad 62.636453 \quad 72.186708$$

$$1{,}000.00/72.186708 = 13.852966$$

Payments before cross-over = 13.85 (rounded)

$$13.85 \text{ pmts 4th year onward}$$
$$13.85/1.06 = 13.07 \text{ pmts 3rd year}$$
$$13.07/1.06 = 12.33 \text{ pmts 2nd year}$$
$$12.33/1.06 = 11.63 \text{ pmts 1st year}$$

Taking these rounded payments, by a DCF calculation, the rate becomes .833091%, providing a nominal rate of 9.997091%. Adding one penny to the cross-over payment, to £13.86, the nominal becomes 10.007% and in both cases the APR (UK) is 10.4%.

To find the loan outstanding

Once again, the only method here is to relate the monthly "blocks" as in the previous example.

To find (say) the LOS(60) the only method is to find the balance at the end of the first 12 months with the first 12 months' payments; and treating the resulting balance as the present value, again find the next year-end (end next 12 months) balance, employing the second year's monthly payments. Again using this balance find the next year-end balance, using the third year's monthly payments — until you reach the cross over period, i.e., when the payments no longer change, here period 36. From there on it's plain sailing! Taking $(10/12)\%$:

With payments of £11.63 the end year balance is £958.58 (12 month)
£12.33   £904.02 ("   "   )
£13.07   (x-over balance)   £834.45 ("   "   )

With £834.45 as the PV, notional "loan amount", and payments of £13.85, at the end of the 60 month period, and the end of the next $(60 - 36)$ 24th period, the balance will be found as:

$$(834.45 \times 1.008333^{24}) - (13.85 \times (1.008333^{24} - 1)/.008333)$$

$$= £652.06$$

Working backwards, between the periods 36–120, after the cross-over point and thus ignoring the changing payment values, is reasonably simple.

To find LOS(108):

$$(13.85a_{\overline{120 - 36}|} \times 1.008333^{(108 - 36)}) - 13.85s_{\overline{108 - 36}|}$$

$$= (834.28 \times 1.817594) - 1358.84$$

$$= \underline{£157.54 \; LOS(108)}.$$

CHAPTER 11

Leasing and hire Purchase

The difference between leasing and hire purchase

The difference between leasing and HP lies not only in the nomenclature, "leasing" as opposed to "purchase" but also in the calculations. At the conclusion of an HP agreement the goods hired belong to, and remain with, the purchaser; whereas in a leasing contract at the end of the term of the agreement the plant leased is returned by the lessee to the lessor. The general rule for calculation is that with HP there is normally a deposit to be made on the goods hired (and ultimately purchased) and if so the following payments required are "in arrears", annuities ordinary (comparable to mortgage-type loan payments); whereas if no deposit is required, this, in effect, is not a case of hire purchase but one of leasing (the plant hired remaining the property of the lessor), in which case the subsequent payments are "in advance", annuities DUE.

In leasing contracts, there being no "deposit", lessors sometimes wish partially to protect themselves by demanding some "advance payments" (usually 3 or 4) as opposed to the normal single payments in advance resulting from the annuities due calculation – and in *that* case all subsequent payments are "in arrears" (annuities ORD).

Also with leasing contracts, because the plant leased belongs to the lessor, the lessor will, naturally, need to assess the terminal value, scrap value or (as it is more usually called) the "residual value" when the plant is returned. This residual value becomes an important part of how the lessees' repayments are calculated. In some contracts the lessee is required to "cover", or guarantee, the difference between the value of the plant after sale and the estimated amount of the residual value. If, for example, the scrap value received was £900 and the residual value was estimated at £1000, the lessee would be liable for £100 at the term-end. Should the sale value be equal to, or greater than, the estimated value the lessee will not be liable for any end-of-term costs other than a small nominal fee for these arrangements. In the event of "advance payments" (as opposed to the conventional one payment in advance) being required, the residual repayments, if any, are normally repaid at the *end* of the full term – not with the final repayment.

Should the lessor company decide not to sell the plant but to "bring it onto their books", namely to rehire the plant elsewhere later, there will be no required residual repayment cover by the lessee, the estimated residual value merely becoming part of the calculations by the lessor to determine the repayments required.

In many countries there are substantial tax advantages to be obtained from leasing *providing* the goods leased are returned to the lessor, there being no "option to purchase" at the lease end. If tax advantages are sought, therefore, the plant must remain at "arm's length" and the lessee, or his agents, must NOT "arrange to acquire" or bid for plant recently leased at an end-of-term auction – although I regret to say some such arrangements through a "third party" are, so I am told, sometimes organised.

HP goods – unit/plant value

In an HP agreement the cost of the goods hired is of vital importance to the purchaser; in a leasing contract it is of little consequence, the lessee's main interest being in the repayments required. The scrap value, important to the lessor in determining his rate of return, and thus the payments, is of interest only to the lessee if, as in some contracts, he is required to "cover", or make up, the value of the scrap if the goods are sold for less than the lessor estimated when calculating the required repayments.

Hire purchase

The mechanism of hire purchase is likely to be well known to those using this useful but often expensive method of acquiring capital goods. A High Street purchase of a washing machine at (say) £350 with a down payment of £50 leaves a hire purchase cost of some £300 to be repaid over (say) 24 months. If the High Street asking (simple) rate is 12% the monthly payments are:

$$300 \times (1 + (.12 \times 2))/24 = £15.50$$

The SI rate becomes a true nominal rate of 21.57% (effective 23.84%):

$$\frac{300.00}{15.50a_{\overline{24}|}} \text{ at } 1.797604\% \text{ monthly}$$
$$21.571245\% \text{ nominal}$$
$$23.837069\% \text{ effective}$$

$$300/((1 - 1.017976^{-24})/.017076) = £15.50 \text{ monthly.}$$

Another slightly more complex example might be related to the hire purchase of the ubiquitous office copier. An office copier costs £1,000 + VAT (at 15%) = £1,150.00 for cash. A vendor offers the purchaser the opportunity to purchase through a 3 years' HP agreement, saying that the interest rate is "only 14%" (as an aside this is the SIMPLE interest rate) but, as the HP vendor is providing a service "exclusively for business purposes" (rather than to a member of the general public), the disclosure of the APR (of 27.3%) is not legally required − and more's the pity! At "only 14%" on £1,150 over three years the monthly payments must be:

$$\frac{1150 \times (1 + (14/100 \times 3))}{36} = £45.36$$

It can be found that the *effective* rate is:

$$\frac{1150.00}{45.36a_{\overline{36}|}} \text{ at } \begin{array}{l} 2.033380\% \text{ monthly} \\ 24.400563\% \text{ nominal} \\ 27.32\% \text{ EFFECTIVE.} \end{array}$$

Assuming the client figures out the true effective rate, in order to allay any client resistance to such high rates, comprehensive literature is then often provided explaining the advantages of HP, as opposed to outright purchase − explaining that there are various tax allowances which can be off-set against corporation tax and that VAT can be reclaimed − which, with the parameters above, would, so we are told, reduce the gross payments, in effect, from £45.36 to "less than £20" net of tax − which if true would be giving it away with a packet of razor blades, for the interest rate in those circumstances would be negative.

In the various schedules provided outlining annual cash flows, what is NOT pointed out is that there is usually some delay in the final off-set of VAT and often a more substantial delay in other allowances related to corporation tax etc. − and incidentally an off-set against corporation tax is only possible if the purchasing company makes sufficient profits to pay corporation tax.

While most HP vendors are highly reputable, providing a useful and legally correct service, the only sensible method to obtain a true cost perspective (whatever the sales pitch) is to make a schedule of all the gross and net cash flows, exactly related to the company concerned − for each company will differ − and in the final analysis it may well be found that the effective cost is not always as attractive as the brochures outline, and that an outright purchase, for a company in profit, is often cheaper in the long run than lumbering the company with series of extremely expensive HP repayments.

Leasing

Plant leasing is somewhat different to HP and all the client, the lessee, is interested in is the precise periodic payments required. Either he accepts them or rejects them.

On the other hand the lessor, to determine the required payments, must know three vital factors, the yield return which he requires, the stand-in cost of the unit to be leased and the value which he places on the plant when it is returned at the end of the leasing term, i.e. the salvage or scrap value.

AN EXAMPLE

Perhaps the simplest way would be to take an example and work right through the scenario.

Assume therefore that a construction company wishes to lease a bull-dozer for five years and, stating the model required, asked a local leasing company for a quotation. The leasing company, enquiring from the dozer makers, discovers the capital cost is £10,000, net of charges and delivery to their clients. And the makers advised that, after 5 years, the scrap value could be in the region of £1,000. The leasing company's policy is that it requires a 15% nominal return with payments made quarterly − and so it figures that:

$15/4 = 3.75\%$ quarterly over $(5 \times 4) = 20$ quarters:

$$\frac{10,000 - (1,000 \times 1.0375^{-20})}{\ddot{a}_{\overline{20}|} \text{ at } 3.75\%} = \text{Pmts}$$

$$\frac{10,000 - 478.89}{((1 - 1.0375^{-20})/.0375) \times 1.0375} =$$

$$\frac{9,521.11}{14.417312} = £660.39$$

$$(\text{say}) = £660.50 \text{ to clients.}$$

While accepting the residual of £1000, when informed of the instalments the construction company demurred, replying that they would prefer payments of £600 per quarter. The leasing company, eager to assist their clients, with whom they had had close relations in the past, decided to re-think the arrangements. There appeared to be two basic options, if the reduced payments of £600 were to obtain, namely to accept a lower return than 15% nominal or to recast, if possible, the time/salvage factor.

$$\frac{10,000 - (1,000 \times 1.0375^{-20})}{600 \ddot{a}_{\overline{20}|}} \text{ at } x\%$$

The quarterly rate is found to equal 2.715439%, namely a 10.86% nominal yield, and one which the leasing company rejected outright.

They then checked to see if the scrap value could be increased in order to obtain their required return; unhappily, to achieve this, the scrap value, after 5 years, would need to be a totally unrealistic figure of £2,716.33, calculated thus:

$$\frac{(10000 \times 1.0375)^{20} - ((600 \times 1.0375^{20} - 1)/.0375) \times 1.0375)}{1.0375} = £2,716.33$$

Recasting the time factor they found that:

$$\frac{\text{LOG}\left[\left(\left(\frac{\text{pmts}}{\text{i/p}}\times(1+\text{i/p})\right)-\text{BAL}\right]\times 1\Big/\left(\left(\frac{\text{pmts}}{\text{i/p}}\times(1+\text{i/p})-\text{PV}\right)\right.}{\text{LOG}\qquad\qquad\qquad (1+\text{i/p})}=\text{np}$$

$$\frac{\text{LOG}\left(\frac{600}{.0375}\times 1.0375\right)-1000\right]\times 1\Big/\left(\left(\frac{600}{.0375}\times(1.0375)-1000\right)\right.}{\text{LOG}\qquad\qquad\qquad 1.0375}$$

= 23.366 quarters

= 5.84 years

The construction company, when they were tentatively approached as to whether they would like to have the use of the dozer for 6 years, and pay £600 per quarter, slightly acidly pointed out that if they had wanted it for 6 years they would have said so in the first place.

Advance payments

As mentioned previously on occasions advance payments are required, and although the construction company was well known to the lessors, and one which would not normally be required to make advance payments, the only way in which the payments could reduce to £600, as postulated by the construction company, was to ask for four "advance payments".

$$\frac{\text{Capital Cost}-(\text{Scrap}\times(1+\text{i/p})^{-\text{np}})}{a_{\overline{\text{np-y}}|}+\text{y}}=\text{Pmts}$$

Where y = the number of advance payments.

The calculations are "in arrears", annuities **ord**inary:

$$\frac{10000.00-(1000\times 1.0375^{-20})}{((1-1.0375^{-(20-4)})/0.0375)+4}=£599.94$$

And so, in order to meet the required payments of £600 per quarter, the following proposition was put to the construction company: that they would pay one year's payments *in advance* (£600 × 4) namely £2,400, thereafter making 16 payments of £600 *in arrears* and, at the end of the 5 years (end of the 20th quarter) guarantee to pay the leasing company £1000 or the difference between £1000 and the scrap value sale price.

It will be seen therefore that the leasing company was assured of a return of 15% nominal and the construction company had to gamble that the scrap value would be not less than £1,000 if the rate cost to them was to be 15% nominal — and providing the scrap value was not less than £1,000, the construction company would not be required to pay anything at the end of the term.

With payments of precisely £600 the nominal interest rate can be found from a simple DCF calculation and will be found to be 15.006372%. If disclosed, the APR would be 15.8%, precisely the same as the APR quoted for the asking nominal rate of 15%.

Suppose that the residual value, in the above example, was to be paid with the **last** payment (here the 16th period) — instead of, as normal, at the lease-end as shown above. In that case the discounting, above, of the residual would be:

$$(1 + i/p)^{-(np-y)}$$ and, above, this is $10000.00 - (1000 \times 1.0375^{-16})$

which would require quarterly payments of £595.15.

In the event, the "advance payments" suggestion was not necessary, for the whole problem was solved when the makers telephoned to say that they had a used dozer, in excellent condition, which they were prepared to sell for £9000. The construction company accepted this plant, with £600 quarterly payments (one payment, normally, in advance) and the lessors reckoned that their IRR would thus be 15.67% — or, if they were prepared to stick to their required return of exactly 15% nominal, they could pass on the benefit to the construction company by asking for quarterly payments of £591.

Skipped payments

Assume that a construction company hired plant but was only able to use it, owing to weather conditions, at certain times during the year. As a result they asked their leasing company whether it was possible for them to pay only when the plant was working, and to skip their payments during the months when it wasn't earning its keep. If the leasing company agreed, it is clear that the value of the lesser number of payments actually made will be greater than the normal payments with no skipped periods. But how are the new values calculated?

First let us assume that the equipment leased is valued at £10,000, that the scrap value is £3,000, that the term is 2 years with 8 quarterly payments and the nominal rate required is 15%.

$$\frac{10,000 - (3000/1.0375^8)}{\ddot{a}_{\overline{8}|} \text{ at } (15/4)\%} = £1,100.23 \text{ pmts quarterly.}$$

If the leasing contract commenced in October, as the quarterly payments are "in advance", the months Oct, Nov, Dec are paid in advance; therefore the next quarter's payments represent Jan, Feb, Mar. Assume that the weather is such that the plant cannot be used during the first quarter of each year (skip months January, February, March).

Let us assume that the correct payments increase from £1,100.23 above to £1,475.69 and for demonstration purposes let us also make a schedule — just to see exactly what "happens to the money".

	LOS	End quarter
Payments in advance	£	
$(10000.00 - 1475.69) \times 1.0375 =$	8843.97	1st (paid Oct – Dec)
$(\ 8843.97 - \ \ \ \ 0.00) \times \ \ ''\ \ =$	9175.62	2nd (skip Jan – Mar)
$(\ 9175.62 - 1475.69) \times \ \ ''\ \ =$	7988.68	3rd (paid Apr – Jun)
$(\ 7988.68 - 1475.69) \times \ \ ''\ \ =$	6757.23	4th (paid Jul – Sep)
$(\ 6757.23 - 1475.69) \times \ \ ''\ \ =$	5479.60	5th (paid Oct – Dec)
$(\ 5479.60 - \ \ \ \ 0.00) \times \ \ ''\ \ =$	5685.09	6th (skip Jan – Mar)
$(\ 5685.09 - 1475.69) \times \ \ ''\ \ =$	4367.25	7th (paid Apr – Jun)
$(\ 4367.25 - 1475.69) \times \ \ ''\ \ =$	3000.00	8th (paid Jul – Sep)

This gives the correct figure of £3000.00 as residual value.

How was the correct payment value of £1,475.69 determined?

Formula for skipped payments

There are various formulae for this slightly complex calculation, some of which are a "mix" between the nominal and effective rates, in that half of the equation is calculated at one rate, the other half at another.

My own formula below is, to my mind, the simplest of a fairly complicated bunch and has one great advantage — which will become apparent later.

$$\frac{(\text{Loan} - (\text{RES} \times (1 + i/p)^{-np}) \times ((1 + i/p)^{p} - 1)}{(s_{\overline{a}|} \times (1 + i/p^{[p-a]})) + s_{\overline{[p-a]-b]}}} \times \frac{1}{1 - (1 + i/p)^{-np}}$$

$$= \text{Pmts (ORD)}$$

where

> a = The number of payments BEFORE the skipping started
>   (above (1) – one quarter – Oct, Nov, Dec)
> b = The number of SKIPPED payments in any one year
>   (above (1) – one quarter – Jan, Feb, Mar)
> p = The number of compounding periods in any one year
>   (above (4) – one year, four quarters)
> np = The number of periods in the term of the loan/leasing
>   (above (8) – two years, eight quarters)
> RES = Residual value.

Calculations are ALWAYS savings ORD and then **convert** for DUE:

$$\frac{\text{Pmts (ORD)}}{(1 + i/p)} = \text{Pmts (DUE)}$$

and

$s_{\overline{np|}}$ (actuarial sign) $= ((1 + i/p) - 1)/(i/p)$

$$\frac{(10000 - (3000 \times 1.0375^{-8}) \times 1.0375^4 - 1)}{s_{\overline{1|}} \times 1.0375^{[4-1]} + s_{\overline{[4-1]-1|}}} \times \frac{1}{1 - 1.0375^{-8}} = \text{Pmts (ORD)}$$

$$\frac{7765.31 \times .158650415}{(1.00 \times 1.116771484) + 2.037500} \times \frac{1}{.2551048} = 1531.03$$

and $1531.03/1.0375 = £1,475.69$ pmts DUE (see above schedule).

To elaborate, and perhaps clarify, the formula "a" and "b" factors above: take another comparable example, the above example but with no residual, a term of 5 years with *monthly* payments, the skipped months being the same as previously.

In this case, there are THREE skipped payments:
a = 3 (payments before skipping started) and
b = 3 (skipped months – Jan, Feb, Mar).

$$\frac{10000 \times 1.0125^{12} - 1}{(s_{\overline{3|}} \times 1.0125^{[12-3]}) + s_{\overline{[12-3]-3|}}} \times \frac{1}{1 - 1.0125^{-60}} = \text{pmts (ORD)}$$

$$= 167.684677 \times 1.903194$$

$$= £319.11 \text{ pmts}$$

and

$319.11/1.0125 = £315.17$ monthly payments in advance (DUE).

The advantage of this particular formula, mentioned at the outset, as compared with others for this type of calculation, is that (providing there is no residual) the term can be varied simply by altering the final factor in the above formula. For instance, in the above example, the term was 5 years, what would be the payments if the term was exactly 12 months instead of 60?

$$167.668467 \times \frac{1}{1 - 1.0125^{-12}} = £1210.68 \text{ pmts}$$

and $1210.68/1.0125 = £1,195.73$ pmts (DUE).

Specific skipped payments

With a loan of £1,000.00 over a period of 300 months at 11/12%, an example frequently used previously, the payments in arrears of £9.80 and in advance of £9.71 are well known. Assume that for some reason the structure of such a loan is that SIX payments are permitted to be missed between periods 201 and 206 (inclusive). What are the required payments over the full term, making allowances for the six missing payments?

$$\frac{1000.00}{a_{\overline{300}|} + a_{\overline{200}|} - a_{\overline{206}|}} = \text{pmts "in arrears" (ORD)}$$

$$\frac{1000.00}{102.03 + 91.50 - 92.44} = £9.89 \text{ pmts adjusted,}$$

or $9.89/1.00916667 = £9.80 \text{ pmts (DUE)}.$

Extra payments as balloon payment

Assume a lease (with payments in advance) over 4 years for £1,000.00 with a residual of £100.00 providing a yield return of 15% nominal with monthly payments required. If, instead of the conventional payments of £25.97, the lessee offered to make 6 extra payments at the END of the term, what would be the required payments?

$$\frac{1000.00 \times (100 \times 1.0125^{-48})}{\ddot{a}_{\overline{48}|} + (6 \times 1.0125^{-48})} = £23.81 \text{ pmts}$$

Calculating the balance at the end of four years,

$$[1000 \times 1.0125^{48}] - [23.81 \times 1.0125(1.0125^{48} - 1)/.0125)] = £242.86$$
                                                                  Balance

and $£242.86 - (23.81 \times 6)$ $= £100.00$
                                                                  Residual.

CHAPTER 12

Savings and Sinking Funds

Savings ordinary and due ($s_{\overline{n}|}$ and $\ddot{s}_{\overline{n}|}$)

In previous chapters the savings factor has been employed as part of other formulae calculations whether they be ORD or DUE, namely payments in arrears or in advance.

In general terms savings calculations assume that a bank or institution will provide interest on credit balances — balances which can be "topped up" every so often by further deposits.

Obviously the sooner a deposit is received by a bank the sooner that amount will be "at interest". Savings DUE therefore, are assumed to be at the beginning of the compounding period (or "in advance", to equate with the terms we have been using for leasings — annuities **due**) whereas "savings **ord**inary" are at the **end** of such periods.

What is the difference in practice?

Let us assume that we deposit £500.00 each year with a bank which agrees to provide 10% interest each year on the credit balances. If the £500 is deposited at the *beginning* of the year, then by the year-end the £500 will be worth $500 \times 1.10 = £550.00$. If at the *beginning* of the following year a further £500 is deposited, then at the end of that year the new £500 will be at interest, as will the previous balance, here £550.

$$£(550 + 500) \times 1.10) = £1155.00 \text{ end of year 2 (DUE).}$$

On the other hand if the £500 was deposited at the *end* of the year, then:

$$£(500 \times 1.10) + 500 = £1050.00 \text{ end of year 2 (ORD).}$$

A schedule over 5 years with both savings ORD and DUE is set out below.

savings DUE $\ddot{s}_{\overline{5}|}$		end of year	savings ORD $s_{\overline{5}|}$	
500.00	$\times 1.10 = 550.00$	1		500.00
$(550.00 + 500) \times 1.10 = 1155.00$		2	$(500 \times 1.10) + 500 =$	1050.00
$(1155.00 + 500) \times 1.10 = 1820.50$		3	$(1050.00 \times 1.10) + 500 =$	1665.00
$(1820.50 + 500) \times 1.10 = 2552.55$		4	$(1665.00 \times 1.10) + 500 =$	2320.50
$(2552.55 + 500) \times 1.10 = \underline{3357.81}$		5	$(2320.50 \times 1.10) + 500 =$	$\underline{3052.55}$

Formulae

$$\frac{\text{Savings (\textbf{due})}}{\ddot{s}_{\overline{np}}} \qquad \text{at } (i/p)\% \qquad \frac{\text{Sinking funds (\textbf{ord})}}{s_{\overline{np}}}$$

$$\frac{((1 + i/p)^{np} - 1) \times (1 + i/p)}{i/p} \qquad\qquad \frac{(1 + i/p)^{np} - 1}{i/p}$$

$$500(1.10^5 - 1)/.10 \times 1.10 = \underline{3{,}357.81} \qquad 500(1.10^5 - 1)/10 = \underline{3{,}052.55}$$

Savings DUE

The type of investment for savings (in advance) could usefully be employed for the building up of a reserve for (say) children's education in future years, and this type of investment is often referred to simply as "savings".

EXAMPLE (A)

In 10 years' time a capital fund of £10,000 is required for a child's future education. If a bank was prepared to pay $(10/12)\%$ monthly interest, on credit balances held, what monthly payments for (10×12) 120 months will be required to fund £10,000? Payments to be made at the beginning of each month.

(Savings **due** – payments "in advance")

$$\frac{10{,}000.00}{\ddot{s}_{\overline{120}}} \text{ at } (10/12)\% \qquad\qquad = \text{Pmts}$$

$$\frac{10{,}000.00}{((1.008333^{120} - 1)/.008333) \times 1.008333} = \text{Pmts}$$

$$= \frac{10{,}000.00}{206.5520156} \qquad\qquad = 48.41395506$$

$$\qquad\qquad\qquad\qquad\qquad\qquad\qquad = \text{£}48.41$$

Recalculating with the rounded-down payments the fund will be:

$$48.41 \times 206.5520156 \qquad\qquad = \text{£}9{,}999.18 \text{ FV}$$

and in that case, if *precise* accuracy is required, the final payment will be a few pennies more (see below).

Savings ORD

Savings (in arrears), sometimes referred to as a "sinking fund", with interest being calculated at the end of the compounding period, could be a method of saving a specific amount for (say) a car.

EXAMPLE (B)

To save for a car, to cost (say) £5000.00 in 2 years' time. The bank will give interest on these savings at 9.5% nominal, with payments and interest charged quarterly. If the instalments are to be made at the **end** of each quarter, what payments are required?

$$\frac{5,000.00}{s_{\overline{8}|}} \text{ at } (9.5/4)\% = \text{Pmts}$$

$$\frac{5,000.00}{(1.02375^8 - 1)/.02375}$$

$$\frac{5,000.00}{8.69754328} = 574.8749775$$

$$= £574.87$$

The balance held at the bank, at the end of 7 quarters, will be £4,425.09 and instead of giving the bank the last payment of £574.87 this will be added to the withdrawn bank balance (4425.09) to provide £5000.00 for the car purchase.

To find "i"

Unhappily, there is no simple method and, like repayment loans, if without computer/calculator facilities the "guess and guess again" interpolation must be used — See Appendix B, "Solve for i".

To find the term for savings

$$\frac{\text{LOG } 1 + \dfrac{FV \times i/p}{pmt \times (1 + i/p)}}{\text{LOG} \qquad 1 + i/p} = \text{term (DUE)}.$$

Taking example (A):

$$\frac{\text{LOG } 1 + \dfrac{10000 \times .008333}{48.41 \times 1.0083333}}{\text{LOG} \qquad 1.0083333} = \frac{\text{LOG } 2.707181}{\text{LOG } 1.083333} = \frac{0.995908}{0.008299}$$

$$= 120.006211$$

Unrounded payments would provide precisely $\qquad = 120$ months

$$\frac{\text{LOG } 1 + \dfrac{FV \times i/p}{pmt}}{\text{LOG} \qquad 1 + i/p} = \text{term (ORD)}$$

Taking example (B):

$$\frac{LOG \ 1 + \dfrac{5000.00 \times .023750}{574.87 \ (\text{rounded})}}{LOG \qquad 1.023750} = \frac{LOG \ 1.206568}{LOG \ 1.023750} = \frac{0.187780}{0.023472}$$

$$= 8.000063$$

$$= 8 \ \text{quarters}$$

Interest and periods not coincident

Sometimes banks will provide interest (say) per quarter irrespective of whether the deposits are made monthly.

In example (B) quarterly deposits, in arrears, of £574.87, over a term of 2 years (8 quarters), at 2.375% quarterly, provided a "sinking fund" (FV) of £5000.00 (less a few odd pence).

Supposing the bank which accepted these quarterly deposits above said that while they would continue to reconcile their accounts quarterly they were prepared to accept monthly instalments. In that case what would the monthly payments be?

Adjust the rate:

$$1200 \times \left[\left(1 + \frac{9.50}{400} \right)^{1/(12/4)} - 1 \right] = 9.425768\%$$

$$\frac{5000.00}{s_{\overline{24}|}} \ \text{at} \ (9.425768/12)\% \qquad = \underline{£190.13 \ \text{Pmts}}$$

It will be seen therefore that this method is of advantage to the lender; for three monthly payments of £190.13 is (×3) some £570.39 each quarter instead of, as above, £574.87 — to provide the same, required, fund of £5,000.

Occasionally, as an added inducement to lenders, some institutions will advertise that interest will be at "continuous compounding", interest from moment to moment. In that event what is the FV, in the above example, if payments are made monthly?

Remember that 9.50% <e> is the EFFECTIVE rate and therefore this must be reduced to its nominal twelve monthly periodic equivalent before any further calculations are contemplated,

$$e^{.095/12} = 1.007948 \ \text{and} \ (1.007948 - 1) \times 100 = .794809\% \ \text{monthly}.$$

Therefore in this case the yet again slightly reduced monthly payments will be:

$$\frac{5000.00}{s_{\overline{24}|}} \ \text{at} \ .794808600\% = £189.92 \ \text{Pmts}$$

Last payments

In the savings example (A) above, with payments of £48.41, over 120 months, with a monthly interest rate of .83333%, the recalculated FV presented as £9,999.18. Assuming that a precise FV of £10,000 is required, what is the value of the final payment, remembering that this is a savings calculation, *savings DUE*, with deposits made at the beginning of (here) each month?

£10,000.00 − 9,999.18 = 0.816699600 (difference);

48.41 + (.816699/1.0083333) = £49.22 Last (120th) deposit required.

With *savings ORD*, payments in arrears, the calculation varies slightly in that the difference is NOT divided by $(1 + i/p)$ prior to adding to the original payment. In example (B) the quarterly rounded instalments, in arrears, of £574.87 over 8 quarters, at a quarterly interest rate of 2.375% will produce a final fund of £4,999.95 (rounded down). If the precise last payment was required to find exactly £5,000:

5,000 − 4,999.95 = .05 and £574.87 + .05 = £574.92 last payment.

To save an exact amount

Assume a savings due calculation, at a rate of 16% nominal, 1.3333% monthly, provided by my bank. My existing credit at the bank is £1000.00. At the end of x number of years I wish to have a fund not exceeding £5,000. I have arranged with my bank to transfer from my current account some £50 each month to my deposit account. How long shall I need to save?

The formula to find the correct FV must be:

$$PV \times (1 + i/p)^{np} + \text{pmts } \ddot{s}_{\overline{np}|} \text{ at } (i/p)\% = FV$$

and in these circumstances, because of the existing credit balance at the commencement of the savings, the previous method of finding the term, set out earlier, will not be valid.

Savings ord (pmts in arrears with an existing credit)

$$\frac{LOG\left(\frac{Pmts}{i/p} + FV\right) \times 1/\left(\frac{Pmts}{i/p} + PV\right)}{LOG \quad 1 + i/p} = \text{term}$$

Savings due (pmts in advance with an existing credit)

Employ above formula but treat pmts as pmts $\times (1 + i/p)$.

And applying the Savings DUE example in question above:

$$\frac{LOG\left(\frac{50 \times 1.0133}{.01333333} + 5000\right) \times 1/\left(\frac{50 \times 1.0133}{.01333333} + 1000\right)}{LOG \quad 1.01333333} = 45.7626$$

Any unrealistic term must be converted to an integer (here 46) which will mean an increased or reduced last payment.

$$1000 \times 1.01333^{46} + 50\ddot{s}_{\overline{46}|} \text{ at } (16/12)\%$$

$$1,839.11 + 3,188.61 = £5,027.72$$

and $5,027.72 - 5,000 = £27.72$

therefore   Last pmt $= 50 - (27.72/1.01333) = £22.65$

Answer: 46 months. $46/12 = 3.8333 = 3$ years and 10 months.

If the term had been taken as 45 months, then the last payment would need to be £137.27 to provide an exact FV of £5,000.

Varying deposits
Find the future value for the following deposits and rate changes.

£100 deposited for 3 years at current rate of 10%
£200   "   " 3 "   "   "   "   " 11%
£300   "   " 4 "   "   "   "   " 12%

Assume a sinking fund transaction, namely savings ORD.

$100s_{\overline{3}|}$ at 10% $= £\ 331.00$

$200s_{\overline{3}|}$ at 11% $= £\ 668.42$

$300s_{\overline{4}|}$ at 12% $= £1433.80$

$((331.00 \times 1.11^3) + 668.42) \times 1.12^4) + 1433.80 = £3,197.88$ FV.

CHAPTER 13

Savings with Percentage Lifts

In the last chapter we examined various calculations related to normal sinking funds and savings (savings ordinary and due). In this chapter we look at variations on the main themes related to deposits which are not constant but which are increased each year by a constant percentage.

First, the more conventional requirement of "savings" (due), with the deposits increased year by year by a chosen percentage. This type of calculation relates more often than not to insurance premiums (payments) and required future values.

Assume that the investment rate is 10%, the term 10 years, and the future value required is £10,000.00. In that case we know that the normal annual deposits (payments), made at the *end*, in arrears, of each compounding period are:

$$\frac{10,000.00}{s_{\overline{10}|}} \text{ at } 10\% = £627.45 \text{ (pmts per year) } \textbf{(ord)}$$

For "due" payments, in advance, the above payments must be less, so divide by $(1 + i)$, here £627.45/1.10 = £570.41 **(due)**.

Assuming the above except that each payment rises each year by 10%, with the investment rate and the percentage uplift rate both being the same, here 10%, what is the "first payment" to ensure that the FV is exactly £10,000.00 (+/– the odd penny)?

$$\text{First Pmt} \times (1 + i)^n \times n = \text{future value (Savings DUE)}$$

$$\text{First Pmt} \times (1 + i)^{n-1} \times n = \text{future value (Savings ORD)}$$

$$FV/((1 + i)^n \times n) = \text{first pmt} \quad \text{(Savings DUE)}$$

$$FV/((1 + i)^{(n-1)} \times n) = \text{first pmt} \quad \text{(Savings ORD)}$$

where n = number of years.

$$10000/(1.10^{10} \times 10) = £385.54 \quad \text{First Pmt (DUE)}$$

$$£385.54 \times 1.10 = £424.10 \quad \text{First Pmt (ORD)}$$

If just for 3 years and the (due) payments were £2,504.38, what is the FV?

$$2504.38 \times 1.10^3 \times 3 = 9999.989340 = £10,000.00$$

If calculations are made with payments rounded there will inevitably be a minor decimal discrepancy when finding the FV.

119

Annual deposits – annual percentage lifts

The more usual requirement, however, for these types of "savings" plans is that (unlike the above example) the percentage uplift rate is different to the investment rate. In these circumstances, to find the "first payment", to provide a required future value, requires a little thought – and a formula.

Assume that the term is 10 years, the investment rate 10%, the annual uplift percentage rate 6%, and the required FV is £10,000.00. What is the value of the first deposit required?

Let us assume the CORRECT first payment (in advance) is £452.91 and make a schedule accordingly, in order to visualise how the calculation runs in practice (i.e., "what exactly happens to the money"). Afterwards we will create a formula.

$$(\ 452.91 \times 1.10) \qquad\qquad\qquad\qquad = \quad 498.20 \,\text{(DUE)}$$
$$(\ 498.20 \times 1.10) + ((452.91 \times 1.06^1) \times 1.10) = \quad 1076.11$$
$$(1076.11 \times 1.10) + ((452.91 \times 1.06^2) \times 1.10) = \quad 1743.50$$
$$(1743.50 \times 1.10) + ((452.91 \times 1.06^3) \times 1.10) = \quad 2511.22$$
$$(2511.22 \times 1.10) + ((452.91 \times 1.06^4) \times 1.10) = \quad 3391.31$$
$$(3391.31 \times 1.10) + ((452.91 \times 1.06^5) \times 1.10) = \quad 4397.15$$
$$(4397.15 \times 1.10) + ((452.91 \times 1.06^6) \times 1.10) = \quad 5543.57$$
$$(5543.57 \times 1.10) + ((452.91 \times 1.06^7) \times 1.10) = \quad 6847.03$$
$$(6847.03 \times 1.10) + ((452.91 \times 1.06^8) \times 1.10) = \quad 8325.79$$
$$(8325.79 \times 1.10) + ((452.91 \times 1.06^9) \times 1.10) = 10000.07 \,\text{FV}$$

Formulae

Converting the above schedule into a formula, to find the first payment from a given FV, we get:

$$\text{DUE: } \frac{FV}{s_{\overline{n}|}} \times (1+j)^{-n} \text{ at } f\% = \text{1st pmt}$$

$$\text{ORD: Pmts (DUE)} \times (1+i)$$

Where:

"i" = interest rate % (here $10/100 = .10$)

"j" = percentage uplift rate % (here $6/100 = .06$)

"f" = $100(((1+i)/(1+j)) - 1)$ = the equation rate %

And for this particular example:

"f" = $100 \times (((1.10/1.06)) - 1 = 3.77358490\%$ (equation rate)

$$f/100 \qquad\qquad = \ .0377358190$$

$$\left[10,000.00 / \frac{(1.0377358^{10} - 1)}{.0377358} \times 1.0377358 \right] \times 1.06^{-10} = \text{1st Pmt (due)}$$

$$10,000.00 / 12.32913667 \times 0.358394777 \qquad\qquad = £452.91$$

Remember the deposits above are at the **beginning** of the compounding period (savings **due**). The payments for a savings **ord**inary calculation, in this example, are £452.91 X 1.10 = £498.20.

A negative "formula (f) rate"

In the event that the percentage uplift is greater than the investment rate the calculated "formula rate" will inevitably be negative. Such an unusual working rate need cause no anxiety — use it:

$$(1.10/1.12) \qquad = (1 + f) = \quad 0.982142857$$

$$(0.982143 - 1) \times 100 \qquad \text{``f\%''} \ = \ -1.7857714290\%$$

For example, if the above example had a required uplift each year of 12% (instead of 6%) the first payment would be £355.04:

$$\frac{10,000.00}{\ddot{s}_{\overline{10}|}} \ \times \ (1.12)^{-10} \text{ at f\%}$$

$$= \frac{10,000.00}{((0.982143^{10} - 1)/-0.017857) \times .982143 \times 1.12^{10}}$$

$$= \ 355.04 \ \text{1st pmt}$$

Periodic deposits — annual percentage lifts

In practice monthly and quarterly deposits are normally uplifted by *annual* percentages; rarely are such periodic payments lifted by periodic percentages.

In the above example, where the investment rate was 10%, the annual uplift percentage rate 6% and the term ten years with a required future value of £10,000.00, assume that the deposits were to be made *monthly* and that each of these monthly deposits would lift by 6% each *year*. What is the amount of each of the first 12 months' deposits?

Before getting involved in the slightly more complex calculations let us determine exactly "what happens to the money". To save a long and un-wieldy schedule ranging over 10 years (120 months) consider a term of 24 months (2 years) and a required FV of £1000.00, with 10% *nominal* investment rate and 6% annual uplift. The correct first year's payments are £36.46 and the year following: £36.46 X 1.06 = £38.65. A schedule therefore:

36.46	X 1.008333	=	38.84
(38.84 + 36.46)	X "	=	75.93
(75.93 + ")	X "	=	111.21

and so on until the end of year 1 $\qquad\qquad$ = 461.96

$$(461.96 + (36.46 \times 1.06)) \times 1.008333 = 504.78$$
$$(504.78 + \quad 38.65) \qquad \times \quad '' \quad = 547.96$$
$$(547.96 + \quad '' \qquad\qquad \times \quad '' \quad = 591.50$$

and so on until the 24th deposit is made $\quad = 1000.04$

Formula

$$\frac{FV}{\ddot{a}_{\overline{p|}} \times (1+j)^n \times \ddot{s}_{\overline{n|}}} = \text{1st pmt}$$

$$\text{(at i/p\%)} \qquad \text{(at f\%)}$$

where:

		here
n	= term	(2 years)
i	= nominal investment rate %	(10.00%)
p	= periods compounded per year	(12 months)
j	= percentage uplift rate % p.a.	(6.00%)

$$1 + f = (1 + i/p^p)/(1 + j)$$
$$= (1 + 10/1200^{12})/(1.06)$$
$$= (1.104713)/(1.06) = (1.042182135)$$

EXAMPLE (A)

Using the data above:

$$\cfrac{1000.00}{\cfrac{(1 - 1.00833^{-12})}{.00833} \times 1.00833 \times 1.06^2 \times \cfrac{(1.04218^2 - 1)}{.04218} \times 1.04218}$$

$$\frac{1000.00}{27.427523} = 36.459727$$
$$= \pounds36.46 \text{ 1st pmt}$$

EXAMPLE (B)

Reverting to the original requirement of an FV of £10,000.00 over a term of 10 years, with monthly deposits in advance, each year's deposits being raised by 6% per annum, the investment rate is 10% nominal. What are the first year's deposits?

$$\frac{10000.00}{((1 - 1.00833)^{-12}/.00833) \times 1.00833 \times 1.06^{10} \times (1.04218^{10} - 1)/.04218 \times 1.04218}$$

$$\frac{10,000.00}{259.620585} = 38.517747$$
$$= \pounds38.52 \text{ (DUE)}$$

Periodic deposits with periodic percentage uplifts

Assuming the above parameters related to semi-annual deposits, arranged as 5% interest paid each half year with a lift of 3% every half year, what is the first half annual payment if the term is just 2 years (4 half year periods)?

In this case "f" = $(1.05/1.03) - 1 = .019417$

$$\frac{10,000}{\ddot{s}_{\overline{4}|}} \times 1.03^{-4} \text{ at } f\% \qquad = \text{1st Pmt (due)}$$

$$\frac{10,000.00/1.03^4}{((1.019417^4 - 1)/.019417) \times 1.019417} = \text{£}2,116.46 \text{ pmts}$$

Check:

2,116.46	$\times 1.05$	= £2,222.29
$2,222.29 + (2,116.46 \times 1.03^1) \times 1.05$		= £4,622.35 **Bal** Year 1
$4,622.35 + (2,116.46 \times 1.03^2) \times 1.05$		= £7,211.09
$7,211.09 + (2,116.46 \times 1.03^3) \times 1.05$		= £9,999.99 FV Year 2

CHAPTER 14

Inflation

General

Inflation is an emotive word, for inflation affects all our lives and the economies of all countries. And because of this it is perhaps a matter of surprise that so often relevant calculations are not always correctly executed or understood.

Already a short comment has been made in Chapter 1 concerning the backroom boys who produced the two political election manifestos with the percentages calculated wrongly! And should overworked backroom boys possibly evoke some sympathy in that perhaps financial calculations were not their forte, and that such errors are unlikely to be repeated, let me say that other equally surprising mistakes continue to occur. When last in Canada, in one of the branches of a leading Canadian bank, picking up one of their AGM reports, I found to my amusement that the President's annual address included a paragraph about inflation and, in providing a simple example for the bank's less experienced readers, got it wrong! I treasure the President's reply to my query!

Adding and subtracting percentages and inflation rates

Colloquial language is sometimes less precise than a mathematician might prefer – hence the possibility of occasional misunderstandings. Investment interest "rates" are usually referred to as "percentages" and inflation percentages as rates!

Supposing there were four years of interest rates, at 10%, 14%, 9% and 14%: the sum of these rates would be 47 and the arithmetic mean would be 47/4 = 11.75% but that information would be useless, for without a time-scale and other relevant information the four rates have no relationship to each other.

But if these were "inflation percentages", say, for the last four years and it was required to know the "average inflation rate" then the correct method is to find the geometric mean:

$$100 \times ((1.10 \times 1.14 \times 1.09 \times 1.14)^{1/4} - 1) = 11.73\%.$$

And should you think that I am stressing the obvious, believe me, I have seen an actuaries' report in which the mean "inflation rate" was attributed to the sum of the percentages — and although, here, the difference might not appear marked, elsewhere it can greatly affect calculations.

More additions

A 10% rate added to a 10% rate is NOT, as you might think, 20% but is 21%. For £100 × 1.10 × 1.10 = £121 and less £100 the interest is £21. By the same token 10% − 10% is NOT zero but is −1%:

$$100\left\{\left[\left(1 + \frac{10.00}{100}\right) \times \left(1 + \frac{-10}{100}\right)\right] - 1\right\} = -1.$$

Inflation, therefore, should always be treated as a percentage, on a percentage, on a percentage, i.e., a growth rate.

An investment rate of 12% with inflation running at 20% is not a negative rate, as some still believe, of $12 - 20 = -8\%$ but is $100((1.12/1.20) - 1) = -6.66666\%$, which in "real terms" is substantially less.

There is no difficulty about employing a negative rate in calculations for the negative aspect "comes out in the wash". Take £100: multiplied by a negative rate of −6.666 compounded over a term of 2 years:

$$100 \times \left(1 + \frac{-6.6666}{100}\right)^2$$

$$= 100 \times ((-6.66667/100) + 1)^2$$

$$= 100 \times 0.933333^2$$

$$= £87.11$$

Discounting

Assume an investment rate of 10% with the expected inflation average running at 8% each year.

A single payment of £100.00 is due at the end of year 5. The present value NOW is:

$$100.00 \times 1.10^{-5} = £62.09$$

and discounted for inflation

$$62.09 \times 1.08^{-5} = £42.26,$$

which could more simply be calculated as

$$100 \times (1.10 \times 1.08)^{-5} = £42.26.$$

Repayment loans

Assume a stream of £200.00 annual payments over the next 6 years with an interest rate of 5.50% with a 6% expected average inflation rate (that is each

year, for the next 6 years, inflation will run at 6%). What is the present value
of the loan amount, in real terms?

$$200a_{\overline{6}|} \text{ at } ((1.055 \times 1.06) - 1) \times 100$$

$$\text{at } 11.83\% \text{ nominal}$$

$$= \text{£}826.26 \text{ loan amount (PV)}.$$

If there had been no inflation factor to take into consideration the Present
Value would be $200a_{\overline{6}|}$ at 5.50% = £1000.

Time factor accuracy

A loan of £100 at 10% over 10 years will provide an FV of £259.37:

$$100 \times (1.10)^{10} = 259.37$$

If inflation was running at 15%, then the inclination is to find the future
value in real terms as:

$$259.37/1.15^{10} = \text{£}64.11$$

$$100 \times \frac{1.10^{10}}{1.15^{10}} = 100 \times \left(\frac{1.10}{1.15}\right)^{10} = \text{£}64.11$$

While this is mathematically correct for percentages per se, it must be remembered that often inflation may not have a bearing on the calculation in
question until after the first year.

For example, if a pension was inflation-proofed, the pension would,
obviously, not be subject to any alteration until the end of the first year.
But if to be adjusted thereafter, the inflation rate, on which the rise would be
based, would be the inflation factor which occurred during the *first* year of
the pension. So it will be seen that sometimes the rate of inflation in the
calculation is not necessarily known until the end of the first year — or even
if known it may be necessary to assume that, like pensions, the first year is,
for calculation purposes, "inflation free".

So one could calculate:

$$\text{£}100 \times \frac{1.10^{10}}{1.15^{9}} = \text{£}73.73 \text{ FV}$$

The following mathematical calculation is a little "technical" — a term
in mathematics usually denoting a "snag" or two on the horizon! While the
differential between the 10th and 9th years above is fully understandable
and easy to calculate manually, what happens if one has the need to input
such values into a computer/calculator — as one rate?

$$100\left(\frac{1.10}{1.20} - 1\right) = -8.33\%,$$

but if this was related to a lesser period of inflation, the calculation needs to be:

$$100\left(\left(\frac{1.10^{10}}{1.20^9}\right)^{1/10} - 1\right) = 100\left(\frac{1.10}{1.20^{9/10}} - 1\right) = -6.646724\%,$$

which of course gives rise to the immediate thought that this must be the method to overcome the problem of monthly, or periodic payments and an ANNUAL inflation rate.

$$£100 \times \frac{1 + 10/1200^{120}}{1.20^9} = £52.46.$$

The annual rate is

$$(52.46/100)^{1/10} - 1) \times 100 \qquad = -6.246742$$

or: $\quad ((1.008333^{12}/1.20^{9/10}) - 1) \times 100 = -6.246742$

As inflation is usually considered as an annual factor it must be realised that 1% monthly inflation is NOT 12% per annum but is:

$$\left(\left(1 + \frac{1}{100}\right)^{12} - 1\right) \times 100 = 12.682503\%.$$

A 12% annual inflation rate finds a monthly rate of:

$$\left(\left(1 + \frac{12.00}{100}\right)^{1/12} - 1\right) \times 100 = .9488795\%.$$

CHAPTER 15

Indexed Pensions and
Golden Handshakes

Since the inception of inflation-proofed, or indexed, pensions they have been a matter of considerable controversy. In a book mainly concerned with calculations the pros and cons have little place here; to those who require a more detailed study the Government Actuary's Report (1979), "Adjustment differences in superannuation benefits" (HMSO) and a trenchant criticism of this report, often called the Chown Report, "Report on the value of Pensions" (1980) (Centre for Policy Studies) are well worth reading. Both reports were called for, and addressed to, the Prime Ministers holding office at the respective dates.

Because the purely factual Actuary's report was drafted by civil servants, themselves subject to indexed pensions, some considered that it was totally biased in favour of indexed pensions and, more unfairly, recalled a remark made some years ago at an inquiry when a witness, asked why she thought certain other witnesses had answered as they did, replied, in words that have now become well enshrined in our legal history, "Well, they would, wouldn't they?".

When indexing was first mooted as possible Government policy, with inflation around 20%, many expressed the view, extremely forcibly at times, that the cost of inflation-proofed pensions was so great that no country could possibly afford such luxuries; others that unless they were introduced the pressure on wages would continue and become so great that the standard of living of pensioners would inevitably be unfairly eroded. The trouble is that there is still a woeful lack of useful data available to the general public on such arcane matters as the long-term cost of pensions in general and public sector pensions in particular. Unlike the private sector, the public sector funding cost is not so immediately apparent, for Governments do not "fund" pensions but pay them, year by year, out of current earnings — paid for by the annual contributions which we all make, usually under protest, to the Revenue authorities. The private sector, save for a few minor exceptions by some of the largest institutions, quickly realised that, even if desirable, indexation was far beyond their funding potential.

Without employing the very detailed methods of actuaries for assessing the probabilities of survival, expectation of life etc., the calculations below, while perhaps not actuarially precise, may be useful in providing some rough costings.

Our civil servant

Our Whitehall worker has retired, after 30 useful years of active service, joining in 1950 and retiring in 1980. He is aged 60, retiring a little before his time. His last appointment had a salary scale of £20,000, including all emoluments, etc.

On retirement he will receive a "lump sum", tax free, of £22,500. This is determined by following the salary scale rule of 3/80th $\times$ the number of years service $\times$ the last salary scale — here it presents as $3/80 \times 30 \times 20,000 = £22,500$.

His pension, as opposed to his tax-free capital gift, is 1/3 of the "lump sum", here £22,500/3 = £7,500, which is paid quarterly in arrears. As a rough assessment let us assume that, unlike Governments, we are "funding" this one civil servant's pension. If we took a rate of 12% and a 20 year "expectation of life", to produce £1,875 quarterly payments, we would have to have as a capital amount a fund of £58,482 (non-indexed):

$$(7500/4) \, a_{\overline{4}|} \text{ at } [100(1 + 12/100)^{1/4} - 1)]$$

$$\text{at } 2.873735\% \text{ quarterly} = £6,990.65 \text{ PV}$$

$$6,990.65 \; \ddot{a}_{\overline{20}|} \text{ at } 12\% = \underline{£58,482.26 \text{ funding}}$$

Now assume that inflation is running at 20% but, hoping that it will fall to (say) 16% — and remain there, we take an arbitrary rate of 16% as our index.

Now do the whole calculation above again but with the negative rate of $[(1.12/1.16) - 1] \times 100 = -3.45\%$:

$$6,990.65 \; \ddot{a}_{\overline{20}|} \text{ at } -3.448276\% = \underline{£199,150.84 \text{ indexed funding}}$$

There are many more civil servants retiring each year . . .

A "print-out" of this particular schedule would be both long and boring, suffice it to say that it begins £(199,150.83 − 1875) $\times$ 1.028737 and so on until the year end when the balance will be £215,219.40. The fund will gradually increase in value to around £375,000 in the 13th year of its life, then it will diminish rapidly to zero at the end of the 20th year.

To find the balance at any year

The formula is:

$$PV \times (1 + i)^n - [(\text{pmts} \times (1 + \text{inf})^n \times \ddot{s}_{\overline{n}|}] \text{ at } x\% = \text{Balance}$$

where:

"inf" = inflation rate % as a decimal fraction,

Above $x\% = 100(((1 + i)/(1 + \text{inf})) - 1)$

$$= 100((1.12/1.16) - 1) = -3.448276\%$$

In year 13:

$$[199,150.83 \times 1.12^{13}] - [6990.65 \times 1.16^{13} \times 965517(.96552^{13} - 1)/(.96552 - 1)]$$

$$= £375,283.15 \text{ Balance 13th year}$$

Golden handshakes

Another controversial subject. In the lower wage brackets redundancy pay is considered right and proper; but when a leading industrialist is dismissed, or becomes redundant, sometimes through no fault of his own, there is often a public outcry, largely due, of course, to the compensation which often appears so extreme as to be far beyond the dreams of the man in the street. In fact it is only compensation for loss of office and in nine cases out of ten it is both fair and just. A company ties an executive to it for a number of years and if it suddenly breaks that contract then it must be liable for a penalty. All that is necessary is to understand how the compensation is calculated. Every case will be different and have individual problems – all one can do here is to provide the general method of calculation.

Compensation is not evaluated, as some still appear to think as a result of the "old boy net", nor as a bribe to prevent the company's dirty linen being exposed to public inspection. The calculation is a simple one of determining a capital sum which will provide the same amount each year as the executive would have received if he/she had not been dismissed. The sum is found from an annuities **due** calculation, the emoluments lost being the payments, the present value found being the compensation due.

Assuming a current market interest rate of 10% p.a., an executive receiving £30,000 per year with 3 years of his contract to run would be due for a capital sum of:

£30,000 $\ddot{a}_{\overline{3}|}$ at 10% = compensation

$$1.10 \times (1 - 1.10^{-3})/.10 \times 30,000 = £82,066.12.$$

Paradoxically, the higher the rate the lower the compensation and it is usually within this narrow field that negotiations, if any, occur: as above, but with a 15% rate = £78,771.27. For a company will doubtless argue that bank lending rates (of say 15%) is the correct level to use in any relevant calculations, whereas the executive's legal advisor will claim that if his client invests the capital sum he is unlikely to be able to obtain an annual return of more than 5% – which, in order to retain his standard of living from an annual income of £30,000, would require a capital sum of £85,782.31.

Inflation could of course be a "talking point" in any negotiations – less important, perhaps, as inflation reduces. If the rate agreed was 10%, and inflation over the next three years accepted as an average amount of 12%, then the compensation above would rise to over £90,000.

The Revenue authorities do not altogether ignore such arrangements and often the shareholder's loss is a benefit, in part, to the Public Purse.

CHAPTER 16

Depreciation

The calculation of depreciation is an accounting tool to value past aquisitions to the present time. The "remaining depreciable value" is the "book value less the salvage value". There are four main methods:

> the straight line method;
> the "sum of the digits" method;
> the declining balance method;
> the reducing value method.

Different requirements often require different methods, for instance business methods of calculating depreciation are usually different to those related to tax write-offs.

The straight line method

This method is both conceptually simple to understand and evaluate and is mainly employed when the asset under valuation is one which remains largely unaltered during its life, such as a lease on buildings and property.

Formula:

$$\frac{\text{Cost} - \text{Scrap value}}{n} = \text{Depreciation per year.}$$

Cost − (Depreciation per year × n) = remaining book value
(after n years' depreciation)

where n = number of years' life.

A machine worth £60,000 has an estimated residual value at the end of 50 years of £10,000. What is the book value at the end of 24 years?

$$\frac{60,000 - 10,000}{50} = \text{£1,000 depreciation each year.}$$

60,000 − (1000 × 24) = £36,000 depreciated value after 24 years. The "remaining depreciable value" is the depreciated value less the estimated residual value, here £36,000 − £10,000 = £26,000.

132

Sum of the years digits method (SOYD)

This practice is used widely in the USA, often for tax reasons. Comment on SOYD, or Rule of 78, methods has already been made earlier in contrast to conventional amortising.

If a term is for 6 years the SOYD factor is $(6 \times 7)/2 = 21$

A truck costing \$2,500 is estimated to have a scrap value of \$400 at the end of 6 years. What is the book value at the end of 5 years?

$$(\text{cost} - \text{scrap}) \times \frac{(n-y)+1}{\text{SOYD}} = \text{Depreciation for the yth year}$$

$$(2500 - 400) \times \frac{(6-5)+1}{21} = \$200 \text{ Depreciation for 5th year}$$

To find the book value (LESS scrap value) at the end of y years:

(y's Depreciation)$/2 \times (n - y) = $ Book value $(-$ scrap) yth year

(see above) $200/2 \times (6 - 5) = \$100$ Book value 5th year

$(2100 \times (6 - 3 + 1)/21)/2 \times (6 - 3) = \$600$ Book value 3rd year

The schedule below will clarify the modus operandi.

Year	Cost $		Annual Dep'n $	(calc)	Book value less scrap $
1	$(2500 - 400) \times 6/21$		600	$(2100 - 600)$ =	1500.00
2	2100	$\times 5/21$	500	$(1500 - 500)$ =	1000.00
3	2100	$\times 4/21$	400	$(1000 - 400)$ =	600.00
4	2100	$\times 3/21$	300	$(\ 600 - 300)$ =	300.00
5	2100	$\times 2/21$	200	$(\ 300 - 200)$ =	100.00
6	2100	$\times 1/21$	100	$(\ 100 - 100)$ =	0.00

A crane costing \$25,000 is considered a "write-off" after 10 years (no scrap value). What is the book value of the crane after 6 years?

$$25000 \times (10 - 6 + 1)/(10 \times 11/2) \times .5 \times (10 - 6) = \$4,545.45 \text{ b.v.}$$

Declining balance method

Depreciation factor $= 2/n = $ "double declining method", where $n = $ the assumed number of years for a total write off.

$$\text{Cost} \left(1 - \frac{\text{dep. factor}}{n}\right)^{y-1} \times \frac{\text{dep. factor}}{n} = \text{Depreciation for yth year}$$

$$\text{Cost} \left(1 - \frac{\text{dep. factor}}{n}\right)^{y} - \text{Residual} = \text{Book value less residual at end of yth year.}$$

In the example above, an item valued at £2,500 had a scrap value of $400. Taking total depreciation over 6 years by the double declining method, the "dd factor" becomes 2/6 = .333. (Employing "double" declining, the basic factor is, not unnaturally, 2 − but this factor could be 1.5 if required to employ just a "declining method" − if so 1.5/6 = .25).

Find the depreciation and book value, less the scrap value, at the end of 4 years.

$$2500(1 - 2/6)^{4-1} \times 2/6 = \$246.91 \text{ depreciation in the 4th year}$$

$$(2500(1 - 2/6)^4) - 400 = \$\ 93.83 \text{ book value (less scrap) at the end of 4th year.}$$

Year	Annual Dep'n $	Book value less salvage $
1	2500.00 × .33 = 833.33 & 2500.00(1 − .33) = 1666.67 − 400 =	1266.67
2	1666.67 × .33 = 555.56 & 1666.67(1 − .33) = 1111.11 − 400 =	711.11
3	1111.11 × .33 = 370.37 & 1111.11(1 − .33) = 740.74 − 400 =	340.74
4	740.74 × .33 = 246.91 & 740.74(1 − .33) = 493.83 − 400 =	93.83

If there was no salvage value, the 5th year's book value would be:

$$(2500 \times (1 - .33)^5) - 0.00 = \$329.22$$

The reducing balance method

When the UK system of writing down for tax purposes one quarter of the cost each year over a period of four years was changed to a "reducing balance method" whereby a write-off was charged at 25% each year on the reducing balance, it meant that the total cost never quite disappears under this form of depreciation.

For example, if plant was purchased for £10,000 (with no salvage value), under the old rules writing down allowances could be charged at £2,500 each year for four years. But under the reducing balance rule, at 25%, the book value after four years is:

$$\text{Cost} \times \left(1 - \frac{\text{rate }\%}{100}\right)^y = \text{Book value at end of } y \text{ years.}$$

$$= \pounds10,000.00 \times .75^4 = \pounds3164.06$$

In other words, £10,000 less 25%, less 25%, less 25% and so on . . .

$$\text{Cost} \times \left(1 - \frac{\text{rate }\%}{100}\right)^{y-1} - \text{Cost} \times \left(1 - \frac{\text{rate }\%}{100}\right)^y = \text{dep year } y.$$

To find the reduced balance: $cost \times .75^n$

To find the annual depreciation: $\dfrac{cost \times .75^n}{3}$

To find 4 years' balance, in the example:

$£10,000 \times .75^4 = £3164.06$

and $£3164.06/3$ $= £1054.69$ depreciation year 4.

The term is:

$$\frac{LOG \dfrac{.01}{10,000}}{LOG \quad .75} = 48.02 \text{ years.}$$

By this method, it will take just over 48 years' depreciation to reduce the book value to one penny!

BIC–J

Part II

CHAPTER 17

Fixed Interest Loans and YTM Formulae

General

Those statisticians well versed in the general methods of calculating fixed interest loans and merely reaching for "Business Interest Calculations" with a view to checking a particular point can usefully skip this chapter and the one following. Others who skipped Part I may yet find a glance over Chapter 2 useful.

Fixed interest loans

In Part I different types of loans and savings were examined in which the periodic interest due varied in each case. Whereas compound interest loans had "interest on interest", the interest amount for repayment loans reduced each payment period commensurate with the reducing capital.

In Part II we shall be dealing exclusively with fixed interest-bearing obligations, that is where the interest received by the lender is the same at each interest due period.

Although the point was never made, the tendency, in Part I, was to regard each loan example from the perspective of the borrower. In Part II the opposite will obtain and, in general terms, the examples outlined will assume the reader is the lender.

Interest rolled up and interest paid per compounding period

A £100.00 loan over 10 years at an interest rate of 10% will have a future value of £259.37, namely £100 capital returned and £159.37 of interest which has been "rolled up" over the ten year term.

Supposing, however, that the interest was not rolled up but was paid to the lender each year, the capital sum would need to be returned to the lender at the end of the term. If the lender required the above return of 10%, the interest paid to him each year would need to be £10 – with the £100 capital amount being repaid at the end of the "term" of the loan, when it "matured". In other words at redemption the last payment will be the £10 interest and the redemption value (the RV), here £100.

In effect that is what all fixed interest loans are, but unfortunately, in the same way as we saw in Part I that there were various different methods

139

of calculating home loans, so also are there many ways — unhappily all too many ways — of calculating fixed interest bond prices and yields. (See "Overview on YTMs in general" at chapter end.)

The "creep up"

In the above example with a 10% gross return on a £100 loan you would expect to receive £10 each year while the loan was running, and your £100 back at maturity, as mentioned above.

The fixed interest loan outlined above could be a personal loan to a friend or by the public to an industrial corporation wishing to raise funds for further development by making a debenture loan issue. The latter would be a promise to repay the original amount lent at a fixed time in the future and an agreement to pay a fixed amount of interest each year, or half year, until the loan matured. Governments make the same type of issues to the general public, except that in their case the interest is usually somewhat less than for a company, however elegant and reputable, for the security of a government loan stock is naturally more assured. Bonds are usually issued in multiples of 100 (sometimes 1,000).

Assume that the above parameters related to a government issue of (UK) loan stock; the terms are that the Government promises to pay £10 per year, per £100 of stock, for the next twenty years and that at the end of the term the repayment on the loan would be 100%, namely £100 would be repaid for every £100 borrowed — or, from the lender's perspective, "subscribed". In that case the gross yield is, naturally, 10% (10 × 100/100).

Now suppose after the issue has been running some 10 years, an investor purchases £100 of this loan stock in the market for £80; on purchase he takes over the role of a "lender" (for this particular amount) and his gross yield becomes:

$$10 \times 100/80 = 12.50\%.$$

The yields to maturity (YTM)

But above, surely, there is a factor which we have not taken into account — and one which must be of great interest to the investor?

If the 20 year loan above has been running for 10 years then it must have a further 10 years to run to redemption, and if £100 of loan stock cost us only £80 and on maturity will be repaid "at par" (parity 100%), then unless our mathematics are wrong we will have a £20 capital gain over a 10 year period — or put another way, there will be a capital lift of £2 a year assuming we hold to redemption. So, whatever the price, it will level out to the maturity value at the end of the term, creeping day by day up to 100% or if purchased above par, inching downward to 100 at redemption.

Our 12.50% gross yield above takes no account of this creep up situation. What the investor really requires in this sort of situation, therefore, is a yardstick or benchmark which will reflect the true value in terms of yield not only of the annual or periodic interest payments but also of the redemption value at maturity — in other words a yield to redemption or maturity.

Thinking in terms of a Part I mortgage type repayment loan we could format the above treating, quite reasonably, the "RV" (redemption value) as the "balance" or "balloon" factor and the loan value as the "cost". In that case the periodic repayments must be interest ONLY — for there is no capital amortisation, for no capital is repaid during the course of the loan — only at the conclusion, at maturity.

Unhappily, as for repayment loans, the interest rate has to be found by guess and guess again interpolation or, more sensibly, by a computer or calculator program. In the above example, with the cost at 80%, RV at 100%, an annual "coupon" (or interest payments) of 10% over a term of 10 years exactly, the yield to maturity (YTM) works out precisely at 13.80515861% — as opposed to the gross yield, quoted above of 12.50%.

$$\frac{80 - (100 \times 1.13805^{-10})}{10a_{\overline{10}|}} \text{ at } 13.805\% \text{ nominal}$$

Check:

To find the cost (price) at maturity:

$100 \times 1.13805^{-10} + 10a_{\overline{10}|}$ at 13.805% $\qquad = \qquad$ cost

$(100 \times 1.13805^{-10}) + [10(1 - 1.13805^{-10})/.013805] =$ $\qquad$ cost

$27.43977314 + 52.56022691$ $\qquad\qquad\qquad = 80$ cost.

The above is an example of a bond price/yield calculation in its simplest form.

Odd days

The reason why the above was in its "simplest form" is because the term was *exactly* 10 years, whereas in practice an integer term is only valid at issue or in the rare event that the bond is purchased and paid for on the precise date that interest is due.

The usual term is a number of periods, either years or half years, plus a number of odd days — and herein lie some of our difficulties; for different "markets", and different statisticians, have different methods of making calculations related to the odd days.

Discounting the maturity value back to the present time

To start with, for the sake of simplicity, let us make certain assumptions — which will be discussed in detail later. Assume that one unit of £100 of a bond has been purchased for a price of £96.1875, with 665 days to run to maturity, with a redemption value (RV) of 100% (£100 per one unit of stock). It has a 5.50% nominal coupon, semi-annual interest of £2.75 paid. The gross or flat yield will therefore stand at $5.50 \times 100/96.1875 = 5.72\%$ (usually expressed to 2 places of decimals).

As the purchase price is 96.1875 there is an obvious maturity lift of 3.81 points $(100 - 96.1987)$ — so a YTM is naturally required.

Since the interest payments are semi-annual, the "life of the stock", in terms of half annual periods and odd days, is $665/182.5 = 3.643836$, some 3 half years and 117.5 odd days (at this stage don't worry about the half day). The resultant (3.643836) of a division of the total number of "life" days by a base (here of $365/2 = 182.5$) is usually referred to as the "n + k" factor (see later), the "n" being the periods (whether years or half years no matter) and the "k" being the odd days fraction.

From an issue prospectus we would always know what the interest, or coupon, is each year, or half year, the dates when payments are to be made and the precise date of redemption when the full capital repayment is due for repayment. Given a YTM, to find the cost (price) we must discount the final repayment value, the RV, back to the present time (purchase payment time), and also discount each payment, as it is made, again back to the present time.

To discount the redemption value and the interest payments, period by period, we must have an interest rate — so assume a nominal 7.777501% yield to maturity which becomes an internal rate of return (IRR) of 7.777501/2 for semi-annual interest payments and presents as 3.888751%, or $7.777501/(100 \times 2) = 0.03888751$ as an "i/p" factor, the "i" representing the interest rate as a percentage and "p" the number of "rests" in any one year. Going forward in time to the redemption date, the investor will expect, on that date, to receive not only the redemption value (£100) but also the last and final interest payment, here £2.75, so the first thing to do is to make a schedule of our discounting process:

$$(\text{RV} + \text{Pmts}) \times (1 + i/p)^{-1} \qquad = \text{first discounting}$$

$$(100 + 2.75) \times 1.03888751^{-1} \qquad = 98.903875 \ (98.91)$$

$$(98.91 + 2.75) \times 1.03888751^{-1} \qquad = 97.848780 \ (97.85)$$

$$(97.85 + 2.75) \times 1.03888751^{-1} \qquad = 96.833179 \ (96.83)$$

(What about the odd days?)

$$(96.83 + 2.75) \times 1.03888751^{-k} \quad (k = 117.5/182.5 \text{ above})$$

(the odd days discounted by COMPOUND INTEREST (CI) methods)

$(96.83 + 2.75) \times 1.03888751^{-.643836} = £97.166952$

> For if simple interest (SI) discounting:
>
> $(96.83 + 2.75) \times 1/(1 + (\quad i/p \quad \times \quad k \quad)) =$
>
> $(96.83 + 2.75) \times 1/1 \ + (.03888751 \times .643836)) = £97.150799$

But surely 96.1875 was the cost of the bargain, not 97.166952, so is the discounting above incorrect?

As the £97.166952 includes the interest accruing between the payment date PRIOR to purchase and the actual purchase date is not (normally) part of the price so this amount must be "cleaned", subtracted, from the 97.166952 amount above. In parenthesis, as the "clean" price (CP) is "less accrued interest" (a/i), not surprisingly the price which includes the a/i is colloquially known as the "dirty" price (DP).

What then is the amount of a/i which needs to be subtracted from the dirty price, here, of 97.166952 above?

With a notional 182.5 days in our half year, and 117.5 odd days, the other interest portion of that half year must be (182.5 − 117.5), some 65 days. 65 days multiplied by the half coupon (2.75) and divided by 182.5 will provide an a/i of 0.979452 which, when subtracted from the dirty price (DP), will present a clean price (CP) of exactly £96.1875 or £96 3/16th.

The basic bond price/yield to maturity formula

With computers doubtless all such calculations could be "scheduled" but this is quite unnecessary, for the requirements shown by the schedule method above can quite simply be converted into a formula which will provide precisely the same answer, namely yield or price.

Bond formula when the periods between SD and RD are greater than 1

$$\frac{RV(1 + i/p)^{-n} + Da_{\overline{n}|} + D}{(1 + i/p)^k} = DP \quad \text{(discounted CI)}$$

Where:

SD = Settlement date
RD = Redemption date
RV = Redemption value (usually 100)
i = The interest rate as a decimal
p = The number of interest periods in any one year
C = Coupon (annual interest payments)
D = $C/2$ (semi-annual interest payments)
n = Total number of interest payment periods
k = ("odd days" between SD and next pmt date)/base factor
a/i = Accrued interest
DP = Dirty price (price +/− accrued interest)
CP = Clean price (price less accrued interest)

$a_{\overline{n}|} = \dfrac{1 - (1 + i/p)^{-n}}{i/p}$ (or any other preferred format − see Chapter 2)

From our knowledge of amortisation calculations in Part I one would expect to see the exponent as "−np" (not "−n") but conventionally the "n" of (n + p) is always understood to be the number of years or half years in the term, dependent on whether the interest payment is annual or semi-annual.

If the calculation relates to a bond's total "life" between issue and maturity (or when settlement falls on a payment date), or for an "ex-div" calculation, delete the last "D" in the numerator. If there is no "k" value delete the denominator.

PRICES can be found from the above formula, given the YTM and the other necessary data.

Yields to maturity can be found, based on this formula, only by assuming a rate and checking whether it meets the required conditions − or by using a computer.

In some cases, for short-dated stock i.e., stock with 5 years or under to run to maturity, some statisticians consider that the discounting in the denominator above should be simple interest (SI) and not, as shown above, by COMPOUND interest methods. In that case the denominator should show:

$$\text{for SI;} \quad \frac{\text{Numerator as above}}{1 + (i/p \times k)} = DP$$

Taking the above example:

$RV(1 + i/p)^{-n} + Da_{\overline{n}|}$ = the discounted amount.

$100(1 + i/p)^{-3} + 2.75a_{\overline{3}|}$ at 7.777501% nominal
at 3.888751%

$100 \times 1.03888751^{-3} + 2.75((1 - 1.03888751^{-3})/.03888751)$ = Balance

$89.185536 + 7.647642 = £96.833179$

Glance back at the schedule above and at this point, namely when we arrived at 96.833179, the comment was "what about the odd days?". At this point we added the last payment amount and discounted this amount by $(1 + i/p)$ to the power of the odd days divided by the base 182.5, namely the "k" factor.

In the same way the formula adds the last half coupon, a "D" (or "C" if annual interest is paid) and discounts accordingly:

$$\frac{RV (1 + i/p)^{-n} + Da_{\overline{n}|} + D}{(1 + i/p)^k} = \text{Price (\textbf{includes} a/i)}$$

So $96.833179 + 2.75 = 99.583179$ discounted by $(1 + i/p)^k$, namely: $1.038888^{.643836}$ provides the "dirty price" £97.166952, as in the schedule above, and "cleaned" to 96.1875, if required, by the method shown above.

$$\frac{100(1.03889^{-3}) + 2.75((1 - 1.03889^{-3})/.03889) + 2.75}{1.03888751^{.643836}} = 97.166952 \text{ DP}$$

$$\boxed{\text{CI} \quad \frac{99.583179}{1.03888751^{.643836}} = 97.166952}$$

$$\boxed{\text{SI} \quad \frac{99.583179}{1 + (.03888751 \times .643836)} = 97.150799}$$

At this point it might be convenient for the beginner to be able to visualise pictorially how the various payments are made and how the odd and accrued interest days fit into the picture.

```
          SD . . . . . . . . . . . . . . 665 days . . . . . . . . . . . . . . RD
              |                                                           |
2.75 ——-|—— 2.75 ———————— 2.75 ———————— 2.75 ———————— 102.75
pmt ——-|—— pmt ———————— pmt ———————— pmt ————— RV + pmt
    65  | 117.5 |                  |                |              |
        (182.5)         (182.5)  |  (182.5)      |  (182.5)      |
days a/i | odd                                                    |
          SD . . . . . . . . . . (n + k = 3.643836) . . . . . . . . . . RD
```

Bonds with less than 1 period interest payment (per < 1)

In the price/YTM formulae above, where there were several payment periods plus odd days, it will be recalled that to find a YTM interpolation and/or a computer program was necessary. Now for the good news!

When a bond has a life from settlement to maturity of so short a period that there are no payments due before redemption (life per < 1) then a shortened formula is available which can find the price or the YTM — and no guessing. Employing the same symbols as above, the shortened formulae present as:

Compound interest method:

$$\frac{RV + D}{(1 + i/p)^k} = DP\,(CI)$$

$$(100 \times p) \times \left(\left(\frac{RV + D}{DP}\right)^{1/k} - 1\right) = YTM\,(CI)$$

Simple interest method:

$$\frac{RV + D}{1 + (i/p \times k)} = DP\,(SI)$$

$$(100 \times p) \times \left(\left(\frac{RV + D}{DP} - 1\right) \times 1/k\right) = YTM\,(SI)$$

For D read C if interest payments are annual.

For UK ex-dividend calculation (see later) delete the numerator D (or C if applicable) from the above formulae:

With such a short period not only must we find the number of odd days, settlement to next payment date (NPD), but also the number of accrued interest (a/i) days, payment prior to settlement Date (PPD) and settlement. These "days" added together are often treated as the "base days" (instead of 182.5). But it is optional whether SI or CI discounting is employed — many statisticians considering that SI is desirable for "short" loans.

To take an example:

Price (clean) $99\frac{28}{32}$nds (99.875). RV 100

Nominal coupon 4.75% with semi-annual interest payments (2.375%)

Settlement   7 February 1984

Redemption 15 May   1984 Days between 98

PPD – SD   Days between 84

PPD – NPD   Days between 182 (incl. 1 leap day)

Options: To include or disregard the leap days

            To use base 182 (in this particular example) or 182.5

                            for both the "k" factor and a/i

            To employ a true or rounded a/i

            To employ compound or simple interest discounting.

k $= 98/182$ $= .538462$

a/i $= [(182 - 98)/182] \times 4.75/2$ $= 1.096154$

The dirty price therefore becomes $99.875 + 1.096154 = 100.971154$

$$(100 \times 2) \times \left(\left(\frac{100 + 2.375}{100.971154}\right)^{1/.538462} - 1\right) = 5.195\% \text{ YTM (CI)}$$

$$\frac{100 + 2.375}{(1 + 5.195/200)^{.538462}} = 100.971154 \text{ DP (CI)}$$

$$200 \times \left(\left(\frac{102.375}{100.971154} - 1\right) \times 1/.538462\right) = 5.164\% \text{ YTM (SI)}$$

or: $$\frac{102.375}{1 + (5.1640/200 \times .538462)} = 100.971190 \text{ DP (SI)}$$

To find the odd days

This is a very rare requirement.

$$\frac{\text{LOG } (RV(1 + i/p)^{-n} + Da_{\overline{n}|} + D)/DP}{\text{LOG} \qquad (1 + i/p)} \times 182.5 = \text{"odd days"}.$$

Taking a previous example:

A "dirty price" of 97.16695205   Redemption Value 100.

YTM   of 7.777501384% (3.88750693% semi-annual)

Coupon   of 5.50%   (2.75%   semi-annual)

3 periods + k odd days.

$$\frac{\text{LOG } \left[(100 \times 1.03889^{-3}) + \left(2.75\left(\frac{1 - 1.03889^{-3}}{.03889}\right)\right) + 2.75\right]/97.167}{\text{LOG} \qquad\qquad\qquad 1.03887507}$$

$\times 182.5 =$ days

$$\frac{\text{LOG } [89.18553641 + 7.647642434 + 2.75]/97.16695205}{\text{LOG} \qquad\qquad 1.038887507} \times 182.5 = \text{days}$$

$$= \frac{\text{LOG } 1.024867}{\text{LOG } 1.038888} \times 182.5 \qquad = \text{days}$$

$$= 0.024563/0.038150 \times 182.5 = \text{days}$$

$$0.64836 \times 182.5 \qquad\qquad = 117.5 \text{ days}.$$

Alternatively, the shortened example above:

$$\frac{\text{LOG } (100 + 2.375)/100.971154}{\text{LOG} \qquad 1 + (5.1640/200)} \times 182.5 = 98 \text{ odd days}.$$

Rounded prices and rounded YTMs call for a little common sense!

Approximate YTMs

Because of the difficulties of finding a YTM without a computer/calculator program it is often useful to be able to make a quick approximate YTM, "on the back of an envelope", as a check or rough guide as to the true value and there are, and have been over many decades, various methods of providing this value.

Perhaps the best and nearest approximation is found as below:

$$\frac{C \times 100}{CP} + \frac{RV - CP}{(n + k)} = \text{Approx YTM \%}.$$

If the $(n + k)$ factor has been derived from a semi-annual base, that is for semi-annual payments, then for C read D in the formula above (the half annual coupon) and multiply the result by 2 to find the nominal approximate YTM%.

A CP provides an approximate YTM usually fractionally greater than the true value, a DP generally fractionally less. Using the figures in the example above "Discounting the maturity value back to the present time":

$$\left(\frac{2.75 \times 100}{96.1875} + \frac{100 - 96.1875}{665/182.5} \right) \times 2 \qquad = 7.810574\%.$$

Whereas, employing a DP of 97.16695205, the resulting approximate YTM would be:

$$\left(\frac{2.75 \times 100}{97.16695205} + \frac{100 - 97.16695205}{665/182.5} \right) \times 2 = 7.215342\%.$$

Readers will recall that the true value for the YTM for this particular bond was 7.778%.

Obviously the above formula/equation will not be valid if the life of the bond is less than one period, i.e., if there is no "n" in the $(n + k)$ factor. But in these circumstances, it will be appreciated, an approximation is quite unnecessary — for the true YTM can be found easily by the shortened $(per < 1)$ formula method without any iteration.

Note for computer programmers

There are various methods employed by experienced programmers to determine interest rates and I would not presume to suggest any particular discipline: nevertheless one such method is set out in Appendix B. This method when employed for finding YTMs (for longer term bonds) needs the calculation of a closely approximate "first guess" in order to commence the iterative, or "looping", process and the formulae above will be found particularly appropriate for this purpose.

Overview of YTMs in general

In olden days, before computers, the difficulties in finding the yield to maturity were considerable, for bond tables or four-figure log tables (themselves not over-precise) had to be employed, as did interpolation. All of which was an immense time-consuming labour which, not surprisingly, led to minimising as much as possible the interpolation – providing only minimal accuracy. As a result redemption yields, in those days, were usually quantified in quarters of one per cent, namely 11%, 11.25% and so on, and were thus considered to be only a rough guide for investment purposes – and nothing more.

But with the advent of the microchip, resulting in computer and calculator programs designed to find yields both rapidly and accurately to 10 or more decimal places, the cult of the YTM appears to have increased out of all proportion, various statisticians and DP managers all apparently vying with each other to produce bigger and better formulae aimed at getting "nearer to the truth" – nearer to the truth in this connection presumably being a formula to equate with, or to be as near as possible to, the result of periodic scheduling – discounting each period on a days-per-period count. As a result nowadays there are an infinite number of ways in which the basic formula above can be interpreted – and herein lies part of the burden of the following chapters.

CHAPTER 18

Some Rules. Some Options. Taxation Formulae

General

The last chapter provided the formulae to find the prices (or YTMs) of fixed interest loans, bonds and debentures. But whereas the basic discounting formulae remain constant, this by no means applies to the various peripheral calculations, as we shall see in Chapters 20, 21 and 22. For although the basic concept is the same in all cases, there is a variety of different ways the required answers can be calculated. And it is these differences that this chapter examines.

Coupons

In the last chapter "coupons" were mentioned to denote the nominal interest rate of bonds. This term derives from bearer bonds which have a detachable coupon for each interest period and which, when presented to an authorised bank, can be encashed for the amount stated on the coupon – a method unremarkable in most countries but less well known in the United Kingdom, for bearer bonds cannot be issued by UK companies and are seldom held in the private hands of a UK national.

Two dates for redemption

An issue of loan stock, whether a government security or an industrial debenture, will state, inter alia, the dates on which the interest will be paid, annually, semi-annually or (rarely) quarterly; and also the date will be given on which the loan will be redeemed i.e., the date the capital previously borrowed will be repaid to the holder of the bond certificate at the time of redemption. In some cases there may be two redemption dates stated and this means that the borrower (government or corporation), CAN repay the loan amount on the first or earlier date but MUST pay on or before the last named date. The rule, for all calculation purposes, is that the LAST date will be taken if the price of the bond (*clean of all accrued interest* – see later) stands below the redemption value (RV).

The logic underlying this convention is that the only reason why a stock will stand above par is that current lending rates must have fallen since the issue of the bond, there being thus more buyers than sellers for the high-income bonds. In that case the assumption is that the borrower will redeem these high income bonds at the earliest possible opportunity in order to borrow more cheaply by another issue with a (lower) coupon more in line with the "going" rates.

Leap days

When calculating the days between settlement date (SD) and redemption date (RD) normally any intervening leap days are ignored in bond price/yield calculations; for the lender receives a fixed interest payment per year or half year irrespective of whether there is an extra day in the payment period or not (unlike bank certificates of deposit, where leap days are included – with a fractional increase of interest paid). To save inaccurate and time-consuming finger-counting, at the end of Chapter 1 will be seen a useful formula for determining quickly and accurately the number of leap years/days between any two dates – providing such dates stand between the years 1901 and 2099.

Settlement

Above we used the terms "purchase" and "cost at purchase"; in fact the correct term should have been "settlement"; for the interest calculations must obviously only reflect the periods from when the money is paid out and received.

Settlement date can be a trap for the unwary, for it varies from market to market and indeed within some markets for different classes of stock. To take two examples, a bargain made in Eurobonds requires settlement 7 days after purchase, whereas on the London Stock Exchange bonds classed as government securities require settlement one day after purchase. But settlement for UK industrial debentures conforms to the settlement days required for ordinary share bargains, namely once a fortnight (unless this "fortnight" is bedevilled by intervening bank holidays – thus extending to a "three week account"). Each year the London SE lists all "acount days" and "days for settlement" throughout the whole year. Therefore it is essential for any statistician working out the number of "days between" settlement date (SD) and redemption date (RD), or in some cases the number of half year payment periods and odd days, to be alert as to **exactly** which day is "settlement" either for the particular market concerned or, indeed, for the class of stock within the market.

Accrued interest

In Chapter 1 only a short mention of the calendar was made, but as nearly all the yields resulting from fixed interest-bearing obligations (bond yields, bank certificates of deposit etc), depend on the number of years, half years, and odd days between settlement and maturity, it is very necessary to understand fully all the various permutations that different calendars present.

In general terms the days between the two dates, settlement and maturity, divided by the required base, provide the (n + k) factor which was mentioned in the last chapter in both the formula and the subsequent calculations. We saw that 665 "days between", divided by 182.5, provided an (n + k) factor of 3.643835616 (which is 3 half years and 117.5 days) and that the accrued interest (a/i) days are "the other half" of the half year. The pictorial discounting chart, in the last chapter, demonstrated the "other portion of the half-year" for the a/i days; from which a mathematician may deduce that he could avoid the labour of finding the actual number of a/i days and find the accrued interest merely by multiplying the coupon by (1 − k).

But this quick (1 − k) method is precisely what the wise statistician must guard against − if the interest is paid semi-annually. For using the (1 − k) method on many occasions the a/i cannot help but be the result of an inexact number of days − which is unacceptable marketwise. Above, the odd days were 117.5 days and therefore the a/i days must be (182.5 − 117.5) = 65 days. If the values were reversed, with 65 odd days, the a/i days would thus be 117.5 days − with the unacceptable fraction. So the *rule* is that when using the actual (365 day) calendar and when semi-annual interest is paid, the correct ACTUAL number of days between prior payment date and settlement date should be found by calendar means and NOT by the (1 − k) method.

Accrued interest true or rounded

In many cases there is a divergence of opinion as to how the accrued interest is to be added or subtracted from the "dirty" price: some consider the a/i in its true value form, to (say) 10 sig.fig. is correct, others that it should be rounded to 2 or 3 decimal places before recalculating. Eurobonds, for example, are always rounded to 2 places of decimals. Remember this is not merely a matter of presentation but one which affects the calculations.

In all the examples above the a/i has been assumed to be "true", eg, $2.75 \times 65/182.5 = 0.979452055$, thus making the "clean" price exactly 96.1875 or 96 3/16ths. If, however, the a/i was rounded to (say) 2 decimal places, namely .98, when subtracting that amount from the dirty price of 97.16695205 we are left with 96.186952 and if a computer program was written (as some are) to round DOWN for a vulgar fraction, the quotation to be quantified in 1/8ths, the price would be 96 1/8th (96.125). Alternatively, if finding a YTM from a DP of 96.1875 + .98, the YTM would be 7.777% instead of 7.778%.

Quoted and listed prices

Remember that the formula/equation MUST always work to a DIRTY price, irrespective of how the price is quoted. In most cases the world over prices are quoted clean, the UK market being an exception, quoting "dirty" for all stock other than UK government securities with a life of 5 years and under.

If determining a price, after calculation, in a market which "quotes clean" the a/i must be "cleaned" before a presentation; alternatively, if a YTM is to be found from a clean quoted price, before any calculations are contemplated the CP must have the addition of the a/i to provide the DP.

Expenses

In the London market brokers in their industrial debenture listings add "expenses", for such bonds attract not only higher commissions than do government securities but also have a modicum of tax added. These expenses are only a guide and are not intended to be an exact representation of the actual expenses incurred – a useful and fairly accurate guide nonetheless.

For example a quoted DIRTY price of (say) 90 for a UK industrial debenture could well have "expenses" added of .9% plus VAT (currently at 15%) before the YTM was calculated.

The calculation for expenses is as follows:

$$90 \times (1 + (.9 \times 1.15)/100) \qquad = 90.9315$$

And if there was an additional (say) 1% stamp duty:

$$90 \times (1 + (1 + (.9 \times 1.15))/100) = 91.8315$$

YTMs as a "guide" only

YTMs are only a GUIDE for investment purposes; useful indeed, but they are not necessarily "practical finance", nor are they intended to be. For example, an irate acquaintance once grumbled that the YTM thrown up by his computer did not equate to that based on his broker's contract note relating to a recent purchase of a UK government security. Of course it didn't! For no conventional bond price/yield computer program is designed to encompass all the different levels of commissions charged.

With a clean price of 96.1875, had the bargain been some £100,000 in a UK government stock, the commission might be (say) £750. If these extra expenses had been added to the dirty price: £97.167 + (750 × 100/100,000) = £97.917 DP and a new calculation of the YTM would have found not 7.778% but 7.319% – for the higher the price the lower the yield. The YTM of 7.778% is the "guide", the 7.319% the "practical yield" on which the investor, having made his purchase, can base his future investment policy.

Calendars

As seen in Chapter 1, the financial calendar (30/360) is often employed for interest-bearing obligations, and fixed interest bonds are no exception. In that case, of course, there is no reason why the $(1 - k)$ method cannot be employed to find the a/i, for obviously, with an integer base $(360 - 180)$ there is no possibility of any unwanted fractional days appearing.

Unfortunately, because many programmed calculators and computer programs emanate from those countries which largely employ the 30/360 calendar for their financial calculations, the $(1 - k)$ method is more than often programmed-in for use with both 30/360 **and** the actual calendars; as a result when the requirement needs actual calendar usage, such programs sometimes provide fractionally erroneous answers.

When calculating accrued interest with the 30/360 calendar the first day's payment is counted but settlement day is NOT, and:

1st – 30th of the same month	= 29 elapsed days
1st – 31st of the same month	= 30 elapsed days
1st – 1st of the following month	= 30 elapsed days
1st – 28th of February	= 27 elapsed days

When interest is payable on the 30th or 31st:

to 1st of the following month	= 1 day's interest
to 30th of the following month	= 30 days' interest
to 31st of the following month	= 30 days' interest

Calculating the days between

The calculation of days between dates in computer programs is merely a matter of finding a "date factor" for each date and then subtracting. There are various formulae but, while they can be determined on a simple calculator, they are an unnecessary labour, for if the statistician has no computer/calculator facilities available the charts in Chapter 1 and/or Appendix E are quite adequate for a few one-off calculations. For instance, the days between 1 January 1980 and 1 June 2000 (in which there are 6 leap days – see Chapter 1) are a matter of some 20 years and the days from Jan 1 – June 1 can be found from Appendix E as 151 days. $(365 \times 20) + 151 = 7451$ days WITHOUT leap days. Add 6 days for the true actual days if required for purposes other than Bond yield calculations.

Appendix C provides methodology for determining payment dates before and after settlement – required for the "quasi-coupon periods" method of calculating bond yields (see below).

At Appendix D will be found more information about "calendars" with details of how to construct a computer program for both actual and 30/360 calendars – (Dates/Dates) = Days and (Dates/Days) = Dates.

Maturity on a Sunday

If a substantial redemption amount, perhaps running to millions of pounds or dollars, cannot be paid immediately into a bank for reinvestment purposes, because of a non-banking day such as a Sunday, inevitably the true return is fractionally reduced. And so, in such cases some statisticians consider that the yield to maturity should be reduced accordingly. The conventional method is to reduce the YTM by one day:

$$\text{YTM} \times \frac{\text{Days between settlement and maturity}}{\text{Days between settlement and maturity} + 1} = \text{YTM (adjusted)}$$

The calculation provides a reasonably accurate adjustment. More than one day is rarely subject to this method of adjustment.

In the same way it could be argued that periodic, semi-annual interest received on a Sunday should also require some adjustment to the YTM. By formula this cannot be achieved and the only method, if this is a specific requirement, is to schedule each interest period, taking the exact number of days in each payment period. But as these amounts are less significant than the total redemption amount any such minor adjustments are ignored.

Scheduling

While on the subject of accuracy it might be worth dwelling for a moment on scheduling – for when dealing in "actuals", with semi-annual interest payments, there is always the ever-present problem of the odd number of days in each half year, namely 181–184, 182–183. One elegant member firm of the London Stock Exchange indeed does schedule all bonds with terms of five and under years, taking the exact number of days in each half year (including leap days), adjusting also for the days (within that period) should the payment fall on a non-banking day. This is the only really accurate method for bond calculations but as the formula method is only fractionally different, and as the YTMs are only a guide, few follow this exemplary method. This is just as well, for without a corresponding computer program there is no possible way of checking the YTM found from such a schedule!

The quasi-coupon period method

This method of calculating the accrued interest and "base" days is used extensively in the United States and indeed forms a required method when calculating US Treasury issues (see Chapter 21) and is used by the Americans to calculate all bonds "foreign" to the USA market. The "base" calculations for these particular bonds are "actual", (not 30/360), and relate only to semi-annual interest payments. By this method the number of periods of the term are found to provide the "n" factor. The (odd) days between settlement and the next payment date are calculated accurately (see Appendix C), as are the number of a/i days between the payment date prior to settlement and the settlement date; in other words the **actual** odd days and the **actual** a/i days are found by calendar methods (and in this case INCLUDE any leap days intervening). They are then added to make the "base" factor (instead of 182.5). The "k" factor is found by dividing the odd days by the new base factor. Taking the pictorial example above, with 117.5 odd days, and 65 a/i days: assume that the true value for the odd days was 117 and, with 65 a/i days, the base would become 182. Thus the k factor would be 117/182 = .642857 and so, with 3 half annual payments periods, the (n + k) would be 3.642857 − the a/i becoming 2.75 × 65/182 = .982143 (cf values above based on 182.5).

Although, admittedly, this quasi-period method of calculation may give statisticians and computer programmers a fraction more to worry about it cannot be denied that this formula provides the closest approximation, compared to other kindred formulae, to what "actually happens to the money".

Taxation

The prices and YTMs so far examined have been the result of calculations with no taxation interference, the YTMs being "before tax" (gross) − not to be confused with the "gross or flat yields". But, inevitably, taxation affects yields − and thus investment management.

There are two main taxes to be considered, income (or corporation) tax and capital gains tax (CGT), and the reader will doubtless already appreciate that there are bound to be "options" as to how the various net calculations are determined.

Income (or corporation) tax

The method to adjust for income (or corporate) tax is reasonably obvious in that if the annual or half annual interest is subject to tax, then the interest employed in any calculations must be net of tax − so the coupon is simply "brought to net" in the normal manner by multiplying the gross interest by (100 − tax rate %)/100. Before 1986, the UK statistician always assumed the a/i to be gross, his US counterpart treating it as net. After February 1986, because of the latest "bond-washing" regulations (Chapter 22), all UK a/i will also be treated as net of tax.

Capital gains tax (CGT)

The capital gain, or loss, is the difference between "cost" (the price) and the "realisation" (the redemption value).

The option, in this category, is whether the cost is the clean cost (price clean of all) or a cost plus accrued interest and, if applicable, with expenses added.

The formula is as follows:

RV − ((Tax rate/100) × (RV − Cost)) = RV (net).

And if RV was 100, the cost 80, and the tax rate 30% the equation would be: 100 − .3(100 − 80) = 94.00 RV (net).

If the price stood above par on purchase, then there is an off-setable loss instead of a gain.

In the CGT calculation, for example, the UK market treats cost as "with all" (a/i, expenses, and anything else that can legitimately be added!), whereas the US markets consider cost as "clean of all". For Eurobonds there is no rule; quite understandably so, for each statistician will tend to calculate as his own national market and tax laws dictate. Taking our original example, a life of 665 days, clean price 96.1875, nominal coupon of 5.50% and an RV of 100: if stemming from the UK market, it is likely that such an example would only have income or corporation tax levied, for a UK Government Security would not attract CGT. Alternatively, if CGT was applicable, it would relate to a different UK class of stock which, as we shall see later, would be calculated differently.

For example purposes only, let us assume that it is not a UK Bond and that income or corporation tax is levied at 50% *and* CGT at 30%. To save looking back, the (n + k) was 3.643836, and the gross a/i (stemming from the half coupon of 2.75 × 65/182.5) was 0.979452. The half-annual gross coupon of 2.75% therefore becomes 2.75 × .5 = 1.375% (NET) for income or corporation tax purposes.

Assume a clean price of 96.1875. Employing the US method of net a/i and clean cost for CGT calculations we have 65/182.5 × 2.75 × .5 = .489726 NET accrued interest. Thus the DP = 96.1875 + .489726 = 96.677226.

For CGT calculations, taking the cost to be CLEAN of all, we find:

100 − .3(100 − 96.1875) = 98.856250 RV (net)

From the above PRICE and other data the NET YTM = 4.336907% (Nominal) derived from an i/p of .02168453420.

To verify:

$$\frac{(98.8563 \times 1.021685^{-3}) + \left(1.375 \times \frac{(1 - 1.021685^{-3})}{.021685}\right) + 1.375}{1.021685^{.643836}} = 96.677226 \text{ DP}$$

which, when cleaned of the a/i *net* after tax (1.375 × 65/182.5), provides a Clean price of 96.1875. The "grossed up net" is 4.336907/.5 = 8.673814

= 8.674%.

Calculations to find the cost from a net YTM with a CGT content

Above the cost was provided, the requirement being to find the net YTM, and the reader had to take my word for the net YTM %, until after verification. Would it not have been simpler to have provided an example with a net YTM and treated the price as the requirement?

If there had been no capital gains tax content in the above example provision of either cost or YTM as data would have been equally applicable. But consider, with a capital gain as part of the problem, how can we find a price when a vital part of that equation is the net RV, i.e., (RV − cost) − when it is the very "cost", or price, which we are trying to find?

It would appear therefore that, given a net YTM for a bond which has a capital gains content, a correct price cannot be determined without considerable difficulty and probably a computer "looping" program. Indeed, some statisticians, when faced with this difficulty, have been known to argue that such a calculation is "quite unnecessary" − thus neatly avoiding the problem! But the requirement, although perhaps not an everyday one, may well be necessary − so what do we do?

The solution can simply be found by adopting one or other of the following formulae below. As the "cost" is not known a notional price (NP) is assumed which, by a short secondary calculation, is converted into the correct required price (RP).

It must be stressed that the correct formula below must be selected to equate with the methods adopted for the particular calculation mode in question. Employing the same symbols as given previously:

Formulae for determining a price where there is a CGT content

First find the correct NOTIONAL RV (RV″):

$$RV - (CGT/100 \times RV) = RV''$$

If the tax rate was 30%:

$$100 - (.3 \times 100) = 70.00 \ RV'' \ \text{(notional)}$$
$$102 - (.3 \times 102) = 71.40 \ RV'' \ \text{(notional)}$$

then apply the correct formula − as below:

$$Per > 1 \ (CI)$$

$$\frac{RV''(1+i/p)^{-n} + a_{\overline{n}|} + D}{(1+i/p)^{k}} = NP \ \& \ NP\bigg/\left(1 - \frac{CGT/100}{(1+i/p)^{n+k}}\right) = RP$$

$$Per > 1 \ (SI)$$

$$\frac{RV''(1+i/p)^{-n} + Da_{\overline{n}|} + D}{1 - (i/p \times k)} = NP \ \& \ NP\bigg/\left(1 - \frac{CGT/100}{(1+i/p)^{n} \times (1 + (i/p \times k))}\right)$$
$$= RP$$

$$Per < 1 \ (CI)$$

$$\frac{RV'' + D}{(1 + i/p)^k} \qquad = NP \ \& \ NP/\left(1 - \frac{CGT/100}{(1 + i/p)^k}\right) \qquad = RP$$

$$Per < 1 \ (SI)$$

$$\frac{RV'' + D}{1 + (i/p \times k)} \qquad = NP \ \& \ NP/\left(1 - \frac{CGT/100}{1 + (i/p \times k)}\right) \qquad = RP$$

where:

NP = Notional price

RP = Required price

For D read C if interest is paid annually.

For UK ex-div calculation delete the single "+ D" from numerators.

Adjusting the notional price

The NP is always "dirty", i.e., price PLUS a/i (and expenses if applicable) and as such reflects the method normally adopted in the particular market to select the "cost" from which the given net YTM stemmed. If the cost was a DP, the NP requires no adjustment. If, however, the cost was "clean of all", then the NP must be cleaned of the a/i (gross or net, depending on the type of calculation mode) PRIOR to employing the conversion formula, i.e., before dividing by the second part of the formula. Taking the example above with a nominal net YTM of 4.336907% and with the connected parameters, find the price. Employing the Per < 1 (CI) converting formula above and, treating the $(1 + i/p)$ as 1.021684535, we get:

$$\frac{70(1 + i/p)^{-3} + 1.375a_{\overline{3}|} + 1.375}{1.021684535^{.643836}} = \frac{70.964192}{1.013908} = 69.990768 \ NP$$

Because the method of calculation employed in this example took the cost as "clean of all" the a/i must be cleaned from the NP, and again as this mode treated the a/i as NET the a/i must be subtracted from the NP, thus:

$65/182.5 \times 1.375 \qquad = \quad .489726 = $ net a/i

$69.9907680 - .489726 = 69.501042$ (adjusted NP)

Now convert:

$$\frac{69.5010420}{1 - (.3/1.021685^{3.643836})} = 96.1875 \text{ Required price}$$

Alternatively assume that the above calculation had related to the UK market, with the a/i assumed to be gross and the "cost" being "dirty", that is a price which includes the gross a/i.

Take a YTM of 4.208077342% with an i/p of 0.021040387. The NP therefore presents as:

$$\frac{70(1.021040)^{-3} + 1.375a_{\overline{3}|} + 1.375}{1.021040^{.643836}} = 70.14672974 \text{ NP}$$

Now convert:

$$\frac{70.14672974}{1 - (.3 \times 1.021040^{-3.643836})} = 97.16695204 \text{ DP}$$

and subtract the a/i to find the CP:

$$97.16695204 - (2.75 \times 65/182.5) = 96.1875 \text{ Required price}$$

Press listings

A word of warning regarding prices and yields as reported in the financial pages of the world's newspapers. Such quotations should be treated with some reserve and should certainly not be employed as a check on any calculations made by the reader! For the data provided in such listings are rarely computed daily, often being received from the market only once or twice a week: the subsequent daily updating being merely by interpolating any price changes.

It will be appreciated that, when considering yields to maturity and fixed interest stock prices, interpolation, as such, will not allow for variations in the number of "days between" the printed date and maturity date — in other words the complete formula calculation is skipped and the printed yield, related to the printed price, is produced pro rata — a most "inefficient" method but nonetheless a useful, quickly produced, approximation often quite sufficient for any but the most critical reader.

In the UK, where settlement is one day after purchase, a price provided by (say) the *Times* newspaper on (say) 2 Jan, a Monday, assumes that settlement is 3 Jan — and the yields are, or should be, determined from that SD date. YTMs, consequent on printed prices on a Friday *should* therefore relate to settlement on the following Monday — but don't always!

Yield conversions according to market perspectives

In Part I we examined, in passing, the conversion between the nominal and the effective rate, pointing out that, as we all knew, if interest payments are made monthly they are more attractive to an investor than those made only once a year and, consequently, the annual return is somewhat higher to the investor/lender and slightly more costly to the borrower.

When we come to lending rates, coupons and yields, whether gross or to maturity, the convention is to refer to them in their nominal terms.

Unfortunately this sometimes causes misconceptions; for, apart from Euro-bonds, interest payments made half-annually are considered, the world over, as the norm for bonds, annual and quarterly payments being the exceptions. Thus the designation "nominal" is conventionally taken to mean those rates provided from a calculation based on semi-annual interest payments. Stupid probably but that is what "conventions" sometimes are!

A 10.25% flat yield or a YTM so based (i.e., the "effective rate" based on semi-annual interest payments) to be mathematically correct should in truth be considered as a 10% nominal (annual) rate

$$200\left(\left(1+\frac{10.25}{100}\right)^{1/2}-1\right) = 10.00\% \text{ Nominal.}$$

But when calculating Eurobonds (see Chapter 20), which normally have annual payments, the coupons and yields stated in their normal or annual terms, of course, stand correct. Some problems, in reverse, arise. When occasionally Eurobonds have "national characteristics" and as such carry semi-annual interest payments, alien to the Eurobond annual concept, these "exceptions", because of their semi-annual payment characteristics, are slightly more valuable than if they were only annually paid. As all "Euro listings" are based on annual payments, naturally such "exceptions" must be "notified" and brought to the attention of the Market. This is done by equating the fractionally greater semi-annual yield to its "annual equivalent". If therefore in a Eurobond listing 10.25% (S) was seen it would denote that the bond yield to maturity, based on semi-annual interest payments, was found as 10.00% but that, being a semi-annual exception in an annual market, it had been converted to its "annual equivalent".

Other conversions

Supposing, however, that instead of the usual semi-annual interest payments the interest payments for a bond were quarterly, four times per year, as sometimes occurs in Australia and very occasionally in the UK, as instanced by the UK Government stock 2½% Consols (UNDATED – no maturity – no YTM), what then is the conversion arrangement?

Assume the above stock was priced at 20 points. The conventional nominal flat or gross yield is:

$$\frac{2.50 \times 100}{20} = 12.50\% \text{ (flat yield).}$$

On the face of it, a 12.50% nominal rate with four interest payments per year SHOULD be converted by:

$$100\left(\left(1+\frac{12.50}{400}\right)^{4}-1\right) = 13.10\% \text{ effective,}$$

but in the UK because the *normal* conventional bond interest payments are *semi-annual*, most brokers relate the quarterly payments to the "norm", thus finding the flat yield as 12.70%:

$$200\left(\left(1 + \frac{12.50}{400}\right)^2 - 1\right) = 12.70\%.$$

Incidently, before computer/calculators, to save time many statisticians, in those circumstances, employed the "800 method" below:

$$\text{Gross yield} \times \left(1 + \frac{\text{Gross yield}}{800}\right) = \text{Flat yield adjusted.}$$

$$12.50 \quad \times \left(1 + \frac{12.50}{800}\right) \quad = 12.70\% \text{ (flat yield)}$$
$$\text{(adjusted quarterly pmts)}$$

For the inquiring mind, why does the 800 rule provide precisely the correct answer?

By transposing the above equation:

$$200 \times \left(\left(1 + \frac{12.50}{400}\right)^2 - 1\right) = 12.70$$

$$200\left(\frac{12.50}{200} + \frac{12.50^2}{160,000}\right) = 12.70$$

$$12.50 \times \left(1 + \frac{12.50}{800}\right) \quad = 12.70$$

Market perspective

So here we have a "market perspective" with statisticians, quite rightly from their point of view, adjusting anomalies THEIR way in THEIR market. The Euro-statistician adjusts anomalies in HIS market HIS way; the statistician accustomed to semi-annual payments adjusting quarterly payments his way. Just suppose, for a moment, that quarterly interest payments were the norm throughout the world, in that case any semi-annual interest payments yield would need to be reduced in value and the Eurobond yield, with its annual payments, reduced still more!

Incidentally, calculations for quarterly payments present no problem, the nominal coupon/4, finds the i/p multiplied by 400 to present the nominal YTM. The base becomes 365/4 and the a/i days must be found by the calendar, not by the $(1-k)$ method.

CHAPTER 19

The Options

The aim of the last two chapters was to give those less experienced in bond yield calculations a general view of formulae and some of the problems which almost inevitably will be encountered if, for example, they wished to write a computer program on the subject. It will be assumed, therefore, that as a result of accumulating knowledge from Part I and the two previous chapters the reader now is familiar with the different actuarial terms outlined in the previous pages, and understands the basic "discounting" concepts of the calculations, the calendars, accrued interest and all the related minor peripheral calculations such as the $(n + k)$ and the $(1 - k)$ factors.

It is hoped, therefore, that when "reading" rather than merely "searching" future chapters he will accept what may appear as an occasional repetition. For a statistician, reaching for the book off the shelf to inform himself as to methods of calculation for a particular market, should receive instant data without the need to search back through various chapters for explanations. The formulae above have all been shown in the "actuarial format" but naturally statisticians in various countries will have their own methods of layout, language and notation. It would obviously be confusing, and indeed quite pointless, to outline all the different methods of setting out the basic formulae, for irrespective of how the formulae are laid out or the format the individual statistician uses and is accustomed to, they must be all the same mathematically — all yielding the same answer as the actuarial format outlined throughout this book. For there can be only one way to discount an RV back to its present value, and only one way to discount each and every coupon payment back to its present value at the time of purchase. For example, the AIBD rule book (see next chapter) sets out various formulae, totally different in format to those shown here, but if "worked through" it will be found that irrespective of format they are precisely the same.

Naturally, too, some terms may vary, for instance most statisticians when dealing in bonds speak of "settlement date" but an alternative term is "value date", used extensively in banking circles. But readers should have no difficulty in translating any such differences into their own familiar terms.

Why then are there any problems concerning the calculation of bond yields and why is any book necessary?

The next three chapters provide a detailed examination of various methods of applying the basic formulae to three main individual markets, the Euro,

UK and US markets, and their particular conventions. In effect these three chapters, with the various options available, cover the whole gamut of bond calculations world-wide. In other words if calculating a bond all the statistician will need to discover is which type of method, Euro, US or UK, is employed in that particular market. At the end of this chapter are some suggestions as to the questions to be asked.

A SUMMARY OF THE VARIOUS OPTIONS

Calendars
"Actual" calendar 365 days/year. "30/360" = 360 days/year.
Base factors $365 - 182.5$: $360 - 180$.

Days between settlement and redemption dates (SD – RD)
Conventionally leap days are IGNORED, but there are exceptions.
(Bank certificates of deposit always INCLUDE leap days).

Number of payment periods + the odd days, SD to next Pmt date
Quasi-coupon period method of calculating.
Usually leap days are included in the a/i and odd days.

(n + k) factor
(1)   (number of days between SD – RD)/base factor.
(2)   (n + odd days)/base factor for quasi-period method.

Coupon (interest payments)
Annual, semi-annual, quarterly.

Accrued interest (a/i) – true or rounded
ACTUAL: (1)   a/i days/base factor X coupon (or 1/2 coupon)
            (2)   As for (1) but base derived by a/i + odd days per quasi-coupon period method
30/360   (3) $(1 - k)$ X coupon (or 1/2 coupon).

Redemption value (RV)
Usually 100 unless bond is "callable" or the result of a NET calculation.

Price
(1)   Clean of all (CP).
(2)   Price +/– a/i (DP).
(3)   Price cum or ex-dividend (UK market only).
(4)   Price with expenses.

Yields
(1)   Gross (flat) yields
(2)   Yields to maturity (YTM)

(3)   NET YTMs
(4)   "Grossed up net" (maturity) yields
(5)   Above based on either compound or simple interest discounting.

Adjustments to above yields
(1)   If Redemption falls on a Sunday
(2)   Conversions to annual equivalent
(3)   Conversions to semi-annual equivalent.

Tax

Income or corporation tax	Accrued interest gross or net
Capital gains tax	Prices clean of all
	Prices with a/i +/− expenses.

Abnormal characteristics

UK Local Authority Bonds (LABs):	see Chapter 22
Split coupons:	see Chapter 25
Delayed first interest payments:	see Chapter 26
Redemption and last payment dates not coincident:	see Chapter 26.

Peripheral calculations

Decimal entry discounted cash flow calculations:	see Chapter 4
Dates fringing settlement:	see Chapter 23
Notional prices (FPPs) and net optimum yields:	see Chapter 24.

The problem

There is nothing difficult about calculating a price from a given YTM, or a YTM from a price by computer — the difficulty arises from the various ways which different statisticians use the basic formula and from trying to calculate the same way as someone else — in a different part of the world.

What questions to ask

On rare occasions when a statistician is not "au fait" with a particular market, he can usually find someone who knows how. And he will find that the problem is not so much which method is employed but which options, with which method, are applicable.

Suppose that our statistician is told that Hong Kong calculates like the London market, semi-annually, actual; immediately he will need to know what their settlement arrangements are, like London for gilts or industrials? Do they employ the quasi-coupon method? Are there "rules" and if so who makes them and are there sanctions if broken? Again, if Japan, following closely the dollar scenario, calculates like the US market, 30/360, semi-annually, do they treat the accrued interest values as net or gross if tax intervenes?

If therefore you are to rely on a telephone call it is sensible to know EXACTLY what questions require answering. Below are some suggestions.

Settlement: How many days after purchase?
                   Same for all classes of stock?
                   Any variations?

Term: Method of determining the term of the Bond, actual or
                   30/360?
                   Annual – semi-annual – both? If both, when/how?

Quasi-Coupon   If "actual" semi-annual, is the quasi-coupon period method
period: employed always, on occasions, or at will?

Quotation: How are prices quoted, clean or dirty? For different classes
                   of stock?

Accrued   Is the a/i rounded, or cut off to x number of decimal
Interest: places, or "true", being allowed to run according to the
                   configuration of the computer/calculator concerned?

Ex-div: Does the market, the stock, bond or annuity concerned
                   have arrangements for closing its books on a certain date
                   prior to periodic payment (cf UK market and see Chapter
                   27 re Zimbabwe annuities), and if so, how many days
                   before?

Taxation: What are the local tax requirements, rates of income or
                   corporation tax? Is there any capital gains tax and if so,
                   when is it applicable?

Tax and a/i: When tax is calculated, is the accrued interest assumed to
                   be net or gross?

Leap days: Are leap days ignored in days between?
                   Are leap days included in a/i period or not?

Non-banking   Are any arrangements made to adjust quoted stock prices
days: in the event that redemption day falls on a non-banking
                   day?

CHAPTER 20

Eurobonds

General

Some years ago, when Eurobonds were first evolved, a number of firms engaged in their marketing formed an association, the Association of International Bond Dealers, more generally known as the AIBD. Realising that here was a new international market, formed since the advent of computers, with no inhibitions about past market conventions or "quill pen" methods, the Association bravely decided to lay down specific rules as to how Eurobond calculations were to be conducted. Indeed there was no reason why this should not be done, and every reason why it should.

After some understandable delays in getting agreement between the then 300 member firms, who all calculated differently according to their 30–40 different markets, a set of "AIBD Rules and Regulations" were drawn up so that nowadays a price and YTM of a Eurobond is quoted in precisely the same terms all the world over, in New York, London, Tokyo and Zurich, a highly desirable state of affairs which is generally agreed to be of great advantage in marketing and overall dealing.

Sadly, such sensible agreements do not obtain anywhere else; some markets lay down general guidelines but unlike the AIBD there is no sanction against non-compliance and all too often liberties are taken and indeed some computer programs, notably in business calculators, attempting to cover all aspects of bond yield calculations, sometimes fail to be precise in any.

Eurobond rules

- Eurobonds are always considered to be on an ANNUAL interest basis, with a calendar base of 30/360.
- The settlement date is seven days after purchase (more than often referred to as the "value date").
- The discounting is ALWAYS by COMPOUND interest.
- Prices are ALWAYS quoted CLEAN of accrued interest.
- The accrued interest is ALWAYS ROUNDED to TWO places of decimals before being added to, or subtracted from, the clean or dirty prices.
- NO VARIATIONS ARE PERMITTED.

Members of the AIBD are expressly forbidden to calculate Eurobonds by any methods other than the AIBD rules. If, for some reason, a member

firm should need to calculate by another method, then this must be so stated
and the method outlined.

Eurobond net calculations

Understandably, however, there are options when it comes to NET calculations, for rules cannot be laid down since any investor requiring a net perspective will inevitably calculate according to his own national tax legislation. For
example, the US statistician will treat the accrued interest for net calculations
as being net of tax, whereas the UK statistician will (until 1986) treat the a/i
as gross. If liable for CGT, the US investor will treat the cost of the purchase
as "clean of all" but his British counterpart will add any extras that he can
legitimately include.

"Annual equivalents"

Above it was noted that Eurobonds are always considered to be annually
based and it is true that the preponderance of Eurobonds pay annual interest
only. Nevertheless there are some bonds which carry their national characteristics and have coupons carrying semi-annual interest payments.

Obviously, from an investor's perspective, payments twice a year are
preferable to payments made only once a year — all other factors being equal
— and adjustments must be made to the yields if they are to be comparable
to the "norm", i.e. annual payments.

The YTMs resulting from semi-annual interest payments, therefore, need
to be converted to their annual equivalent, i.e. brought to their "effective
rate". A resulting 10% YTM from a semi-annual interest paid Eurobond is
"converted" to its "annual equivalent" (nobody ever talks, more correctly,
about converting to an "effective rate") by:

$$100\left(\left(1 + \frac{10.00}{200}\right)^2 - 1\right) = 10.25\% \text{ annual equivalent.}$$

Alternatively,

$$10 \times \left(1 + \frac{10.00}{400}\right) = 10.25\%.$$

(and in this case compare the method employed in the "800 Rule", Chapter
18).

Once this calculation has been made it should always be shown as 10.25%
(S) which denotes that the yield stems from a semi-annual coupon and that
it has already been converted. It is essential to understand the full import
of the (S); for if it is required to find a price from a QUOTED yield to
maturity of (say) 10.25%(S) before any calculations commence the "annual

equivalent" rate must be (re)converted to its true semi-annual structure, (or in banking terms converted to its "nominal value"):

$$200\left(\left(1 + \frac{10.25}{100}\right)^{1/2} - 1\right) = 10.00\% \text{ semi-annual status.}$$

Comment

There is no rule concerning presentation of the YTM, the most customary method being to round to THREE places of decimals.

The accrued interest, which is always rounded to two places of decimals, is determined by the number of financial calendar days between the payment date prior to settlement and settlement day — never the "actual" number of days, (AIBD Rule 225).

The AIBD formula for calculating bond yields, given in the AIBD Rule Book, although totally different in format, is EXACTLY the same as the actuarial formulae outlined throughout this book.

EXAMPLE: *Eurobond (DSM Holland) 8.75%*

Redemption Value 100.
Yield to Maturity 8.88%.
Purchase   9 September, 1976
Settlement   16 September, 1976 (7 days after purchase)
Maturity   1 August,   1988
Days Between Actual   4337
                 30/360   4275
$(n + k)$ factor $4275/360 = 11.875$
The i/p is $8.88/100 \quad = .08888$

To find the price:

$$\frac{100(1.0888^{-11}) + 8.75a_{\overline{11}|} + 8.75}{1.0888^{.875}} = DP$$

$$\frac{100(1.0888^{-11}) + (8.75(1 - 1.0888^{-11})/.0888) + 8.75}{1.0888^{.875}} = DP$$

$$\frac{39.225706 + (8.75 \times 6.843952) + 8.75}{1.077282} = 100.122566$$

The $a/i = 8.75 \times (1 - k)$
$\quad = 8.75 \times .125 \qquad = 1.093750$
$\qquad\qquad\qquad\qquad = 1.09$ (rounded to 2 places decimals)

$100.122566 - 1.09 \quad = 99.03$ Price

Because of the probable "rounding" of the YTM (from 10 sig.fig. to 2 places of decimals) it would be reasonable to assume that the true (clean) price was 99. In that case the necessary DP would become 99 + 1.09 = 100.09, and the precise YTM 8.884576%.

EXAMPLE
As above, assume semi-annual interest payments. Find the price.

In this case the half coupon will become 8.75/2 = 4.375%. The (n + k) will become 4275/180 = 23.75.

The YTM, however, would have been marked 8.88%(S), the (S) as explained above to denote that the interest payments were semi-annual and in that case before any calculations are contemplated, this rate, having previously been adjusted for its "annual equivalent", must be reduced to its nominal semi-annual state:

$$200 \left(1 + \frac{8.88}{100}\right)^{.5} - 1 \qquad\qquad = 8.6911594\%$$

$$\text{YTM}/200 \qquad\qquad\qquad\qquad\qquad = .043455797 \text{ i/p}$$

$$\frac{100(1.0435^{-23}) + (4.375(1 - 1.0435^{-23})/.0435) + 4.375}{1.0435^{.75}} = 101.506868$$

and deducting the a/i of 4.375 × (1 − .75) = 1.09 (rounded) we get a clean or quoted price of 101.51 − 1.09 = 100.42.

EXAMPLE
Alternatively, assume a Eurobond with a short life to redemption of 250 days only with a coupon of 10%, an RV of 100 and a price of 99.90. Find the YTM %.

In this case we can use the shortened formula because the term is less than one year. The k becomes 250/360 = .694444 and as the reader will recall from Chapter 17, the shortened compound discounting formula (because Eurobonds are NEVER at simple interest) is:

$$100\left(\left(\frac{\text{RV} + \text{Coupon}}{\text{Price} + \text{a/i}}\right)^{1/k} - 1\right) = \text{YTM}\%$$

First convert the CP of 99.90 to its DP, namely the price + a/i:

$$99.90 + ((10 \times (1 - .69444445))$$
$$99.90 + 3.055556$$
$$99.90 + 3.06 \textbf{ (rounded)} = 102.96 \text{ DP}$$

$$100\left(\left(\frac{100 + 10}{102.96}\right)^{1/.6944} - 1\right) = 9.992425\% \text{ YTM}$$

In this case if the YTM had been exactly 10% then the price would be fractionally different:

$$\frac{RV + Coupon}{(1 + i/p)^k} = DP$$

$$\frac{110}{1.10^{.69444}} = 102.955076 \ DP$$

and $\quad 102.955076 - 3.06 = 99.89507630$
$$= 99.90 \ (clean \ price)$$

Before leaving Eurobond calculations there is one peripheral calculation which we must fully understand.

"Average life" – sinking funds

Some institutional borrowers sometimes partially redeem their issues at various periods during the life of the bond. In these circumstances the conventionally calculated yield to maturity will be of limited value, for the normal redemption value of 100% at maturity will not obtain. What is required, therefore, is a weighted mean yield, usually referred to as the "average life" yield, found by a calculation designed to provide a suitable (n + k) factor. This yield will provide a true perspective by taking into account when, and by how much, each partial redemption occurs.

The calculations to determine the average life, and consequently the average life yield, require the exact data of the redemption structure and this often means checking back to the original loan issue details – and indeed an alert statistical department for the borrower may alter the rules half way through the life of the loan, sometimes increasing the partial repayments; changes which, of course, are notified from time to time in the financial press.

The conventional market method of calculating the average life is often regarded as complicated, largely, perhaps, because such methods are usually computer-presented owing to the necessary library data required. But the calculations are not complex once the methods are fully understood and perhaps the best way of grasping the essentials is to follow through an example. One such example is provided below which will, it is hoped, save a long explanation.

EXAMPLE

Assume a Eurobond at issue with a loan amount of $20 million. The issue is dated 15 December 1969 with maturity 20 years later, 15 December 1989.

The issue structure is that on each 15 December the following repayments will be made to bond holders:

(Years)	(Dollars)
1978 & 1979	500,000 will be redeemed (2 years)
1980 – 1986 (incl.)	1,000,000 will be redeemed (7 years)
1987 & 1988	1,250,000 will be redeemed (2 years)
1989 Maturity	the residual

The residual amount, which will be paid at the final maturity date, is therefore the $20 million loan less the funds already redeemed of $10.50 million – which leaves a residual of $9.50m. A quick calculation:

$$20 - ((.5 \times 2) + (1 \times 7) + (1.25 \times 2)) = £9.50 \text{ millions to be paid in the}$$
final maturity year, 1989.

Making a schedule of each of the repayments, working BACK from maturity, with the required calculations produces:

Year	Years SD–RD	Repayment		Calculated value
1989	20	X 9,500,000 (residual)	=	190,000,000
1988	19	X 1,250,000	=	23,750,000
1987	18	X 1,250,000	=	22,500,000
1986	17	X 1,000,000	=	17,000,000
1985	16	X 1,000,000	=	16,000,000
1984	15	X 1,000,000	=	15,000,000
1983	14	X 1,000,000	=	14,000,000
1982	13	X 1,000,000	=	13,000,000
1981	12	X 1,000,000	=	12,000,000
1980	11	X 1,000,000	=	11,000,000
1979	10	X 500,000	=	5,000,000
1978	9	X 500,000	=	4,500,000
		20,000,000		343,750,000

1977 to 1969: 8 years – no capital repayments during these years.

343,759,000/20,000,000 = 17.1875 Average life (n + k)

A quick method of calculating average life (n + k), "on the back of an envelope", is to employ an arithmetical progression calculation, namely:

$$\frac{\text{The first term (F)} + \text{the last term (L)}}{2} \times \text{number of periods (n)} = \text{SUM}$$

or $\dfrac{F + L}{2} \times n$ = S

where n = L – F + 1 .

Taking the example above:

$$20 \times 9.5 \qquad\qquad = 190.00$$

$$2 \times \frac{19 + 18}{2} \times 1.25 \qquad = 46.25$$

$$(17 - 11 + 1) \times \frac{17 + 11}{2} \times 1.00 = 98.00$$

$$2 \times \frac{10 + 9}{2} \times .50 \qquad = \underline{\quad 9.50}$$
$$343.75$$

$$\underline{343.75/20 = (n + k)} \qquad \underline{= 17.1875 \text{ Average life}}$$

Assuming that the above Eurobond issue had a coupon of 10% over a life of 20 years the conventional YTM, at issue, would be, naturally, 10% — providing the issue price was not at a discount.

$$100(1.10)^{-20} + 10a_{\overline{20}|} = 100.00 \text{ CP}$$

But a yield based on the average life calculation above would be 9.782865%:

$$\frac{100(1.097829)^{-17} + 10a_{\overline{17}|}}{1.097829^{.1875}} = 100.00 \text{ CP}$$

It may seem, at first glance, surprising to have a denominator at the time of issue but, in fact, the calculation of the average life, with the consequent average life yield, is designed to provide an overall picture of the partial redemption structure during the whole life of the loan. In effect, therefore, the average life yield becomes operative, and of interest and value for investment purposes, once the settlement date is determined and once the partial repayments are known — and in this context the issue date is equivalent to settlement.

Settlement before partial repayments commence

Suppose settlement occurred on 15 December 1977 with exactly the same repayment structure and Maturity as above.

Because settlement is *before* partial repayments commence the new average life is simply calculated, as shown below.

Average life at issue — years from issue to settlement = Avg Life

17.1875 (the n + k above) — (years 1977—1969)

17.1876 − 8   = 9.1875

but just to prove the point:

SD 15 December 1977 – RD 15 December 1989 = 12 Years life.

Year	Years SD–RD		Repayment		Calculated value
1989	12	X	9,500,000 (residual)	=	114,000,000
1988	11	X	1,250,000	=	13,750,000
1987	10	X	1,250,000	=	12,500,000
1986	9	X	1,000,000	=	9,000,000
1985	8	X	1,000,000	=	8,000,000
1984	7	X	1,000,000	=	7,000,000
1983	6	X	1,000,000	=	6,000,000
1982	5	X	1,000,000	=	5,000,000
1981	4	X	1,000,000	=	4,000,000
1980	3	X	1,000,000	=	3,000,000
1979	2	X	500,000	=	1,000,000
1978	1	X	500,000	=	500,000
			20,000,000		183,750,000

183,750,000/20,000,000   = 9.1785 average life

or, by arithmetical progression:

$$
\begin{aligned}
&\$m \\
12 \times 9.50 &= 114.00 \\
(11 + 10) \times 1.25 &= 26.25 \\
(9 + 3)/2 \times 7 \times 1 &= 42.00 \\
(2 + 1) \times .50 &= \underline{1.50} \\
&= \overline{183.75}
\end{aligned}
$$

183.75/20 = 9.1875 Average life (n + k)

Settlement after partial payments have commenced

If settlement, however, occurred *after* some redemption amounts have been partialy repaid, the calculation requires the dates/days between settlement and maturity.

If, for example, the above Eurobond was traded at a Euro quoted price of 99 (CP) with settlement on 29 May 1984, the yield to maturity will be 10.214% and the average life yield will be 10.253%.

The yields derive from the calculation shown on the facing page.

Yield to maturity:

29 May 1984 − 15 December 1989 = 1996 days (30/360)
(n + k) factor = 1996/360   =   5.544444
a/i = (1 − .544444) × 10   =   4.56 (rounded)
DP = 99 + 4.56   = 103.56

$$\frac{100(1.102144648)^{-5} + 10a_{\overline{5}|} + 10}{1.102144648^{.5444444}} = 103.56 \text{ DP}$$

$$= 10.214\% \text{ YTM.}$$

The average life at settlement:

Year	Years SD–RD		$ Millions		Calculated value
1989	5.5444444	×	9.50 (residual)	=	52.672222
1988	4.5444444	×	1.25	=	5.680556
1987	3.5444444	×	1.25	=	4.430555
1986	2.5444444	×	1.00	=	2.544444
1985	1.5444444	×	1.00	=	1.544444
5.29.	1984 settlement		14.00	=	66.872222

66.872222/14 = 4.776587 average life (n + k)

Average life yield:

(n + k) factor   =   4.776587
a/i = (1 − .776587) × 10   =   2.23 (rounded)
DP = 99 + 2.23   = 101.23

$$\frac{100(1.102531980)^{-4} + 10a_{\overline{4}|} + 10}{1.102531980^{.776587}} = 101.23 \text{ DP}$$

$$= 10.253\% \text{ Average life yield.}$$

EXAMPLE

40 million Swiss Fr. issued	20 April 1970
Redemptions Fr. 2 millions commencing	20 April 1978
Residual amount Fr. 26 millions	20 April 1985

There are 15 years between 1970−85, and 7 years between 1978−85.

15 × 26   = 390.00

$$7 \times \frac{8 + 14}{2} \times 2 = \underline{154.00}$$
$$544.00$$

Average life 544/40 = 13.60 (n + k).

CHAPTER 21

US Dollar Calculations

General

Unlike the inflexible AIBD rules for calculating Eurobonds, the US calculations of bond prices/yields have no "rules", as such, but there are advisory calculations as set out in "Standard Securities Calculation Methods", published by the Securities Industry Association. Therein are numerous examples outlining the various "required" methods of US market conventions for calculating yields to maturity for different classes of money market instruments. These advisory methods are, it is stated, consistent with those previously outlined (1962) by the Bankers' Association of America.

When in financial calendar mode (30/360) with semi-annual interest payments the US calculations are precisely the same as for AIBD semi-annual Eurobond calculations, save that the accrued interest is "true" — not rounded to 2 decimal places.

But in actual mode, with semi-annual interest payments, it is customary for the US statistician to employ the quasi-coupon periods method of calculation (Chapter 18). (This mode is invariably employed for bonds foreign to the US market, except, of course, Eurobonds, which have their prescribed method of calculation).

In parenthesis, it must be noted that often some statisticians ignore this required quasi-coupon period method and simply employ base 182.5 and find the a/i by $(1 - k) \times$ coupon. The reason is that because most US bond calculations are based on the financial calendar (30/360 — semi-annual interest paid), and because the $(1 - k) \times$ coupon method is thus in everyday use, many programmable calculators are so designed. And it is simpler to superimpose 182.5, for 180, than to switch to a quasi-coupon period program — or calculate manually!

In effect, it will be seen therefore that the various US methods of calculations cover all the conventional methods and any differences, compared to other market methods, lie in the peripheral calculations. For example, when employing the financial calendar, 30/360, the only difference between the US and the AIBD calculations, as noted above, is that the AIBD round the accrued interest to 2 places of decimals and the US statistician does not.

176

US market conventions

The problem arises, therefore, of how to calculate the different classes of interest-bearing obligations – for seldom does the nomenclature of the instruments concerned provide any clue as to the method of calculation required, namely semi-annual interest paid, or interest paid at maturity, or whether the note, bill, or bond is discounted back from maturity to settlement. Nor is the base mentioned, Actual, 30/360, Actual/360, or Actual/ Actual. In Appendix A the different categories are set out for guidance; those above the line relate to main-theme calculations outlined in this book. For the remainder, if in doubt, refer to the SIA publication, mentioned above. Remember, in the same way as the New York Stock Exchange regulations for calculating client commissions are constantly changing, so also over the years existing conventions *may* be altered and developed.

US bond conventions

Interest payments are annual or semi-annual (very occasionally annual).

Mode is either Actual or 30/360. (A mix is only applicable for certificates of deposit and other forms of "commercial paper").

Leap days In Actual mode leap days are ignored, except for the odd and a/i days when employing the quasi-coupon period method.

Discounting is ALWAYS by compound methods for a life greater than 5 years; for less than 5 years discounting by simple interest is OPTIONAL except that with under one period to run to maturity SIMPLE INTEREST discounting is ALWAYS the "required" method.

Quoted prices are always clean of accrued interest.

Presentation YTMs are rounded to 3 decimal places. Gross (flat) yields are usually presented to 2 decimal places (user optional).

Net calculations The accrued interest is always treated as a net value and when capital gains tax has a bearing on the net calculations the cost (price) is treated as "clean of all".

Settlement
For Treasury Bonds – one day after purchase.
For other bonds – five days after purchase.
Private arrangements for delayed settlement are not uncommon.

Concessions In the same way as the New York Stock Exchange permits brokers to allow discounts on clients' commissions, concessions on either the yield or price are sometimes included in transactions. Such concessions in no way affect the basic calculations. On yields the concession is a decimal value and as such .05 or .1 might be added to the YTM, the price, after recalculation, thus being automatically lowered. Alternatively, 0.25 or 1.50 can be subtracted from the price, thus automatically raising the yields. Sometimes the price concessions are quoted as (say) "ten" or "five and a half": if the price is in multiples of $1000 subtract the concession from the price, or divide by 10 for the more usual $100 range – and then deal as outlined above (e.g., 985 – 5.5 = 979.50 or 98.50 – (5.5/10) = 97.95).

EXAMPLE (30/360)
In Chapter 18 an example was outlined and calculated using the "actual" base of 182.5. The price was 96.1875 clean of a/i and the YTM presented as 7.778%. The parameters were 665 actual days between SD and RD, 65 days between payment date prior to settlement and settlement date and the nominal coupon was 5.50% (with semi-annual interest payments).

If this example was calculated for a dollar bond, using the 30/360 calendar base, the calculations would differ in some features and would present as follows:

Assuming 656 days (equivalent in 30/360 mode to the actual days) the (n + k) therefore becomes 656/180 = 3.644444 and thus the a/i would adjust to $2.75 × (1 − 3.644444) = .9777778 and DP is thus $96.1875 + .9777778 = $97.165278.

$$\frac{100(1 + i/p)^{-3} + 2.75a_{\overline{3}|} + 2.75}{(1 + i/p)^{.64444}} = \$97.165278 \text{ DP}$$

The i/p will be found as .03888571838 and thus the YTM is 7.777%.

EXAMPLE (Quasi-coupon period method)
US Treasury Note, 4.75%
Price 99\frac{28}{32}$ ($99.875)
RV 100
Settlement   7 February 1984
Maturity   15 May 1984
Pmt Dates 15 May/November

The "required calculation" for this class of note is by the quasi-coupon semi-annual period method with the actual calendar. The days between SD and RD are 98 (and in this case, with this type of calculation, leap days ARE counted) and the days between 15 November 1983 and settlement are 84 days. The base, therefore, by the quasi coupon method, is 98 + 84 = 182 days.

Remember, too, that as the convention is for a life of less than one period the calculation is SIMPLE interest discounting. As the bond life is less than one period the simpler calculation (Chapter 17) can be employed to find the YTM (instead of the long basic formula which requires the iterative method with interpolation).

The price + a/i is found as 99.875 + (84/182 × 4.75/2) which becomes $100.9711538 DP:

$$200\left(\frac{100 + 2.375}{100.9711538} - 1\right) \times \frac{1}{98/182} = 5.164\% \text{ YTM (SI)}$$

Out of interest, suppose that the calculation was determined on a computer/calculator program which was not specifically designed for quasi-coupon period calculations: in that case as the program would employ base 182.5 and ignore leap days throughout the whole life of the bond, the YTM, in this example, would be found as:

$$200\left(\left(\frac{102.375}{99.875 + (2.375 \times 84/182.5)} - 1\right) \times \frac{1}{97/182.5}\right) = 5.243\%.$$

Using the (1 − k) method (non valid but sometimes employed in programmable calculators) the YTM becomes 5.169%.

EXAMPLE (Yield to call calculations (30/360))
A US semi-annual coupon bond at a rate of 5% nominal matures on 6 February 2003. The bond was purchased at a price of 99 with settlement on 15 November 1983. If the bond was callable at 101 on 6 February 1990, what is the yield to call and the yield to maturity?

The base is 30/360 and so the (n + k) for the call term is 2241/180 which = 12.45, and the life is 6921/180 = 38.45 (n + k). The DP therefore becomes 99 + ((1 − .45) × 2.50) = $100.375.

$$\frac{101(1 + i/p)^{-12} + 2.50a_{\overline{12}|} + 2.50}{(1 + i/p)^{.45}} = \$100.375 \text{ DP}$$

The yield to call will be found as 5.326892568% rounded to 5.33%.

The yield to maturity will present as above except that the n will be shown as 38(n + k = 38.45) and the RV will, of course, be 100 (and not the call value of 101). In this case the YTM will be found as 5.08%.

If the purchaser in the above example had a tax bracket of 40% and was subject to a gains tax at 25%, what is the net YTM?

The coupon is brought to net: 2.50 × (100 − 40)/100 = 1.50% net and the accrued interest is also treated as NET (unlike UK and other calculations which treat the a/i as gross):

99 + ((1 − .45) × 2.50 × .6) = $99.825 DP.

The capital gains adjustment must now be considered. US calculations treat the cost as clean of all, so this will be 99 and the adjusted RV will thus become:

$$100 - .25(100 - 99) \qquad = \$99.75 \text{ RV.}$$

$$\frac{99.75(1 + i/p)^{-38} + 1.50a_{\overline{38}|} + 1.50}{(1 + i/p)^{.45}} = \$99.825 \text{ DP (net a/i)}$$

The NET YTM will be found as 3.059345022% rounded to 3.06%.

EXAMPLE: ((Actual/365) Quasi-coupon period method)
Assume a US calculation of a "foreign bond" which matures on 4 June 1996 and which is purchased on 28 April 1982. The bond has a semi-annual coupon of 6.75% nominal with an RV of 100 and a yield to maturity of 8.25% precisely. What was the price paid?

The days between SD and RD are 5151 which includes leap days. 1982/4 = 495.5 and 1996/4 = 499, so 499 − 495 = 4 leap days. The life in days less leap days is 5147. There are 28 half annual periods (see Appendix C) and as the quasi-coupon period method is to be employed, the next calculation is to find the number of days between 4 June 1982 and 4 December 1981 which results in 182. This 182 is the base and the number of days between SD and next coupon period is 37 days; thus the (n + k) = 28 + (37/182) = 28.20329670 and the a/i days are 182 − 37 = 145.

Employing an i/p of 8.25/200 = .04125 to find the price the equations present as:

$$\frac{100(1.04125)^{-28} + 3.375a_{\overline{28}|} + 3.375}{1.04125^{.2033}} = DP$$

$$\frac{32.2448 + 3.375((1 - 1.04125^{-28})/.04125) + 3.375}{1.008251499} = \$90.31067 \text{ (DP)}$$

$$\$90.31067 - (145/182 \times 3.375) = \$87.62 \text{ clean price.}$$

CHAPTER 22

The London Market

General

Within the compass of market conventions, such as always employing the actual calendar and all issues with a maturity value having interest payments twice a year, the British have no rules, advisory or mandatory, as to how calculations for prices or yields to maturity should be calculated. Any such calculations are therefore largely at the whim of the individual statistician or data processing manager – which has certain disadvantages for the interested student!

The London market structure

To those unfamiliar with the British market structure there are, at the present time, two main differences to other markets. In the first place brokers trade in shares, on behalf of clients, not marrying up sellers and buyers but dealing only with stock jobber firms who make a market in most of the shares quoted on the Exchange. Jobbers therefore compete among themselves to provide attractive bargains for brokers. There are advantages and disadvantages in this system but comment on that aspect has no place here; indeed after 1985 the jobber system may no longer be current.

The other main difference is that bearer shares are largely unknown to the investing British public, for the owners of ordinary shares and corporate fixed interest debentures are registered with the company's "registrar" and dividends and/or interest are posted on the due date to the holder. Trading in stock or bonds can only be through a broker, through the market. An excellent system obtains for marrying purchases against sales and little difficulty on this score is experienced by either broker or client. As far as government securities are concerned, the Bank of England is the "registrar".

As a result of this system there is inevitably a period when a purchaser, the new owner, is not registered in sufficient time to receive a dividend, which instead is posted to the previous owner, the seller. In such event the dividend is collected from the market, the seller surrendering the dividend, which the broker passes on to the buyer.

The nearer the time that interest or dividends are due the more adjustments and the more surrenders would be likely so each registrar regularises the whole matter by deciding at a certain point in time, prior to the payment

181

date, that any purchaser, the newly registered owner, will *not* receive the dividend for the period on which interest was due.

The price of the shares/stock naturally falls slightly (roughly commensurate with the value of the dividend) and the stock is considered, and therefore purchased, as "ex-dividend" — and remains in that form until such time as the new payment period commences.

The Bank of England, registrar for government securities, has specific rules as to when government stock goes ex-div (XD) and these are outlined in more detail in Chapter 24 in which net optimum yields are examined.

Settlement dates

For government and local authority loans settlement is one day after purchase.

For ordinary shares and corporate fixed interest loans settlement is "according to date". Each year the London Stock Exchange provides a list showing the dates of the "account days" throughout the following year. These "accounts" are usually on a fortnightly basis; settlement is for bargains made during the previous fortnight. In other words, the "account" commences on a Monday and closes on Friday week, a trading fortnight. Settlement follows on the Monday 10 days after the close of the account.

When the "account fortnight" is interrupted by Bank Holidays the account is extended to a "three week account". Therefore for any statistician calculating yields related to industrial debentures, it is essential to be clear exactly as to which day settlement is effected. Later the method of calculating YTMs for "ex-div" securities will be examined in detail.

Market conventions

- Actual calendar (leap days ignored), **never** 30/360.
- Semi-annual interest paid.
- All classes of stock are quoted in the market as a DP, price WITH accrued interest, EXCEPT government securities with 5 years or under to run to redemption.

Options

- Compound discounting is normal.
- Simple interest is sometimes employed for securities with 5 years and under to run to maturity.
- One well-known "house" calculates all government securities with 5 years and under to run to maturity by schedule methods, should periodic repayments fall on a Sunday, Saturday or Bank Holiday, adjusting the YTMs accordingly.

- Usually, but not obligatorily, simple interest discounting is employed for securities with less than one period (Per $<$ 1) to run to maturity.
- As the quasi-period coupon method is (unfortunately) NOT normally used it is essential to calculate the correct number of actual a/i days. The $(1 - k) \times$ coupon method is not valid.
- If redemption falls on a Sunday some statisticians adjust YTMs by: YTM $\times$ (Number of life days)/(Number of life days + 1).
- With corporation (industrial debenture) stocks most brokers add expenses before calculating YTMs; for instance with a price of 90 and a current (1985) ratio of .9% plus VAT (currently 15%) a DP of 90 = 90 $\times$ (1 + (.9 $\times$ 1.15/100)) = 90.93150 DP + expenses. If stamp duty of (say) 1% was levied the expenses would thus become 90 $\times$ (1 + ((1 + (.9 $\times$ 1.15))/100)) = 91.8315 DP. One broking firm adds expenses for a buyer and subtracts for a seller.
- If there are two maturity dates quoted, for calculation purposes take the longest date if the *clean* price is below "par" (100) (See Chapter 18).
- **For net calculations**: the accrued interest, previously always treated as gross, will from 1986 be net. For capital gains tax purposes the cost is treated as DP + expenses (if applicable) i.e., "cum all".

General

The a/i days are, or should be, calculated from the calendar, although some still employ the $(1 - k)$ method.

All calculations are usually made to 10 significant figures, or greater according to the computer/calculator configuration. The a/i is never normally rounded prior to adding or subtracting to/from the DP. But there is no rule and for all I know some broker may do so!

Some London jobbers and brokers have combined into various consortia to share computer facilities — the consortia programs are not identical. Other brokers have their in-house computers — their programs are not necessarily compatible with others.

Many years ago one UK broker suddenly changed his method of calculating UK government securities, with under five years to maturity, from compound to simple interest discounting. I have no quarrel with the reasons, which were understandable at that time, but I question the fact that changes can be made simply at will without any notification to clients, the recipients of their daily lists. Caveant investment managers whose desks are littered daily with brokers' listings.

Recently, discussing quasi-coupon period methods of calculation with a talented young statistician, employed by one of the most elegant "houses" in the City of London, I advanced the opinion that it was, after periodic scheduling, perhaps the best and most accurate formula method of calculating bond yields to maturity. I doubt that their long employed existing computer program will be altered but you never know — and if it was I'm sure no one would be informed!

Government securities with under ONE PERIOD to maturity

In the last chapter the US Treasury Note was calculated by the same "quasi-coupon period method". If a bond with precisely the same characteristics was quoted on the London market it would be calculated in the same way, not because anyone knew the US method, or indeed what it was called, but simply because as it was necessary to find the number of odd days and the a/i days it seems absurd not to join them together! In the UK while simple interest discounting would be the most likely, there is no rule and compound interest discounting and a base of 182.5 days must not be ruled out.

Government securities greater than one but less than five periods

EXAMPLE: Treasury Stock 5½% (semi-annual interest)

Price 96-3/16th (96.1875) quoted "clean"
RV 100
Settlement   18 September 1981
Redemption 15 July   1983
(Days between 665 — no leap days intervening)
(n + k) factor 665/182.5 = 3.643836
a/i = 65/182.5 × 2.75   = .979452
Calculated by **compound** discounting and employing 1.038887507 as the 1 + i/p, the YTM presents as 7.778%:

$$\frac{100(1 + i/p)^{-3} + 2.75a_{\overline{3}|} + 2.75}{(1 + i/p)^{.643836}} = 97.166952 \text{ DP}$$

If this example had been discounted by **simple** interest and employing 1.038838030 the YTM would reduce to 7.768%:

$$\frac{100(1 + i/p)^{-3} + 2.75a_{\overline{3}|} + 2.75}{1 + (i/p \times .643836)} = 97.166952 \text{ DP}$$

Because the odd days are .643836 × 182.5 = 117.5 some statisticians take the "actual" odd days, here 119, and find the (n + k) as 3 + 119/182.5 = 3.652055 providing a YTM of 7.759%.

Some comparisons

Before continuing with other methods of calculating UK bond yields, this might be a convenient time to make some interesting comparisons.

Suppose the above bond was recalculated by the other market methods previously examined; it will be found that all the YTMs are different.

Market	Method	YTMs	(n + k)
UK	182.5 base	7.778% (CI)	665 (Actual)
		7.768% (SI)	(no leap days)
	182.5 base	7.759% (CI)	3 periods, 65 a/i days
		7.749% (SI)	119 odd days
	by schedule	7.777% (CI)	(181−184−181−119)
		7.766% (SI)	
Eurobond	Annual	7.805% (CI ONLY)	657 (30/360)
	Semi-annual	7.927% (S)	
US Corporate	180 base	7.774% (CI)	657 (30/360)
		7.764% (SI)	
US Treasury	quasi-coupon	7.776% (CI)	3 periods, 65 a/i days
	184 base	7.766% (SI)	119 odd days

TWELVE different YTMs for precisely the same bond parameters!

But this is not all: if the maturity date was a Sunday then some statisticians might slightly reduce some, or all, of the above yields (YTM X 665/666). Furthermore, if the example above had been a UK industrial debenture, some brokers would then have added expenses which would have reduced the YTM substantially (from 7.778% above to 7.164%).

Such a crazy situation perhaps confirms the earlier comment that YTMs should be considered as only a guide for investment purposes and not a law unto themselves: nevertheless if there was ONE way only of calculating (cf the AIBD Rules), to which all conformed, how much simpler life would be!

EXAMPLE: UK Industrial Debenture 6% (CUM div)

RV 100
Days between SD−RD 4065 days
(n + k) = 22.273973
The YTM = 6.801% nominal (*after expenses*) and .03400450 is the i/p.
Find the (dirty) price:

$$\frac{100(1.034005)^{-22} + [3(1 - 1.034005^{-22})/.03405] + 3}{(1.034005)^{.273973}} = 95.983250 \text{ DP}$$

As the given (broker listed) YTM was "after expenses" the market "floor" price will be the above price LESS expenses, namely: 95.983250/(1 + (.9 X 1.15)/100) = 95.000 DP (clean of expenses).

UK ex-dividend calculations

In these circumstances not only is there no accrued interest due from payment date prior to SD and SD, but a "dirty price" will be the clean price LESS the a/i for the period settlement to next payment date. Therefore, for calculation purposes there is no last half coupon value in the numerator of the normal actuarial formula: and the a/i value becomes the *odd days*/base × half coupon.

Before continuing with a full example of an XD stock it might be useful to examine an ex-div schedule, in the same manner as a cum div schedule was outlined in Chapter 17.

Assume a clean price of 96.1875 with a half coupon of 2.75% and an RV of 100. The days between are 557 days providing an (n + k) of 3.052055 and an XD accrued interest factor of 2.75 × 9/182.5 which equals 0.1356164. Thus the DP = 96.1875 LESS 0.1356164 = 96.051884 DP. These parameters will provide a YTM of 8.205624% giving us a working i/p of 8.205624/200 = .041028122.

The XD schedule will therefore present as follows:

$$(100.000000 + 2.75) \times 1.041028^{-1} \quad = 98.700504$$

$$(\ 98.700504 + 2.75) \times 1.041028^{-1} \quad = 97.452222$$

$$(\ 97.452222 + 2.75) \times 1.041028^{-1} \quad = 96.253137$$

$$(\ 97.253137 + 0.00) \times 1.041028^{-.052055} = 96.051884 \text{ DP}$$

and $\quad$ 96.051884 *plus* (2.75 × 9/182.5) $\quad = 96.1875 \text{ CP}$

EXAMPLE: UK industrial debenture 6%

Price (DP) 54.50 (XD)
RV 100.
Tax Rate 52%.
Gains tax equivalent 52% (because with corporate tax the profit uplift between purchase and realisation will (ultimately) attract tax)
Settlement $\quad$ 13 June 1979
Redemption 17 June 1990 (SUNDAY)
Days between SD and RD are 4022 and as there are 3 leap days intervening the working (n + k) = 4019/182.5 = 22.021918
There are 4 days between SD and next following payment date, providing both the odd days (k) and the a/i days.

The DP of 54.50 must have expenses added, namely:

$$54.50 \times (1 + (.9 \times 1.15)/100) = 55.064075 \text{ DP + expenses}$$

$$\frac{100(1 + i/p)^{-22} + 3a_{\overline{22}|}}{(1 + i/p)^{.021918}} \quad = 55.064075 \text{ DP + expenses}$$

The i/p will be found as .07082915211 and the YTM therefore presents as (X 200) 14.166% YTM.

As redemption day was a Sunday some statisticians will adjust the YTM as:

$$14.166 \times \frac{4019}{4020} = 14.162\%.$$

What is the gross yield?

Gross yields are always calculated from a CLEAN price, so the a/i must be removed from the DP (54.50), and, if the yield "with expenses" is required, the DP + expenses (55.064075) must also be cleaned of a/i. As the mode is EX-div the a/i must be ADDED to the above prices.

$3 \times 4/182.5$	=	.065753 (a/i)
$54.50 + .065753$	=	54.565753 (CP)
$600/54.565753$	=	11.00% gross yield
$55.064075 + .065750$	=	55.129828 (CP + exp)
$600/55.129828$	=	10.88% gross yield (with expenses)

The gross yield is, of course, the one yield which is never adjusted for a Sunday redemption day — for maturity has nothing to do with the flat yield.

Taxation

In the data line above the tax was stated to be 52% for both income and CGT (or its equivalent); therefore the half coupon above becomes $3 \times .48 =$ 1.44 NET half coupon, and the RV' becomes

$$100 - .52(100 - (DP + exp))$$

$$100 - .52(100 - 55.064075) = 76.633319 \text{ RV}'$$

$$\frac{76.633319(1 + i/p)^{-22} + 1.44a_{\overline{22}|}}{(1 + i/p)^{.021918}} = 55.064075$$

The i/p = .03782512064 and the NET YTM is 7.565% (net 52% tax)

The grossed-up net = 7.565/.48 = 15.76%.

If these values above were *adjusted for Sunday redemption* the rates, having been multiplied by 4019/4020, would be 7.563% and 15.76% respectively.

If a schedule was made for the above (gross value) loan:

$$(100 + 3) \times 1.070829^{-1} \qquad = 96.187146$$

$$(96.187146 + .3) \times 1.070829^{-1} = 92.626490$$

et seq until a further 21
discountings have been made.
The balance would be $\qquad = 55.146728$

Also found from:

$$100(1.070829^{-22}) + (3 \times (1 - 1.070829^{-22})/.070829 = 55.146728$$

and because of XD mode:

$$(55.146728 + 0) \times 1.070829^{-.021918} = 55.064075 \text{ DP + expenses.}$$

If these pre-1986 yield values above were adjusted for *Sunday redemption*, the rates, having been multiplied by 4019/4020, would be 7.563% and 15.76% respectively.

If a schedule was made for the above (gross value) loan:

$$(100 \qquad + 3) \times 1.070829^{-1} = 96.187146$$

$$(96.187146 + 3) \times 1.070829^{-1} = 92.626490$$

et seq until a further 21 discountings have been made. The balance would be:

$$= 55.146728$$

Also found from:

$$100(1.070829^{-22}) + (3 \times (1 - 1.070829^{-22})/.070829 = 55.146728$$

and because of XD mode:

$$(55.146728 + 0) \times 1.070829^{-.021918} = 55.064075 \text{ DP + expenses.}$$

"Bond washing"

Bond washing, or "dividend stripping" denotes the practice, peculiar to the London market, of assuming that any accrued interest due at point of sale is part of the capital realisation, the object being that the combined amount, the capital return and the small amount of interest due from the past payment date, can be treated as liable for a lower amount of capital gains tax instead of the income portion being taxed separately at (possibly higher) income or corporation tax rates. As a corollary to the above, when the realisation is not due for CGT, then bond washing presupposes that any interest accruing also escapes any tax.

Over many decades there has been a running battle between the Inland Revenue and investors, both private and institutional, in regard to the perspective of various fixed interest stocks in the UK. If a Government security is free of CGT, if held for 366 days, the argument has been that whereas tax is paid on the first half year's interest payments, the last half year's interest is part of the capital lift (or loss) between purchase and sale — and as such all the realisation should be considered as capital.

Early in 1985 the Chancellor of the Exchequer stated that, inter alia, such an argument would no longer be acceptable and that, with certain minor exceptions, all such a/i must be treated as net. When the necessary regulations come into force in February 1986, therefore, the LAB calculations below are likely to be of value only if an individual's portfolio is £5,000 or less.

Net accrued interest calculations

In view of the February 1986 regulations designed to prevent dividend stripping, unless the London market changes its method of quoting prices (DP, a price + gross a/i) for both medium and long-term gilts and industrial debentures, difficulties will arise when calculations are set in train to obtain a NET YTM, requiring the accrued interest to be treated as net of tax.

At first glance the calculations to convert a DP with gross a/i to one having a net perspective may appear somewhat cumbersome; but the simplest method is to ignore all the complications and in order to reduce a gross a/i cum or ex-div dirty price (with or without expenses) to a net a/i DP (+/– exp) simply calculate the TAX value of the a/i and SUBTRACT that amount from the gross value.

In the previous ex-div industrial debenture example above, with a quoted DP of 54.50, with a half coupon of 3% and with 4 odd days, if the tax rate is 52%, the DP(XD) + expenses of 55.0564075, will become a net value of:

$$55.064075 - (3 \times .52 \times 4/182.5) = 55.029883 \text{ (price which includes a/i net of 52\% tax and expenses)}$$

And employing these values in the previous ex-div example above:

$$100 - .52(100 - \text{net DP incl exp}) =$$

$$100 - .52(100 - 55.029883) \qquad = 76.615539 \text{ RV (net)}$$

$$\frac{76.615539(1 + i/p)^{-22} + 1.44a_{\overline{22}|}}{(1 + i/p)^{.021918}} = 55.029883$$

The i/p will result as .03785366 hence the net YTM = 7.570732% with a grossed up net of 15.77%.

Taking a cum div example and assuming a gross a/i cum div DP of 97.166952

and a half coupon of 2.75 and 65 a/i days, if the DP is 97.166952 then
97.166952 − (2.75 × 65/182.50) = a CP of 96.1875. Assuming a 30% income
tax rate, the DP with net a/i must be 96.1875 + (2.75 × .7 × 65/182.5) =
96.873116 DP (with net a/i) but this value could far more easily have been
calculated by:

$$\text{DP (gross) } 97.166952 - (2.75 \times .3 \times 65/182.5) = 96.87116 \text{ DP (net)}$$

UK local authority bonds

These types of loans (yearlings) were based on the premise (which is now
no longer valid, except for a very minor investment), that since UK government securities and local authority loans, if held for 366 days, are not liable
to UK capital gains tax when the security is realised, if the final realisation was arranged to fall on a date which was just greater than 365 days
since issue, tax on the interest could be avoided. Often, therefore, there is a
few days difference (+/−) between redemption date and the last (final)
payment date; as a result the holder will have a few days' gross interest
accruing or due, this being added to or subtracted from the redemption value.
The section above explains the likely limitations of this type of investment in
the future.

If redemption falls (say) 2 days after the final payment date then the
holder is, in effect, short of 2 days' interest which, under the issue terms, is
added to the RV. Alternatively if redemption falls 2 days before the final
interest payment date (FIPD), as the interest will be paid in full on that date
the RV will be paid with the 2 days' interest deducted − you can't win!

Following the conventional method of calculating these "yearlings" the
RULE is, should the RV fall after the FIPD, then ADD the days' interest
between FIPD and the RD − the converse is true.

EXAMPLE: LAB 11.375% (11.375/2 = 5.68750)

Price (CP)	102.393
RV ***	99.9377 (usually issue quoted − see method below)
Settlement	17 November 1977
Redemption	12 April 1978
Pmt Dates	14 April/October (− 2 interest days)
Days between	SD−RD = 146 days
a/i days	= 34 days
a/i	= 5.6875 × 34/182.5 = 1.059589
102.393 + 1.059589	= 103.4526589 DP

To prevent any possible confusion over dates and base days the calculations
are usually made with base 182.5 and by simple discounting. No rules − and

compound interest can be used as can the quasi-coupon period method (here base 180) if desired.

The conventional calculation for such a short term interest "difference" is to determine the RV thus:

$$100 - (2/182.5 \times 5.6875) = 99.9377 \text{ RV } ***$$

$$200 \left(\frac{99.9377 + 5.6875}{103.452589} - 1 \right) \times \frac{1}{146/182.5} = 5.2503 \text{ YTM \% (SI)}$$

$$200 \left(\left(\frac{105.625171}{103.452589} \right)^{1/.8} - 1 \right) \qquad = 5.2640 \text{ YTM \% (CI)}$$

The Irish market

Irish government securities (gilt stocks) are occasionally dealt in the London market. As from November 1984 ALL Irish gilts (longs, mediums and shorts) are quoted clean of accrued interest.

CHAPTER 23

When Settlement Is Near Next Payment Date

The problem

When dealing with semi-annual payments, for calculation purposes, a year of 365 days is often divided into two — sometimes causing difficulties which, if care is not taken, can produce erroneous results.

Assume a clean price of 90, an RV of 100, a coupon of 5.50%, and that the calculation, to find the YTM, is based on half annual interest payments and that the days base is 182.5. Assuming that settlement day is 14 November 1976 and that maturity is on 15 November 1979 it will be found that between settlement and redemption there are 1096 days and the (n + k) factor in this case becomes 1096/182.5 = 6.005479, namely 6 half years and one odd day.

If maturity was moved exactly six months earlier, to 15 May, 1979, one could confidently expect that there should thus be 5 half year periods and one odd day and that the new (n + k) factor would thus be 5.005479. However, the number of actual days between 14 November 1976 and 15 May 1979 will be found as 912 which when divided by 182.5 will find an (n + k) factor of 4.997260 **not** 5.005479 — and obviously any YTM (in the above example 8.795%) so found will consequently be spurious, for if settlement was a day later with exactly 5 half annual periods and no odd days, the YTM would be 10.128%. But employing the days between method another erroneous (n + k) (of 911/182.5 = 4.991781) will provide yet another invalid YTM of 8.864%.

If the quasi-coupon method is unavailable and the computer facilities are such that the obvious term error cannot be adjusted, the calculation being correctly XD mode based, the best method to overcome the difficulty is to:

  (i)   Retain the erroneous (n + k) value
  (ii) Employ the ex-div price
  (iii) Treat the calculation as cum div.

Taking a practical example, with settlement on 18 September 1984 find the YTM of a UK government security, Treasury 11.50% 2001/2004 (payments 19 March/September) priced at 106.125 XD. As the term is over 5 years the price is a DP, and because the price less accrued interest stands above par, treat the earlier date (2001) as the maturity date. By looking at settlement and the next following payment date we see that there is just one "odd" day. But after finding the days between and subtracting four leap days we get 6022 days which when divided by 182.5 provides an (n + k) factor of 32.997260. It is clear that this is an erroneous term, for the true term is 33 payment periods and one day (see Appendix C).

The correct YTM (XD) therefore is *10.698%:*

$$\frac{100(1.053489)^{-33} + 5.75a_{\overline{33}|}}{1.053489035^{1/182.5}} = 106.125 \text{ DP (ex div)}$$

The *alternative* solution provides a YTM of *10.703%*:

$$\frac{100(1.053517)^{-32} + 5.75a_{\overline{32}|} + 5.75}{1.053517^{.997260}} = 106.125 \text{ DP (ex div)}$$

One of the most elegant City consortiums, awash with the latest computers and innumerable programmers, to this day still use the alternative method!

It must be accepted, therefore, that whenever the 182.5 base days method is used to find the (n + k) factor for bond calculation purposes, there will always be the likelihood of the occasional problem; so users of all bond yield programs should ensure they fully understand exactly how their particular programs are written, with special reference to the (n + k) finding sub-routine.

Undoubtedly, the soundest method, and the one strongly recommended to anyone purchasing such a program (or indeed writing one for a PC), is to insist on methods to determine the (n + k) as outlined in Appendix C, namely that of determining the correct "number of periods" between settlement and maturity and the precise number of a/i and odd days — a method entirely divorced from "finding the days between".

If the "days between/182.5 base" method is to be employed (as opposed to the Appendix C method), try and ensure that the resulting (n + k) is screen-flashed before the remaining computation of yields or prices displays — so that, if the (n + k) is obviously invalid, a correction, or calculation adjustment, can be made before an erroneous YTM is provided.

The tables following, employing the original clean price (90) example above, provide a perspective of the various methods employed to adjust the bond parameters in order to find the YTM. It will be seen, incidentally, that when using the quasi-coupon period method the yields run concurrently with no peaks and troughs.

SD 14 Nov 1976   Clean Price 90   RD 15 May 1979

The schedule unadjusted (cum-div)

| | | | days | | | |
Nov	Days	(n + k)	a/i	a/i	DP	YTM%
12	914/182.5	5.008219	181	2.727397	92.727397	10.120
13	913/182.5	5.002740	182	2.742466	92.742466	10.125
14	**912/182.5**	**4.997260**	**183**	**2.757534**	**92.757534**	**8.795**
15	**911/182.5**	**4.991781**	**––––**	**––––––**	**90.000000**	**8.864**
16	910/182.5	4.986301	1	.015068	90.015068	10.150
17	909/182.5	4.980822	2	.030137	90.030137	10.155
18	908/182.5	4.975342	3	.045205	90.045205	10.160

The schedule unadjusted (ex-div)

| | | | days | | | |
Nov	Days	(n + k)	a/i	a/i	DP	YTM%
12	914/182.5	5.008219	−3	−.045205	89.954795	10.132
13	913/182.5	5.002740	−2	−.030137	89.969863	10.137
14	**912/182.5**	**4.997260**	**−1**	**−.015068**	**89.984932**	**8.861**
15	**911/182.5**	**4.991781**	**––––**	**––––––**	**90.000000**	**8.864**
16	910/182.5	4.986301	1	.015068	90.015068	10.150
17	909/182.5	4.980822	2	.030137	90.030137	10.155
18	908/182.5	4.975342	3	.045205	90.045205	10.160

The schedule if merely corrected (cum-div calculations)

| | | | days | | | |
Nov	Days	(n + k)	a/i	a/i	DP	YTM%
12	914/182.5	5.008219	181	2.727397	92.727397	10.120
13	913/182.5	5.002740	182	2.742466	92.742466	10.125
14	**912**	**5.005479**	**183**	**2.757534**	**92.757534**	**10.112**
15	**911**	**5.000000**	**––––**	**––––––**	**90.000000**	**10.128**
16	910/182.5	4.986301	1	.015068	90.015068	10.150
17	909/182.5	4.980822	2	.030137	90.030137	10.155
18	908/182.5	4.975342	3	.045205	90.045205	10.160

The schedule if merely corrected (ex-div calculations)

Nov	Days	(n + k)	days a/i	a/i	DP	YTM%
12	914/182.5	5.008219	−3	−.045205	89.954795	10.132
13	913/182.5	5.002740	−2	−.030137	89.969863	10.137
14	**912**	**5.005479**	**−1**	**−.015068**	**89.984932**	**10.123**
15	**911**	**5.000000**	——	—————	**90.000000**	**10.128**
16	910/182.5	4.986301	1	.015068	90.015068	10.150
17	909/182.5	4.980822	2	.030137	90.030137	10.155
18	908/182.5	4.975342	3	.045205	90.045205	10.160

The quasi-coupon period schedule

Nov	Days	(n + k)	days a/i	a/i	DP	YTM%
12	914	5 + 3/184	181/184	2.705163	92.705163	10.113
13	913	5 + 2/184	182/184	2.720109	92.720109	10.118
14	**912**	**5 + 1/184**	**183/184**	**2.735054**	**92.735054**	**10.123**
15	**911**	**5 +** ——	————	—————	**90.000000**	**10.128**
16	910	4 + 180/181	1/181	.015193	90.015193	10.132
17	909	4 + 179/181	2/181	.030387	90.030387	10.137
18	908	4 + 178/181	3/181	.045580	90.045580	10.142

The alternative method

Retain the erroneous (n + k) factor. Calculate cum-div but SUBTRACT the a/i from the clean price to determine the DP.

Nov	Days	(n + k)	days a/i	a/i	DP	YTM%
12	914/182.5	5.008219	181	2.727397	92.727397	10.120
13	913/182.5	5.002740	182	2.742466	92.742466	10.125
14	**912**	**4.997260**	**−1**	**−.015068**	**89.984932**	**10.141**
15	**911**	**4.991781**	(see below)		**90.000000**	**10.146**
16	910/182.5	4.986301	1	.015068	90.015068	10.150
17	909/182.5	4.980822	2	.030137	90.030137	10.155
18	908/182.5	4.975342	3	.045205	90.045205	10.160

CHAPTER 24

Notional Price. Forward Projected Price. Net Optimum Yields

Notional price

Readers may recall that in Chapter 17 it was mentioned that a fixed interest bond, with a redemption value, will "creep up" in price day by day from the buying price to the maturity value, irrespective of market forces. The example taken earlier was a stock purchased at 80 with an RV at 100 with a ten year life — making an annual lift of two points per year. Ignoring then any price movements resulting from market forces, the price resulting from this time-lift outlined above is in effect a "notional price". For a variety of reasons it is sometimes required to be able to determine this notional price, the market lift between two dates irrespective of price movements resulting from the buying and selling of stock. One reason could be whether the current price has "beaten the index" — and if so how much was this due to market forces and how much was it due to the normal time-lift price rise mentioned above. The notional price found from such a calculation is usually called the forward projected price. The nomenclature, while correct, might appear at first glance to be peculiar, for the discounting process required is BACK from the redemption date to the earlier date.

Forward projected price

The forward projected price (FPP) cannot be found by any calculation based on the purchase price: for the whole raison d'être of a fixed interest bond with a redemption value is precisely the point, that there *is* a redemption value — and so any notional price must be worked BACK from the RV to the date of the required FPP.

Taking our oft-used example of a bond with a CP of 96.1875, a 5.50% coupon, an RV of 100 and a term of 665 days with a YTM of 7.777501%; assume that the price of the stock was quoted 98.75 some 500 days after purchase (SD). The yield to redemption is all-important (i/p = .038887507) for it is on the current YTM that the calculation must naturally be based. The time factor for the calculation is therefore $665 - 500 = 165$ days and the $(m + t)$ factor (to differentiate from the $(n + k)$ factor) becomes $165/182.5 = .904109589$, and from this we can find the FPP by a normal bond price calculation.

196

Because the life is less than a complete half year the shortened (Per <1) formula can be applied:

$$\frac{100 + 2.75}{1.03889^{.90411}} = 99.26635 \text{ FPP (notional price} + a/i)$$

As a result of cleaning the price (by $1 - t$ for example purposes):

$$99.266 - (2.75 \times (1 - .90411) = 99.00 \text{ CP}.$$

The forward projected price is 99.00 and it will be seen therefore that although the quoted price (98.75) has risen since purchase (96.1875), it has not risen commensurately with its "creep up" value (99.00) and, as the market price naturally reflects the fact that 100 will be repaid 165 days hence, the quoted price shows that there are other factors in the market adversely affecting its value. Admittedly, in this example only a fractional difference, nevertheless the point is made. (As the calculations relate to a "notional" price, the $(1 - k)$ method of determining the a/i is acceptable).

Two points to remember: the FPP, as a result of any such calculation, is always a "dirty" FPP and is not a true price until cleaned of its a/i; and again the $(m + t)$ must always be calculated *back* from the redemption date and not from the SD. The yield requirement following provides another use for the forward projected price method of calculations.

Net optimum yields

The following claculations are peculiar to the UK market for they stem from the British tax system (if indeed the present conglomeration of tax structures can be called a system). The methods outlined, however, may well be applicable, if adapted, to the tax requirements of other nations.

Net optimum yield calculations, although not widely recognised, have a small but enthusiastic following in Britain, arising, as they do, from UK capital gains tax legislation. In the UK, at the present time, if a government security is sold within one year of purchase it is liable to capital gains tax, or if sold at a loss, an offset. If held for longer, no CGT is payable. If, therefore, there is a substantial profit on such a bond, if held for a year and a day, the usual inclination is to sell immediately and reinvest elsewhere. But the more astute investor, however, delays his sale, reasoning that the best (optimum) time to sell is when the stock is "full of accrued interest". Readers of Chapter 22, The London Market, will appreciate the UK laws relating to registration with the Bank of England, and the fact that Government securities are declared "ex-dividend" by the Bank at a fixed time prior to the "next payment date" (NPD). The optimum sell date therefore is one day before the stock goes XD.

The Bank of England rules that all government securities are "ex-dividend" exactly 37 days prior to the NPD — unless declaration date falls on a Saturday, Sunday or Bank Holiday, in which case D-day falls on the "next day for dealing" in the market, i.e. 35 or 36 days prior. As settlement for government securities is one day after purchase the net optimum sell date is 37 days (or 35 or 36 days) *prior to the next interest payment date.*

Net optimum yield calculations

In the first place why "net"? The reason is that, although there is no CGT to be considered, normal income or corporation tax will be levied on any interest received during the period when the stock was held. The resulting yield for the period held must therefore be a net yield which is useful for comparison purposes with either the net yields to maturity or the net yields resulting if the security was sold exactly one year and one day after purchase.

The "grossing up" of such net yields is also useful for comparison with other yield returns based on other tax-structured investments.

The method is:

    (a) to find the normal YTM

    (b) to find the optimum sell date

    (c) to find the FPP

    (d) to find an interest rate which will discount the FPP back to the DP to include the additional net interest (net half coupon).

It will be clear, when the discounting schedules are examined below, that a computer or programmable calculator program is necessary. Such a program is not difficult and can easily be superimposed on the normal bond yield program.

Formula to find the (m + t)

In the same way as, above, the date for the notional price (or FPP) was found by tracing it back from redemption date, so the term between redemption date and the optimum sell date must be correctly determined. But the statistician and computer programmer will require a more suitable method than "finger counting"! The solution lies below:

    (Total number of days SD–RD) − (3 × 182.5) + 37 + the a/i days

and   the above resulting days divided by 182.5 = (m + t) factor.

For an "ex-div" calculation the a/i days are *subtracted*, not added.

    The above method can be formula-formatted as follows:

    Cum div: $((n + k) - 3) + (37/182.5) + (1 - k) = m + t$

    Ex div: $((n + k) - 3) + (36/182.5) + (\ -k) = m + t$

As the UK calculations are "actual" the normal rule, often stressed above, is that the correct number of a/i days should be calendar found and that the $(1 - k)$ method is invalid; however while there is no reason why the actual a/i days cannot be calendar calculated, or for that matter the quasi-coupon period method employed, the minimal difference is relatively unimportant as the FPP is only a **notional** price. And the $(1 - k)$ method greatly simplifies the calculations — and will doubtless be welcomed by statisticians and computer/calculator programmers!

EXAMPLE: A UK Government Security. 9¼% (cum-div)

Price (Clean) 99.375
RV 100
Tax at 40%
Settlement   29 December 1983
Redemption   22 September 1988
Payment dates 22 March/September
Days between 1727 (excluding 2 leap days)
$(n + k) = 9.463014$

The first necessary calculation is to find the *precise* YTM%, for a quoted YTM will probably be only accurate to 2 or 3 decimal places.

Taking this case, the YTM will be found to be 9.409653%, the i/p becoming .047048265 and checking we get:

$$\frac{100(1 + i/p)^{-9} + 4.625a_{\overline{9}|} + 4.625}{(1 + i/p)^{.463014}} \qquad = 101.858562 \text{ DP}$$

$$101.858562 - (4.625 \times (1 - .463014)) \qquad = 99.375 \text{ CP}$$

Then:

$$1727 - (3 \times 182.5) + 37 + 98 \qquad = 1314.5 \text{ days}$$

or $\quad (9.463014 - 3) + (37/182.5) + (1 - .463014) = 7.202740 \text{ (m + t)}$

Now find the FPP:

$$\frac{100(1.047)^{-7} + 4.625a_{\overline{7}|} + 4.625}{1.047^{.202740}} \qquad = 103.191769 \text{ FPP}$$

The discounting schedule

Before netting the 1/2 coupon or trying to find the interest rate which will discount the FPP of 103.19 back to the DP of 101.86, let us retain the existing 1/2 YTM, namely 4.7048265% and the gross 1/2 coupon and discount period by period. Providing the schedule outlined below does indeed discount the FPP *exactly* to the DP, then we will know that the schedule has been structured correctly; we can then net the coupon and a computer program will find the i/p which, when multiplied by 200 will provide us with the net optimum yield per cent:

FPP

$$103.191769 \qquad \times\ 1.047^{-(182.5-37)/182.5} \ = \ 99.477852$$

$$103.191769 \qquad \times\ 1.047^{(t-1)} \qquad\qquad = \ 99.477852$$

$$103.191769 \qquad \times\ 1.047^{-.797260} \qquad\ = \ 99.477852$$

$$(99.477852 + 4.625) \times\ 1.047^{-1} \qquad\quad = \ 99.425075$$

$$(99.425074 + 4.625) \times\ 1.047^{-k} \qquad\quad =$$

$$(99.425074 + 4.625) \times\ 1.047^{-.463014} \qquad = \ 101.858562 \ \text{DP}$$

Q.E.D.

If, therefore, the 1/2 coupon is brought to net $4.625 \times .6 = 2.775$ and substituted for 4.625, in the schedule above, it will be found that an i/p of .03027204830 is required to discount the FPP precisely to the DP and thus the net optimum yield is the i/p $\times$ 200 which finds 6.054%:

$$\text{FPP }103.191769 \qquad \times\ 1.0303^{-.797260} \qquad = \ 100.767157$$

$$(100.767157 + 2.775) \times\ 1.0303^{-1} \qquad\quad = \ 100.499822$$

$$(100.499822 + 2.775) \times\ 1.0303^{-.463014} \qquad = \ 101.858562 \ \text{DP}$$

The net optimum yield = $6.054/.6 = 10.09\%$ grossed up.

**

It will be appreciated that the a/i shown above is net of tax and therefore does not conflict with Inland Revenue requirements that dividends must not be stripped of tax.

The institutional investor

While there is no CGT as such, if held for over a year, an institution will make a "profit" — or loss — on the difference between purchase and sale and this will, in due course, be corporation tax liable. Therefore, the gross FPP must be "netted" in the same way as an RV is brought to its net value for CGT purposes.

Assume that, for the purposes of this example, corporation tax for a particular company was at 52%. In this case the net half coupon would become $4.625 \times .48 = 2.220\%$.

The FPP will be adjusted as follows:

$$FPP - Tax/100(FPP - DP) = FPP'$$

$$103.191769 - .52(103.191769 - 101.858562) = 102.498501 \ FPP'$$

and the net optimum yield will adjust accordingly.

Example ex-dividend

The system for ex-dividend calculations requires the same method save that the original calculation to find the YTM must be made in XD mode but the *calculation to find the FPP is ALWAYS in CUM div mode.* The discounting structure becomes slightly different. Assume that the days between RD and settlement are 1112 with the (n + k) becoming 1112/182.5 = 6.093151.

A nominal coupon of 11.50%, a clean price of 105-5/8th and an RV of 100. The DP = the CP LESS the a/i for XD calculation so $105.625 - (11.5/2 \times k) = 105.089384$ DP. Assume tax at 40%.

First find the precise YTM:

$$\frac{100(1 + i/p)^{-6} + 5.75a_{\overline{6}|}}{(1 + i/p)^{.093151}} = 105.089384 \ DP$$

The i/p = .04670544665 and the YTM is therefore ($\times$ 200) 9.341%.

The FPP will be found from this i/p and an m + t of:

$$(6.093151 - 3) + (37/182.5) - .093151 = 3.202739726 \ (m + t)$$

Don't forget that the FPP calculations are ALWAYS cum div method even if the YTM calculation for the bond itself is XD mode, so:

$$\frac{100(1.047)^{-3} + 5.75a_{\overline{3}|} + 5.75}{1.047^{.202739726}} = 107.706462 \ FPP$$

Incidentally it is worth noting that the t factor is ALWAYS 37/182.5 — or should be! (unless using 35 − 36 if applicable).

Having found the FPP, net the coupon 5.75 $\times$ .6 = 3.45 and discount back to the DP. In this case the net optimum yield is 6.265% derived from an i/p of .031325841:

$$FPP \ 107.70646 \quad \times 1 + i/p^{t-1} \quad =$$

$$107.70646 \quad \times 1.0313^{-.797260} = 105.090085$$

$$(105.0901 + 3.45) \times 1.0313^{-1} = 105.243252$$

$$(105.2433 + 3.45) \times 1.0313^{-1} = 105.391766$$

$$105.3918 \ + 0.00 \ \times 1.0313^{-k} \quad =$$

$$105.3918 \ + 0.00 \ \times 1.0313^{-.0931507} = 105.089384 \ DP.$$

CHAPTER 25

Split Coupon Bonds

Many years ago the board of a UK industrial company issued a prospectus for a debenture loan and, for reasons best known to themselves, decided that the coupons, semi-annual interest paid, would be varied during the course of the loan life. They decided to split the coupons so that the first 9 years would be at a rate of 8% nominal and the remaining 16 years at 12%. The price (95) was at a discount but the prospectus provided no indication as to the yield to maturity at issue.

As this structure was a newcomer to the market, such an omission caused no little concern in statistical circles for no formula was immediately apparent, and no computer program was available. Some statistical departments of various brokers and jobbers spent angry hours converting existing programs to find ultimately the YTM.

The more astute statisticians suddenly realised that as the requirement was a YTM *at issue*, with no "odd days" intruding, by using a simple conventional discounted cash flow program (on even a simple hand-held calculator with such facilities) the IRR (the half YTM) could easily be determined.

Reverting thus to a DCF calculation (see Chapter 4) and employing a YTM of 9.99% derived from an i/p of .04993604046:

$$\text{Investment} = -95.00$$
$$4 \times \ddot{a}_{\overline{18}|} \times 1.04994^{-1} = 46.78$$
$$6 \times \ddot{a}_{\overline{31}|} \times 1.04994^{-19} = 38.95$$
$$(100 + 6) \times 1.04994^{-50} = \underline{\quad 9.27}$$
$$\text{NPV} = 0.00$$

And in case the reader has forgotten the DCF group calculation the annuities DUE factor is:

$$\ddot{a}_{\overline{n}|} = ((1 - (1 + i/p)^{-n})/(i/p)) \times (1 + i/p)$$

and taking the second series to demonstrate:

$$6 \times [(1 - 1.04994^{-31})/.04994] \times 1.04994 \times 1.04994^{-19} = 38.95$$

As soon as trading commences, however, this method is no longer valid and therefore formulae were evolved and programs written. However, by

202

using the **decimal entry** DCF method, outlined previously (see Chapter 4) no special program is necessary for this rather specialised and rarely issued type of loan.

Nevertheless, I set out below the full split coupon formula and its method of calculation for, as will be seen below, this formula and computer program, if available, has uses other than that solely related to variable coupon bonds as outlined above.

Formula for split coupons

$$\frac{RV(1 + i/p)^{-n} + Da_{\overline{n}|} - (D - D')a_{\overline{n'}|} + D'}{(1 + i/p)^k} = DP$$

Where:

  n = Number of periods during the life of the loan
  n' = Number of periods BEFORE change
  D' = 1/2 coupon value BEFORE change
  D = 1/2 coupon value AFTER change.

Taking the example above, and assuming the issue price was a **Clean** price of 95, the above formula would convert to:

$$100(1 + i/p)^{-50} + 6a_{\overline{50}|} - (6 - 4)a_{\overline{18}|} = 95 \; CP$$

and the i/p will as above = 0.049936046, making the YTM 9.99%.

The gross (or flat) yield

There is a minor problem here, which needs a moment's thought.

The coupons must first be calculated as a *weighted mean:*

$$(8 \times 9/25) + (12 \times 16/25) = 10.56\% \text{ mean coupon}$$

$$10.56 \times 100/95 \qquad\qquad = 11.12\% \text{ gross (flat) yield.}$$

EXAMPLE: A split coupon debenture loan

Coupons 8% for the first 9 years; 12% for the remaining 16 years.
Semi-annual interest paid.
RV 100.
Price, at settlement, 95 (dirty price).

As this was a London issue it must be calculated by UK methods, the base being 182.5, and it will be appreciated that the price quoted is the DP, price + a/i.

Assume that the days between settlement and redemption are 6662 and that, therefore, the (n + k) factor is 36.50410959.

As there were 32 half year periods at 12% nominal there must be $36 - 32$ periods, plus some odd days, at 8% nominal. See equation below.

This type of debenture loan on the UK market (see Chapter 22, The London Market) would have expenses included in the price before calculating the YTM. Assuming the current expenses ratio (not that of some years ago when the issue was actually made) of .9% plus VAT at 15% we find the DP + expenses becomes: $95 \times (1 + (.9 \times 1.15/100)) = 95.983250$ DP.

Taking an i/p of .05882772025 (which provides a YTM of 11.766%) we follow the equation through:

$$\frac{100(1.0588)^{-36} + 6a_{\overline{36}|} - (6 - 4)a_{\overline{4}|} + 4}{(1.0588)^{.50410959}} = 95.983250 \text{ DP.}$$

Decimal entry discounted cash flow calculation method

Earlier, in Chapter 4, when DCF and DEDCF calculations were outlined, it was stated that the DEDCF method could take the place of a number of individual computer program calculations for a number of one-off requirements or any bonds with abnormal characteristics.

Although above there is a useful formula for "split coupons", which indeed can be used for other bond calculations with abnormal structures, it is perhaps worth examining how the YTM% in the above example could be determined by the DEDCF method.

Taking the same i/p and working through the cash flows, the NPV must result in 0.00. With the investment amount (here the DP) and the respective cash flows (here the respective half coupon values — and the last CF of redemption value + the half coupon) a computer program would continue to "loop" until satisfied that the NPV was exactly 0.00 and at that point would "throw up" the periodic IRR — which multiplied by 2 finds the YTM.

Investment (DP) $\qquad\qquad\qquad\qquad = -95.983250$

Cash flows:

$4 \times 1.0588^{-.50410959}$ $\qquad\qquad = \quad 3.886380$

$4 \times \dfrac{(1 - 1.0588^{-4})/.0588 \times 1.0588}{1.0588^{1.504}}$ $\quad = \quad 13.502947$

$6 \times \dfrac{(1 - 1.0588^{-31})/.0588 \times 1.0588}{1.0588^{5.504}}$ $\quad = \quad 65.439243$

$106 \times 1.0588^{-36.504}$ $\qquad\qquad = \quad 13.154680$

$\qquad\qquad\qquad\qquad\qquad$ NPV $= \quad\ \ 0.00$

Periodic IRR $\quad = \quad 5.882772025\%$
YTM (IRR $\times$ 2) $= 11.766\%$

There are various other applications in which the split coupon formula is useful — one such is below.

Convertibles

EXAMPLE: Bond 9% Semi-annual interest paid
Actual
Issue Price 100
Maturity 100
Redemption March 1980
Convertible into a 9% stock at 110, redemption March 2000.

Every 100 units held before conversion, if converted, would be worth 10% more. Thus after conversion the 9% coupon would be valued at 9.90 and in the same way the 100 RV would be worth 110.

An investor purchased his stock at 94.75 (DP) some 1412 days PRIOR to conversion and wishes to calculate his YTM% IF he converts.

The $(n + k)$ from SD to conversion date = $1412/182.5 = 7.736986$.

As conversion to final redemption is 20 years the total $(n + k)$ becomes 47.736986.

In effect this requirement becomes a calculation with two differing coupons for varying periods and so employing the "split coupon" formula:

$$\frac{110(1 + i/p)^{-47} + 4.95a_{\overline{47}|} - (4.95 - 4.5)a_{\overline{7}|} + 4.50}{(1 + i/p)^{.736986}} = 94.75$$

The precise i/p will be found as .052065885 and therefore the YTM presents as 10.413%.

Currency revaluations

When investing in bonds not of the currency of the (domiciled) investor the concern is always what effect a currency revaluation will have on the investor's return (yield). For if the revaluation is against the investor, his interest payments and his redemption value will be adversely affected in terms of his own currency, i.e., the amount that finally is credited to his domiciled bank account. The converse is also true.

The split coupon calculation here applies to the interest received before and after revaluation: and whereas the coupon calculation is a straight adjustment of the percentage valuation, the difficulty arises when determining the equation for revaluation of the maturity value (RV). For it cannot be the original RV before revaluation (100), or the original value adjusted by the revaluation percentage $(100 \times (1 + i/p))$, for there will be some periods relating to the RV "before and after" revaluation. So the calculation must be a weighted mean. The example below will elaborate this important point.

EXAMPLE: A Eurobond 10%
This bond was issued in XYZ currency at 100, with a maturity value of 100
in 12 years' time (12 × 360 = 4320 days). After some 3 years (360 × 3 =
1080 days) from issue XYZ currency was revalued 5% upward against the US
dollar. A US investor, for one reason at least, found this revaluation not un-
welcome for he had purchased the Bond at 89.56 some 700 days after issue.
From the chart below it will be seen that he held the stock for 380 days at
10% and for 3240 days at 10.50%.

```
                        |       4380 days
   ID ------------------+----------------------------------- RD
         10%       re   | val     10.50%
         1080          |         3240 days
   ID ------------------+----------------------------------- RD
         |              |
        10% |    10%   |         10.50%
   ID ----- SD --------+----------------------------------- RD
        700 |    380   |         3240 days
            |
           SD ----- 3620 days ------------------------------ RD
```

His YTM at purchase was 11.825% and he naturally now wishes to know
what the revalued YTM is from settlement (SD) to redemption (RD), a
matter of 3620 days or 10 years and 20 days.
   Therefore:

$$3620/360 = 10.055556 \,(n+k)$$

As explained above the RV cannot be either 100 or 105 (derived from 100
× 1.05) but because 380 + 3240 = 3620 the weighted mean RV becomes:

$$(100 \times 380/3620) + (105 \times 3240/3620) = 104.4751381 \text{ RV adjusted.}$$

As a Eurobond quotation price is a CP converting to a DP, we get 89.56 +
(10 × (1 − .055556)) = 89.56 + 9.44 = 99.00 DP.
   The YTM calculation now presents as:

$$\frac{104.4752(1+i/p)^{-10} + 10.50a_{\overline{10}|} - .5a_{\overline{1}|} + 10}{(1+i/p)^{.0555556}} = 99.00$$

The precise i/p will be found as .125399624 and therefore the YTM presents
as 12.540% against the original YTM, before revaluation, of 11.825% − and
incidentally please note that 11.825% × 1.05 does NOT equal 12.54!

Inflation

The above split coupon formula, having facilities for incorporating different
coupon values during the life of a bond, permits various modelling to be
undertaken if required − currency revaluations being merely one of them.

Some statisticians include inflation factors in such evaluations, but because these are inevitably loaded with assumptions, some scepticism as to their true usefulness persists. My own view is, generally, that the inflation indices of different countries are usually of more value for assessing the likelihood, or not, of re- or de-valuation in future years, rather than being part of a consequently imprecise and often complex calculation.

Nevertheless, if evaluations are to be made for investments in countries with high annual inflation then this fact, obviously, cannot be totally ignored and any related calculation should include some suitable factor or comment — even if only to the extent that some countries may be best avoided for investment purposes! Certainly for example, if evaluating investments in Israel (with run-away inflation of around 1000% in 1984), it would be a serious omission if no such comment was made.

CHAPTER 26

Abnormalities at Issue

The "abnormalities" under examination are bonds with minor differences in their structure; the slightly abnormal characteristics being stated at the time of issue and thus requiring minor adjustment in calculations to determine the price/YTM. The differences fall under two heads:

A. First interest payment abnormality.
B. Final interest payment abnormality.

A. FIRST PAYMENT ABNORMALITY

A(i)

EXAMPLE: A UK bond at 13.25%

Semi-annual interest paid
Actual (182.5 base)
Issue Price 94.50
RV 100
Issue date   17 July 1975
Redemption date 22 July 1997
Payment dates   22 Jan/July.

Studying the above data it would obviously be unreasonable for the first payment to be on the anniversary of the maturity date (as is normal), namely 22 July 1975, only 5 days after issue. In such circumstances the first payment is "skipped" and the "extra" days of interest are carried forward to the next payment date, 22 January, which in effect becomes the "first" payment date.

The value of the "first" payment must therefore include the extra five days' interest and from the dates given above the period from issue to the "first" payment date is 189 days. Therefore the total interest for that extended period is: $13.25/2 \times 189/182.5 = 6.860959\%$.

The convention is that the lender benefits if the fraction is greater than 2 places of decimals when the value is rounded up to 2 places of decimals — here the first payment becomes £6.87, per £100 worth of stock, as stated in the prospectus.

How is the yield to maturity calculated at issue? *In practice*, in this case, because the number of "extra days" are so few at issue they are ignored and the only reason why the YTM is not the coupon value, namely 13.25%, is because the issue price (here) is at a discount.

$$100(1 + i/p)^{-44} + 6.625a_{\overline{44}|} = 94.50 \text{ CP}$$

and the YTM will be found as 14.06%. The logic behind ignoring the five days' difference is that the extra time delay in waiting for the five days' interest is considered to equate roughly with the extra interest due.

But as soon as trading occurs in the period between issue and the "first" payment, then the correct YTM must be correctly calculated. The formula is set out below:

$$\frac{RV(1 + i/p)^{-(n-1)} + Da_{\overline{n}|} + D \text{ (adjusted)}}{(1 + i/p)^k} = \textbf{Clean} \text{ price.}$$

It must obviously be a clean price, instead of the normal DP when odd days intrude, because in this case not until the "first" payment date is reached is any interest paid — therefore there can be no accrued interest.

Assume that a purchase was made at a price of 96, resulting in settlement on 1 October 1975, which provides 7959 days between SD–RD with an (n + k) factor (7959/182.5) of 43.6109589:

$$\frac{100(1 + i/p)^{-(43-1)} + 6.625a_{\overline{42}|} + 6.87 \text{ (adjusted)}}{(1 + i/p)^{.6109589}} = 96.00$$

The YTM will be found as 14.268% (1 + i/p = 1.071341532).

Finding the first payment

To find the "first actual" interest payment is not always as easy as in the above example. For if partial payments, at issue, are permitted the calculation becomes less straightforward.

For example, a UK Treasury 10.25% convertible stock 1987 was issued on 2 June 1983 with a price of 98.25. Interest payment dates 10 Feb/Aug.

Issued 2 June   1983 20% payment required per £100 of stock.
          18 July   1983 50% payment required per £100 of stock.
          15 August 1983 the balance.

Because the issue date (2 June) was so close to the normal, expected, first interest payment date (10 August), the Bank of England noted in the issue documents that the first "actual" interest payment date would be 10 February 1984 and that the interest value on that occasion would be 5.8499% (and not 10.25/2%) on £100 of stock.

The 5.8499% was derived as shown overleaf.

$$(20\% \text{ of}) \; 10.25 \times \frac{20}{100} \times \frac{46 \,(\text{days Jun } 2 - \text{Jul } 18)}{365} \times \frac{100}{98.25} = .262958$$

$$(70\% \text{ of}) \; 10.25 \times \frac{70}{100} \times \frac{28 \,(\text{days Jul } 18 - \text{Aug } 25)}{365} \times \frac{100}{98.25} = .560215$$

$$(100\%) \; 10.25 \times \frac{179 \,(\text{days Aug } 15 - \text{Feb } 10)}{365} = 5.026712$$

$$= 5.849885$$
$$= 5.8499\%.$$

A(ii)

Above the first payment dates were so close to the issue date that payments were delayed: another abnormality is when the true first payment date is sufficiently far away from the issue date to warrant a payment — but not the full amount.

EXAMPLE: A UK Bond 9.50%

Semi-annual interest paid
Actual (182.5 base)
Issue Price 93.25
RV 100

Issue date	14 January 1976	Days between Issue–RD
Redemption date	14 May 1980	1580 (excl. 2 leap days)
Pmt dates	14 May/Nov	Days between 14 Jan–14 May
		120 (excl. 1 leap day)

Find the YTM at issue.

In this case the first payment is on the due date, 14 May, but must be reduced to only 120 days' interest, namely, $9.50/2 \times 120/182.5 = 3.123288$, which is rounded to 3.13.

The same formula as above is employed, save that in this case there is the (full) normal number of (n) periods, providing an (n + k) factor of $1580/182.5 = 8.657534247$.

Again, as the requirement is at issue, and as there have been no payments as yet made, the price stands as a CP.

The calculation presents therefore as:

$$\frac{100(1 + i/p)^{-8} + 4.75a_{\overline{8}|} + 3.13 \,(\text{adjusted})}{(1 + i/p)^{.657534}} = 93.25 \; CP$$

and the YTM will be found as 11.535% at issue and as 11.54% as provided in the prospectus. $(1 + i/p = 1.057676039)$.

If trading occurs between issue and the first payment date, the above formula must be used with the interest days and the (n + k) factors suitably amended. Once the first payment date (here May 14) is passed the normal formula is of course used, with no adjustments, to find the YTM.

B. WHEN MATURITY FALLS AFTER FINAL INTEREST PAYMENT DATE

Whereas the anomalies, in A above, are by no means exceptional, the following example occurs more rarely, and perhaps because of this the necessary calculations are not in everyday use. Occasionally for some reason a bond issue may be structured in such a way that the maturity date falls some time AFTER the final interest payment – sometimes, for example, irrespective of interest payment date a corporation might decide to redeem at a year-end. In cases such as this there must obviously be some interest due for the period between the final normal interest payment and the redemption date, for the holder will be "out of the money" until such time as the redemption value is repaid on the delayed redemption date.

If the difference between maturity and the last interest payment is only a week or two, then, usually, the Registrar will pay both the final interest payment, and the small interest due, together with the redemption value at the maturity date. We have already seen the type of calculation necessary for UK and local authority bonds at the end of Chapter 22, and in such cases the formula below is not necessary.

But when the delay is sufficient for the final payment to be made on one date and the delayed RV plus extra interest to be paid on another date then the following formula is required. It is not complicated and the "verification" methods, both by schedule and by decimal entry discounting cash flow, are provided to assist in the general understanding of the "rearrangements" that must be made in order to obtain a YTM by formula.

EXAMPLE: Bond 10%

Semi-annual interest paid
Price 95 (DP)
RV 100
Settlement 18 June 1983
Redemption 1 Sept 1992
Payment Dates 1 *May*/Nov
FIPD is on 1 May 1992 (FIPD = final interest payment date).

Rounding

When "adjusted interest" is due it is customary for any rounding benefit to be passed on to the lender. Rounding, in such cases, is not merely the conventional "rounding to 2 decimal places" but reflects any decimal value fraction greater than exactly 2 decimals. For instance, assuming that interest due is calculated as (say) 5.250001 the interest paid would be 5.26.

Some values in the equation below are, for convenience, shown in a shortened form but all the calculations have been worked to 10 decimal places.

In this example the "days between" are:

SD   − FIPD 3237 days (with FIPD on 1 May 1992)
FIPD − RD   123 days (with Maturity on 1 September 1992)

$3237/182.5 = 17.736986300 = (n + k)$
$123/182.5 = \quad .673972603 = t$

Formula when RD is after FIPD

$$\frac{RV(1 + i/p)^{-(n+t)} + Da_{\overline{n}|} + D + (Dt \times (1 + i/p)^{-(n+t)})}{(1 + i/p)^k} = DP$$

The interest due (the "D × t" factor) should be rounded UP:

$5 \times .673972603 = 3.37$

The YTM presents as 11.11031735% and $1.055551587 = (1 + i/p)$:

$$\frac{100(1.0556)^{-(17+.6740)} + 5a_{\overline{17}|} + 5 + (3.37 \times 1.0556^{-17.6740})}{1.055551587^{.7369863}} = 95.00 \text{ DP}$$

Verification

$(RV + Dt) \times (1 + i/p)^{-t} = A$

$(A + \text{pmts}) \times (1 + i/p)^{-1} = B$

$(B + \text{pmts}) \times (1 + i/p)^{-1} = C$

(Continue to discount to a total of n times to find the balance Z.)

$(Z + \text{pmts}) \times (1 + i/p)^{-k} = \underline{\text{Price (DP)}}.$

And for the above example:

$(100 + 3.37) \qquad \times 1.0556^{-.6740} = 99.67126868$

$(99.67126868 + 5.00) \times 1.0556^{-1} \quad = 99.16262221$

Continue discounting until a total of 17
periods have been completed, when the
balance will be $= 93.86160674$

$(93.86160674 + 5.00) \times 1.0556^{.7370} = 95.00 \text{ DP}.$

DEDCF

Price (DP)   = –95.00

$5 \times 1.0556^{-.73698630}$ =   4.804696333

$5 \times \dfrac{(1 - 1.0556^{-17})/.0556 \times 1.0556}{1.0556^{1.73698630}}$ = 51.99073064

$(100 + 3.37)(1.0556)^{-.674} \times 1.0556^{-17.7370}$ = 38.20451323

NPV =   0.00

In all the examples in this chapter the (n + k) has been determined by finding the days between SD and RD, or SD and FIPD, divided by 182.5, but, when using the above formulae, there is no reason why the quasi-coupon period method could not be employed or the actual number of odd days divided by 182.5 — or indeed annual payments calculated.

Employing the 30/360 calendar, it is optional whether the "extra days' interest" is actual or 30/360 based. Of course this option could never apply to Eurobonds for their interest is never "actual". But then I have never seen a Eurobond so structured — still there's obviously a first time for everything....

CHAPTER 27

Zero Coupon Bonds and Annuities

Zero coupon bonds and notes

In the early 80s a new type of money instrument appeared on the world markets — the zero coupon bond. This type of bond is geared to capital appreciation, there being no annual or semi-annual interest due to the lender. The calculations are quite simply compound interest with "rolled up" interest.

EXAMPLE

On 21 April 1981 J. C. Penney Company, Inc. issued a prospectus on the following lines (I paraphrase):

Notes would be issued on 1 May 1981 in denominations of $1,000 and any integral multiples of $1,000, to mature on 1 May 1989. There would NOT be any periodic payments of interest on the notes which could be exchanged or transferred without payment of any service charge other than tax or other Governmental charges payable in connection therewith. The price of the notes was 33.247% (which means that for calculation purposes the Redemption Value is 100).

The prospectus stated that the "price to the public represents a yield to maturity of 14.25% computed on a semi-annual basis".

To check these figures — as the term between issue and maturity is exactly 8 years or 16 half years:

$$200\left(\left(\frac{100}{33.247}\right)^{1/16} - 1\right) \ = 14.24982040\% \\ = 14.25\%$$

or, alternatively,

$$\$33.247 \times \left(1 + \frac{14.25}{200}\right)^{16} = \$100.0013406$$

or 100×1.07125^{-16} = $ 33.2465528

A straight compound/discount interest calculation — no problem.

Incidentally, to find the term:

$$\frac{\text{LOG} \ (100/33.2465528)}{\text{LOG} \ \ \ \ 1.07125} = 16 \text{ (term)}$$

Assume that after the issue the notes were actively traded "over the counter" and that on 1 January 1984 the price was $60. Assuming that settlement was 2 January, the days between SD and RD (1 May 1989) are (actual) 1946 or (30/360) 1919 providing an (n + k) factor of 1946/182.5 = 10.66301370 or 1919/180 = 10.661111 respectively — being half year periods because the notional (non) interest was considered to be semi-annual.

$$200\left(\left(\frac{100}{60}\right)^{1/10.663} - 1\right) = 9.81447240 \text{ YTM\% (actual)}$$

$$200\left(\left(\frac{100}{60}\right)^{1/10.661} - 1\right) = 9.81626620 \text{ YTM\% (30/360)}$$

With an (n + k) of 16 − 10.661 = 5.33889 the seller's gross yield would be:

$$200 \times ((60/33.247)^{1/5.33889} - 1) = 23.39\% \text{ gross.}$$

Tax considerations for zero bonds

Throughout the previous chapters any question of taxation has been studiously avoided, unless specific to the particular calculation under examination, for each country has its own taxation structures and therefore each national (investor) has different problems. But it is clear that zero coupons, if not tax-free, are "tax-incentive" in that when/if tax is liable it is in the form of delayed tax payments. In some countries the borrower can obtain each year tax credits for the annual interest which in fact is not paid until redemption; alternatively the lender avoids annual income tax in some countries but is later taxed on the annual interest accruals either at redemption or at point of sale. In any event, there is a capital lift and in those countries where capital gains tax is applicable some tax will be levied on the difference between purchase and realisation.

Buying and selling annuities

"Annuities" are occasionally sold "on the market" and as such it is necessary to know the correct calculations.

To take one such example, Zimbabwe, in mid-1980, issued an annuity over a period of eight years, with a first, semi-annual, payment of £50 on 15 April 1981. As payments are "in arrears" the issue commenced officially on 15 October 1980. The final payment is on 15 October 1988. The annuity rate of interest is 10.25% nominal, hence the semi-annual interest rate is 5.125% which makes the capital value of the annuity:

$$50a_{\overline{16}|} \text{ at } 5.125\% = 537.099259 = £537.10 \text{ PV.}$$

A schedule

With this data available readers of Part I will be aware of how such an annuity schedule would present, providing a balance or loan outstanding (LOS) each half year.

PMTS made		LOS	INT	CAP	PMTS
[537.10 X 1.05125 = 27.53 et seq]					
15 Oct 80	Issued	537.10	27.53 +	22.47 =	50.00
15 Apr 81	537.10 + 27.53 − 50 =	514.63	26.37 +	23.63 =	50.00
15 Oct 81	514.63 + 26.37 − 50 =	491.00	25.16 +	24.84 =	50.00
15 Apr 82	491.00 + 25.16 − 50 =	466.16	23.89 +	26.11 =	50.00
15 Oct 82	466.16 + 23.89 − 50 =	440.05	22.55 +	27.45 =	50.00
15 Apr 83	440.05 + 22.55 − 50 =	412.60	21.15 +	28.85 =	50.00
15 Oct 83	412.60 + 21.15 − 50 =	383.75	19.67 +	30.33 =	50.00
15 Apr 84	383.75 + 19.67 − 50 =	353.42	18.11 +	31.89 =	50.00
15 Oct 84	353.42 + 18.11 − 50 =	321.53	16.48 +	33.52 =	50.00
15 Apr 85	321.53 + 16.48 − 50 =	288.01	14.76 +	35.24 =	50.00
15 Oct 85	288.01 + 14.76 − 50 =	252.77	12.95 +	37.05 =	50.00
15 Apr 86	252.77 + 12.95 − 50 =	215.72	11.06 +	38.94 =	50.00
15 Oct 86	215.72 + 11.06 − 50 =	176.78	9.06 +	40.94 =	50.00
15 Apr 87	176.78 + 9.06 − 50 =	135.84	6.96 +	43.04 =	50.00
15 Oct 87	135.84 + 6.96 − 50 =	92.80	4.76 +	45.24 =	50.00
15 Apr 88	92.80 + 4.76 − 50 =	47.56	2.44 +	47.56 =	50.00
15 Oct 88	47.56 + 2.44 − 50 =	0.00			
			262.90	537.10 =	800.00

As will be seen from the above schedule this type of interest-bearing obligation is therefore quite different from a conventional bond in which the redemption value (RV), the original loan amount, is redeemed in toto at maturity. A further important difference is that the repayments made each half year are not "coupons", in the accepted sense, for here the £50 semi-annual annuity payments comprise both interest AND capital so that after the last repayment on 15 October 1988 the transaction is concluded − all the capital having been repaid.

Naturally during the course of the term of the annuity prices will change with the varying views of the investing public as to the stability, or not, of the country concerned − and the normal variation in world-wide interest rates.

How then do we calculate the yield related to the price paid at purchase (settlement)?

The whole structure of the loan can be treated, for calculation purposes, as if it was a conventional bond with the proviso that some adjustment must be made for the fact that as the semi-annual repayments reflect portions of both capital and interest there will be no redemption value to be considered — i.e., no final maturity payment.

Yields to maturity (YTMs) and redemption yields (RYs) mean precisely the same thing, but in order constantly to remind ourselves, in the text below, of the difference between bonds, which have a final capital payment, and annuities, which haven't, the term redemption yield (instead of the conventional YTM) will be used for those yields related to changing prices.

EXAMPLE
If the market quoted the redemption yield as 13%, with settlement 23 February 1984, what is the market price?

There are 1696 days between settlement and maturity (22 February 1984 — 15 October 1988) with two leap days intervening, so the operative "days between" are 1694.

With these rather rarely quoted annuity-loans the price spread is such that most statisticians consider that employing a base of 182.5 is sufficiently precise; but there is no reason why the odd days calculations cannot be based on the "quasi-coupon period" method if preferred:

The $(n + k) = 1694/182.5 = 9.282192$ and the price therefore is:

$$\frac{\text{Pmts } a_{\overline{n}|} + \text{Pmt}}{(1 + i/p)^k} = \text{quoted (dirty) price}$$

$$\frac{(50 \times (1 - 1.065^{-9})/.065) + 50}{1.065^{.282192}} = 376.06 \text{ DP}$$

It will be observed that the only difference in calculations between annuities and conventional bond yields is that in the above equation the term $RV(1 + i/p)^{-n}$ is omitted, there being no final capital repayment to be discounted — and, because of this, difficulties can obviously arise if attempting to calculate annuities on a conventional bond price/yield computer program.

The "quoted" price, "as set out", is one which includes any interest due — and is therefore a "dirty" price.

Ex-div calculations

The Zimbabwe prospectus advised all annuitants that "balances would be struck" one month prior to payment dates, in other words the stock would go "ex-div" on the 15th day of each month prior to the payment date, namely March and September.

Assume that the (gross) RY is 13% with settlement 2 April 1984, what is the price quoted in the market?

There are 1657 days between settlement and maturity, with ONE leap day, the (n + k) thus becomes 1656/182.5 = 9.073972603.

$$\frac{50 \times (1 - 1.065^{-9})/.065}{1.065^{.07397}} = £331.26 \text{ price.}$$

Annuity capital

In all previous calculations it has been assumed that the annuitant holds a £100 annuity (£50 per half year), represented by Annuity Capital of £537.10. Therefore, an annuity capital of £98.01 will entitle the accepting holder to an annuity of £18.25 (£9.13 per half year).

£98.01 × 100/537.10 = £18.25

Annuity payments

A holder of a £55.78 annuity (receiving £27.89 gross per half year) would have purchased a capital value of:

£55.78 × 537.10/100 = £299.59,

equally well found by:

$27.89a_{\overline{16}|}$ at 5.125% = £299.59

To find LOS and capital and interest values by formulae

In the cum-div example above, with an (n + k) of 9.282192, the price was, naturally, found by "working backwards" from the maturity date. To find a balance or LOS at any particular period of an annuity, however, we must work from the front end (issue period).

So, to find the balance at 15 April 1984 (the first payment after our settlement on 23 February 1984) we must determine the correct period(s) for calculation — here:

16 − (n + 1) = 16 − 10 = 6 (period).

The method of finding the loan outstanding (LOS), for annuities ordinary, has already been fully outlined in Part I and the calculation thus becomes:

£537.10 × 1.05125^6 − $50s_{\overline{6}|}$		= LOS(6)
£537.10 × 1.05125^6 − $[50 \times (1.05125^6 - 1)/.05125]$		= LOS(6)
724.92 − 341.17		= £383.75

To find the capital and interest portions for this 6th period, that is, the values standing between 15 October 1983 − 15 April 1984, we must first find the balance for the *next* (7th) period:

$£537.10 \times 1.05125^7 - 50s_{\overline{7}|}$ = LOS(7)

$£537.10 \times 1.05125^7 - [50 \times (1.05125^7 - 1)/.05125]$ = LOS(7)

762.07 $- 408.65$ = £353.42

(383.75 − 353.42) = capital repaid for period 6   = £30.33

50 − (383.75 − 353.42) = gross interest for period 6   = £19.67

(Compare schedule above)   £50.00

Net yields

We have seen previously that to provide a bond with a net YTM (ignoring any CGT complications) a statistician will merely "net the coupon" and then recalculate a new (net) YTM from the gross coupon suitably reduced in value by the tax deduction.

Unhappily, this simple method cannot be employed for annuity loans because all the semi-annual repayments include a portion of capital − and are thus not solely an "interest" coupon suitable for "netting". Equally unsuitable would be the employment of the MIRAS method (Chapter 7) to net the RY, for again this would be frustrated by the capital content of the repayments.

Reverting to the cum-div example above, if the interest between a specific period was taxed and then subtracted from the payment factor, would that serve? Unfortunately, no! For this would assume mathematically that ALL the net interest values, for the periods from maturity right back to the period under review, were all the same − which they obviously aren't.

Formula for NET redemption yields

At the end of this chapter will be shown a useful and quick method of finding an approximate net RY − but this is only an approximation and cannot replace the two correct methods outlined below, namely the formula method or schedule. First the formulae.

Cum-Div formula

$$\frac{(\text{at } i/p)\ \text{Net Pmts } \ddot{a}_{\overline{n+1}|} + B\ddot{a}_{\overline{n+1}|}\ (\text{at } j\%)}{(1 + i/p)^k} = \text{Price}.$$

Where:

i = the NET RY (as a decimal)

p = the number of compounding periods in one year (2)

g = the annual interest rate (10.25%)
t = the tax rate as a decimal (.30)
B = Pmts $\times (1 + g/p)^{-(n+1)}$

$$(1 + j) = \frac{(1 + i/p)}{(1 + g/p)}$$

Taking a net RY of 9.2593806% with an $(1 + i/p)$ of 1.046296903 $(1 + j)$ becomes:

$$\frac{1 + (9.2593806/200)}{1 + (10.250000/200)} = \frac{1.046296903}{1.05125} = 0.995288374 \quad = (1 + j)$$

$$= 100(.99529 - 1)$$

$$= -0.47116262\% = \text{"j"}$$

B becomes $50 \times 1.05125^{-10} \times .3 \qquad = 9.099785829$

The $(n + k)$ is, if the reader glances back,

$$1694/182.5 \qquad\qquad\qquad = 9.282192.$$

$$\frac{(\text{at } i/p)\ 35\ddot{a}_{\overline{10}|} + 9.099786\ddot{a}_{\overline{10}|}\ (\text{at } j\%)}{1.046297^{.282192}} = 376.06$$

$$\frac{[(35(1 - 1.046297^{-10}) \times 1.046297]}{.046297} + \frac{[(9.099786(1 - .995288^{-10}) \times .995288]}{-.004712}$$
$$\overline{\hspace{10cm}}$$
$$1.012853$$

$$\frac{287.927939 + 92.961032}{1.012853} = 376.06 \text{ Price}$$

Ex-div formula

For an ex-div calculation the above formula alters in that the two annuities **due** calculations, in the formula above, become annuities **ord** and their term employed is (n) — instead of (n + 1) as shown above.

Taking the above ex-div example where the (n + k) was 1656/182.5 = 9.073972603 and the price was 331.26, the net RY is 9.8308870% and therefore taking the $(1 + i/p)$ as 1.049154435:

$$\frac{[(35(1 - 1.049154^{-9})/.049154] + [(9.099786(1 - .998007^{-9})/-.0020)]}{1.049154435^{.073972603}}$$

$$\frac{249.71 + 82.72}{1.003555848} = £331.26 \text{ (Price)}$$

It will be seen, when comparing the two cum and ex-div calculations above, that the B factor (9.099785829) is constant to both calculations, as of course it should be, and the $(1 + j)$ is determined as shown opposite:

$$\frac{(1 + i/p)}{(1 + g/p)} = (1 + j)$$

$$\frac{1.049154435}{1.051250} = .998006597$$

Below are the two schedules, cum and ex-div, which demonstrate that, with the respective net RYs above, the interest portions brought to net and subtracted from the semi-annual payments in both cases provide a zero NPV. Both the net schedules can be compared with the original gross schedule to observe the various interest calculations etc.

Because the term length of these types of annuities is comparatively short, most net RYs are found from computer programs by the schedule method, rather than the formulae above — for, as can be seen below, a schedule can provide many other features "on screen" or in print-out form. A quick approximation method to determine the net yields, cum or ex div, is set out at the end of the schedules.

Cum-dividend schedule

"Investment" $= -376.06$

(net payments)

PMT $-$ (INT $\times$ .3) $\qquad\qquad \times (1 + i/p)^{-k}$

$50 - (19.67 \times .3) = 44.10 \times 1.046296903^{-0.282191781} = 43.54037117$

$50 - (18.11 \times .3) = 44.57 \times 1.046296903^{-1.282191781} = 42.05728483$

$50 - (16.48 \times .3) = 45.06 \times 1.046296903^{-2.282191781} = 40.63823574$

$50 - (14.76 \times .3) = 45.57 \times 1.046296903^{-3.282191781} = 39.27966240$

$50 - (12.95 \times .3) = 46.12 \times 1.046296903^{-4.282191781} = 37.99470498$

$50 - (11.96 \times .3) = 46.68 \times 1.046296903^{-5.282191781} = 36.75442949$

$50 - (\ 9.06 \times .3) = 47.28 \times 1.046296903^{-6.282191781} = 35.57962501$

$50 - (\ 6.96 \times .3) = 47.91 \times 1.046296903^{-7.282191781} = 34.45840171$

$50 - (\ 4.76 \times .3) = 48.57 \times 1.046296903^{-8.282191781} = 33.38736326$

$50 - (\ 2.44 \times .3) = 49.27 \times 1.046296903^{-9.282191781} = \underline{32.36992113}$

$$\text{NPV} = \quad 0.00000030$$

Ex-dividend schedule

"Investment"   = −331.26

(net payments)

44.57	X 1.049154435$^{-1.073972603}$	= 42.33130596
45.06	X 1.049154435$^{-2.073972603}$	= 40.79160555
45.57	X 1.049154435$^{-3.073972603}$	= 39.32051703
46.12	X 1.049154435$^{-4.073972603}$	= 37.93063112
46.68	X 1.049154435$^{-5.073972603}$	= 36.59250973
47.28	X 1.049154435$^{-6.073972603}$	= 35.32640119
47.91	X 1.049154435$^{-7.073972603}$	= 34.11997300
48.57	X 1.049154435$^{-8.073972603}$	= 32.96941115
49.27	X 1.049154435$^{-9.073972603}$	= 31.87764492

NPV = 0.00000040

An averaging method for calculator users to find a rough net RY

While the correct schedule method can be found on a calculator, neverthe-less, sometimes even a rough idea of particular net RY can be useful, and the method outlined below is a "possibility" providing it is realised and accepted that the answer is bound to be fractionally incorrect.

Roughly the idea is that instead of computing each of the applicable net payments and working through the required term of the loan, period by period, we add all the gross interest portions applicable to the term in question. Then after determining the tax on the sum of these payments we find an "average net payment" by dividing the net amount by the (n + k) and subtracting the result from the gross payments, here £50.00. Having found the "average net payments" the yield can be found by the conventional means and methods.

Taking the cum-div example above, which found a price of £376.06 from a gross RY of 13% over a term of 1694 days, the (n + k) being 9.282192, to find the sum of the interest between a required date and final maturity, first find the loan outstanding at the date required (see Section LOS(n) above where LOS(6) = £383.75). Then subtract this amount from the sum of the total payments made between the required date and maturity.

[pmts X (n − y)] − LOS(y) = interest between NPD − RD

50 X (16 − 6) − 383.75   = £116.25 gross interest (see above)

(between April 84 − Oct 88)

Where:

  NPD = Next Payment Date after settlement
  RD = Redemption Date
  Tax = 30%

To convert gross interest to an "average" net value

Gross pmts − (gross int × .30/(n + k))   = Average net payments

50   − (116.25 × .30)/9.282192

50   − (3.757195 tax average)   = 46.24280549

$$\frac{46.242805 \times ((1 - 1.046^{-9})/.046) + 46.242805}{1.046^{.282192}} = 376.06 \text{ DP}$$

the i/p here equals .04600002498   = 9.20% NET RY.

The correctly calculated net RY, as we saw above, was only fractionally greater, namely 9.259380600%.

If the imprecise, "average net RY" of 9.20%, and an i/p of 0.046000025, (instead of the correct net RY of 9.26%) was employed in a DEDCF calculation (see the cum-dividend schedule above) it will be found that the NPV will present as −.481772 which will alert the user to the fact that the "average" periodic interest rate is fractionally too small and requires a slight mental adjustment.

The ex-div net RY approximation

Taking the previous ex-div calculation above, with a gross RY of 13% providing a price of £331.26 for a term of 1656 days, (n + k) = 9.073973, it will be seen that the settlement *period* is the same as that in the previous cum-div example. But being "ex-div", however, the sum of the gross interest due must be less the April interest, namely £116.25 (as above) less £19.67 = £96.58.

The tax on £96.58 = 96.58 × .3 = 28.9740 and this divided by the (n + k) of 9.073972603 = 3.193088768 which subtracted from the gross payments of £50 provides an "average net payment" of 46.80691123:

$$\frac{46.80691123 a_{\overline{9}|}}{(1 + i/p)^{.073972603}} = 331.26 \text{ DP}$$

at 5.015786555% semi-annually, hence 10.03157311% NET RY.

The correct net RY was, as seen above, 9.830887000% and so the difference, here, is slightly greater, and consequently the approximation slightly less accurate than the comparisons previously made between the correct cum-div and approximate RY above.

CHAPTER 28

Discounting Bills and
Bank Certificates of Deposit

Bills

Readers will be aware that the concept of discounting bills is based on the old adage that "a bird in the hand . . .".

A manufacturer, with terms of sale "payment within 90 days", selling equipment for $1000 (or £1000) might well prefer to receive the $1000 less a small fee (or discount) NOW rather than to wait for 3 months. If the "discount rate" was 15%:

Bill (simple interest) discounting

$$£1000 \times 15/100 \times 90/365 = £36.99 \quad \text{discount amount}$$
$$1000 - 36.99 \quad\quad = £963.013699 \quad \text{discounted value}$$
$$\$1000 \times 15/100 \times 90/360 = \$37.50 \quad \text{discount amount}$$
$$1000 - 37.50 \quad\quad = \$962.500000 \quad \text{discounted value}$$

Note

As seen above, for dollar discounting, the mix, ACTUAL − 30/360, actual days and base 360, always obtains (unless otherwise stated) throughout ALL dollar discounting and dollar certificates of deposit calculations. This method differs from previous calculations relating to bond price/yield calculations where the calendar is either actual or 30/360. Incidentally, from the experience of date examples in earlier chapters the temptation might be to assume that the 30/360 days are always less than the actual days − but this is by no means the case. For 1 February 1983 − 9 March 1983 is 36 (actual) days and 38 days (30/360).

The banker's return (or yield)

Above the banker received £36.99 for his trouble and his client received £963.01 on settlement, or value day, instead of having to wait 90 days for the £1000 payment. The banker's perspective is therefore a little different: for a £963.01 outlay after 90 days he receives £1000 and consequently his resulting yield is not 15% but is:

$$£((1000/963.013699) - 1) \times 365/90 \times 100 = 15.576102$$
$$15.58\% \text{ yield}$$

$((1000/962.500000) - 1) \times 360/90 \times 100 = 15.584416$
$$= 15.58\% \text{ yield}$$

The rate can also be found from:

$(15.00 \times 360)/(360 - (15.00/100 \times 90)) \quad = 15.584415\%$

Conversely:

$(15.58 \times 360)/(360 + (15.58/100 \times 90)) \quad = 15.000000\%.$

Simple interest to yield basis

A banker may decide to discount a bill on a "yield return" basis and, assuming that he was prepared to accept a yield of 15% (and not 15.58%) for the above $1000 bill, the manufacturer benefits as he receives, not $962.50 for his $1000 bill, but:

$$\frac{1000}{(1 + (15/100 \times 90/360))} = \$963.86 \text{ value}$$

$\$1000 - 963.86 \qquad = \$ \ 36.14 \text{ amount}$

and for the sterling bill the values are £964.33 and £35.67 respectively.

Simple interest to yield basis with a term exceeding one year

Assume the capital value, or face value, of a bill is £/$1000, the term is 500 days and the required return is 15%. The banker would deem the term to be (500 − 365), some 1 year and 135 actual days, and so the bill would be discounted first for one year and then the balance found re-discounted for the 135 odd days. Remember that, should a leap day intervene, the above term would be either 366 days + 135 days or 365 days + 136 days; for leap days are always counted and, as we shall see in CD calculations later, substantially affect all the calculations.

Dollars:

$$\frac{1000}{1 + (15/100 \times 365/360)} = 867.99$$

$$\frac{867.99}{1 + (15/100 \times 135/360)} = \$821.77 \text{ value}$$

$$= \$178.23 \text{ amount}$$

Sterling:

$$\frac{1000}{1 + (15/100 \times 365/365)} = 868.57$$

$$\frac{869.57}{1 + (15/100 \times 135/365)} = \$823.86 \text{ value}$$
$$= \$176.14 \text{ amount}$$

Semi-annual discounting to yield basis

Some dollar orientated bankers prefer their return to be calculated on a semi-annual basis and in that case the exact number of actual days must be determined between each half year. Assuming the above $1000 bill and the required nominal 15% return:

$$\frac{1000}{1 + (15/200 \times 181/180)} = 929.87$$

$$\frac{929.87}{1 + (15/200 \times 184/180)} = 863.66$$

$$\frac{863.66}{1 + (15/200 \times 135/180)} = \$817.660 \text{ value}$$
$$= \$182.34 \quad \text{amount}$$

Bank certificates of deposit

A CD is a receipt for a deposit made with an issuing bank. This receipt states the principal amount loaned, the nominal rate of interest, the issue date, and the date on which the loan is to be redeemed. Banks take care that the maturity date never falls on a weekend or bank holiday.

A CD is in bearer form and is negotiable without endorsement; therefore it should be lodged, for safe custody, with an authorised depository.

A CD can be traded on the secondary market, thus providing instant liquidity — one of the attractions of this form of money instrument. There are thus no penalties for early realisation: no tax is withheld and so all payments are gross: and so far as the author is aware, no government levies any stamp duty. The Max/Min permissible borrowing varies with different markets and the required life of the loan.

Short-term CDs Life is between 3 months and one year. Interest due is paid at the same time as the principal is repaid.

Medium-term CDs Life is greater than one year but not more than 5 years. Interest is paid annually, or semi-annually, the final interest payment being made with the return of the principal amount.

Currencies CDs can be in any required currency and different banks and markets have their own conventions as to whether the discounting will be annual or semi-annual.

Actual 30/360, Actual/360 The calculating base employed is either 365 or 360, or 180, BUT the "days between" value (settlement) date and maturity are ALWAYS "actual" and leap days are ALWAYS included.

Rounding Presentation is usually to 2 places of decimals, for example $/c or £/p, but the intermediate calculations are seldom rounded, being true to the full capabilities of the computer/calculator employed. Even if the intermediate discounted values are rounded the difference is not significant.

Simple interest discounting Simple interest discounting (SI) is the ONLY permissible method of calculating CD values.

Values discounted (divided) by $1 + (i/p \times k)$, NEVER $(1 + i/p)^k$.

Note

Sterling CDs (365 days based) are annual interest paid, as are Eurodollar CDs (360 days based), but US dollar CDs, sometimes colloquially referred to as "Yankee" dollar CDs, being both annual or semi-annual interest paid, are 360 or 180 days based. In all cases the "actual" days are employed to obtain the life of the loan – and any leap days are always included.

Short-term certificates

Formula:

$$\text{Principal} \times \frac{1 + \dfrac{\text{Int Rate } \% \times \text{life (days)}}{100 \times 360}}{1 + \dfrac{\text{Yield Rate } \% \times \text{Remaining days}}{100 \times 360}} = \text{Price}$$

The above formula can usefully be transposed to:

$$\text{Principal} \times \frac{36000 + (\text{Int } \% \times \text{Life Days})}{36000 + (\text{Yield } \% \times \text{Rem Days})} = \text{Price}$$

For sterling CDs: for 360 read 365, and for 36000 read 36500.

EXAMPLE

A certified deposit (principal) of $50,000 (the "face value").
Nominal interest rate 16%.
Period of issue 90 days.
The CD is held for 60 days and traded on the secondary market with 30 days to run to maturity at a yield to maturity rate of 15%. What is the price, or "proceeds"?

$$\$50,000 \times \frac{36000 + (16 \times 90)}{36000 + (15 \times 30)} = \$51,358.02 \text{ proceeds.}$$

For a Sterling CD: for 360 read 365, the proceeds presenting as £51,339.65.

In effect the above CD means that the original $50,000 would be repaid in 90 days together with 90 days' interest at 16%, namely:

$$50,000 + (50,000 \times (16/100 \times 90/360)) = \$52,000.00.$$

The purchaser in the secondary market having paid $51,358.02 (30 days before maturity), receives at maturity, $52,000, so his "profit" is $641.98.
Check yield:

$$\frac{641.98 \times 360 \times 100}{51,358.02 \times 30} = 15\%.$$

Note to computer programmers

Reverting to the main formula, not the transposed equation used above, remember that although *in practice* the actual days appear to be divided by 360 in fact the true perspective is (here):

$$\frac{16 \times 365 \times 90}{100 \times 360 \times 365} = \frac{16 \times 365 \times 90}{100 \times 360 \times 365} = \frac{16 \times 90}{100 \times 360}$$

If this over-simplification in the equation calculation is not fully appreciated, erroneous results may follow from incorrect programming. Whereas, above, it may appear obvious, later with more complex semi-annual CDs, et al, with leap days intervening, etc, mental clarity of thought on this point is essential.

Medium-term certificates

Perhaps an example at the outset will provide a clearer picture than a long explanation; for formulae, as we shall see later, will be replaced by schedules. A sterling CD with a face value of £50,000 has a term of three years to maturity at an interest rate of 17%. This CD was sold on the secondary market on a yield to maturity basis of 16.50% with exactly 2 years and 300 days to run to redemption from settlement. The annual interest therefore becomes 50,000 × 17/100 = £8,500.

Reflecting on this data, and having digested the YTM methods of calculation earlier, why could not this be calculated as a bond to fix the price? As redemption will be the face value, namely £50,000, surely the whole problem could be placed on percentage basis; the coupon is therefore 17% and the term, the $(n + k)$ is $2 + (300/365) = 2.821918$ and the RV 100 with the price when found divided by 100 and multiplied by the face value. Indeed it could be, providing, and only providing, that the simple interest method of finding bond yields is employed and, more important, that the term has no leap days intervening.

Assuming therefore that the term is clear of leap days, the bond equation would present as follows:

$$\frac{100(1.1659)^{-2} + 17((1 - 1.165^{-2})/.165) + 17}{1 + (.165 \times 300/365)} = 103.7300794$$

(proceeds %)

and

$$103.7300794/100 \times 50,000 = \text{Proceeds} \qquad = £51,865.04.$$

For a Eurodollar CD exactly the same calculation would obtain except that *both* the interest factors will have to be multiplied by 365/360 namely $16.5 \times 365/360 = 16.729167\%$ YTM and the coupon $17 \times 365/360 = 17.236111\%$. Note that the term in *actual* days is NOT altered, namely $2 + 300/365$, which may help to explain the note above addressed to computer programmers. In this case the proceeds would present as $51,886.79.

Unfortunately, the bond formula is a *formula* and even if leap days were included in the $(n + k)$ factor, as of course they could be, the period in which they occurred, the precise year or half year, would not be apparent in the calculations – and therefore would not equate exactly with the requirement. Readers may recall that previously, when discussing the various methods of calculating bond yields, I said that the only true calculation was by schedule – but that as bonds often have a life of over 20 years or 40 half year periods, the labour, even on a computer, is hardly worth the problems which a schedule would entail. But for CDs with only five years to run little difficulty is encountered from that aspect: also, of course, with CDs the proceeds or price is the requirement – NOT the yield.

As medium-term CDs have an issued life, usually, of 5 years, it is more than likely that a leap year will occur somewhere during the period between settlement and maturity and so, regrettably, the bond yield formula method for calculating CDs must be relegated to a "near check method" and schedules must be made in all cases.

Note
Eurodollar CDs, medium term, are always annual interest payments, whereas US (Yankee) dollar CDs are semi-annual interest paid.

The method to calculate medium-term certificates of deposit

First find the annual (or half-annual) interest due both for the normal period term and for an extra day occasioned by an extra leap day (see calculation below:

$$£50,000 \times 17/100 \times 365/365 = £8,500.00 \text{ (365 days)}$$
$$£50,000 \times 17/100 \times 366/365 = £8,523.29 \text{ (366 days)}$$

$$\$50,000 \times 17/100 \times 365/360 = \$8,618.06 \text{ (365 days)}$$
$$\$50,000 \times 17/100 \times 366/360 = \$8,641.67 \text{ (366 days)}$$

The above example was a life of 2 years and 300 days — assume NO leap days.

Sterling

$$(50000.00 + 8500.00) \times 1.1650^{-1} \qquad\qquad = \quad 50,214.59$$
$$(50214.59 + 8500.00) \times 1.1650^{-1} \qquad\qquad = \quad 50,398.79$$
$$(50398.79 + 8500.00) \times (1 + (.165 \times 300/365))^{-1} = £51,865.04$$
$$\text{(Proceeds)}$$

(compare £ bond calculations above)

Dollars

$$(50000.00 + 8618.06) \times (1 + (.165 \times 365/360))^{-1} = \quad 50,217.15$$
$$(50217.15 + 8618.06) \times (1 + (.165 \times 365/360))^{-1} = \quad 50,403.18$$
$$(50403.18 + 8618.06) \times (1 + (.165 \times 300/360))^{-1} = \$51,886.80$$
$$\text{(Proceeds)}$$

(compare $ bond comment above)

If, however, the first full year nearest redemption contained a leap day (366 days), the the calculation would be amended:

$$\text{Sterling } (\ldots 8,523.29) \times (1 + (.165 \times 366/365))^{-1}$$
$$\text{Dollars } (\ldots 8,641.67) \times (1 + (.165 \times 366/360))^{-1}$$

and the proceeds would become £51,865.42 and $51,887.19 respectively.

Should a leap day fall in the odd days period the same addition of one day would obtain.

Dollar CDs with semi-annual interest payments

Note

Semi-annual (Yankee) $ CDs are not traded in the London Market.

Exactly the same discipline is employed to calculate semi-annual CDs as is employed for annual interest paid CDs, except that the nominal rates are halved and the correct number of days in each half year period must be found from the calendar.

EXAMPLE: A dollar semi-annual CD

Face value	$500,000.00
Interest rate	7.75% nominal
Yield to maturity	7.625% nominal
Settlement	2 July 1983
Maturity	10 December 1985

Date/Days/Interest schedule

Dates	Days	Loan	Rates	½ Yr Int
(RD)				

$$\underline{10 \text{ Dec } 85} - 10 \text{ Jun } 85 = 183 \quad 500{,}000 \times \frac{7.75 \times 183}{200 \times 180} = \$19{,}697.92$$

$$10 \text{ Jun } 85 - 10 \text{ Dec } 84 = 182 \quad 500{,}000 \times \frac{7.75 \times 182}{200 \times 180} = \$19{,}590.28$$

$$10 \text{ Dec } 84 - 10 \text{ Jun } 84 = 183 \qquad\qquad\qquad\qquad = \$19{,}697.92$$

$$10 \text{ Jun } 84 - 10 \text{ Dec } 83 = 183 \text{ (incl. leap day)} \qquad = \$19{,}697.92$$

$$10 \text{ Dec } 83 - \underline{2\,Jul\,83} \;\; = 161 \text{ (odd days SD)}$$
$$\phantom{10 \text{ Dec } 83}\;\; 2 \text{ Jul } 83 - 10 \text{ Jun } 83 = -22 \qquad\qquad) \, 183 \qquad = \$19{,}697.92$$
$$(914 - 22 = 892)$$

Discount schedule

$$(500{,}000.00 + 19{,}697.92) \div \left(1 + \frac{7.625 \times 183}{200 \times 180}\right) = 500{,}305.86$$

$$(500{,}305.86 + 19{,}590.28) \div \left(1 + \frac{7.625 \times 182}{200 \times 180}\right) = 500{,}598.75$$

$$(500{,}598.75 + 19{,}697.92) \div \left(1 + \frac{7.625 \times 183}{200 \times 180}\right) = 500{,}882.26$$

$$(500{,}882.26 + 19{,}697.92) \div \left(1 + \frac{7.625 \times 183}{200 \times 180}\right)^{***} = 501{,}155.20^{***}$$

$$(501{,}155.20 + 19{,}697.92) \div \left(1 + \frac{7.625 \times 161}{200 \times 180}\right) = \$503{,}677.37$$
$$\text{(Proceeds)}$$

***Leap day intervenes in this half year.

The above example calculated by bond yield methods

Given the coupon, rate of return, the yield required, and the term, the normal requirement is to calculate the proceeds (or "cost"). Rarely is the requirement to find the rate of return or in other words the yield to maturity: fortunately — for the only correct method would be to employ the above schedules, "guessing" various yield rates, interpolating and re-guessing. Employing a computer program would achieve this end but, even so, some little time might elapse, for "looping a schedule" is somewhat more complex than interpolating a formula. Certainly on a programmed calculator looping a schedule would be far too time-consuming.

However, with a little imagination a CD yield can be found by employing the bond YTM formula method. Taking the above example, and assuming that the data as provided above are the same, save that in this instance the proceeds are given as $503,677.37 and the yield to maturity (of 7.625%) is NOT known, find the YTM.

Days between settlement (2 July 1983) and maturity (10 December 1985) are 878 (30/360 days base) and so the $(n + k) = 878/180 = 4.877778$. The price percentage is found by: $503,677.37/500,000 \times 100 = 100.735474$, and looking at the schedule it will be realised that this value represents the price AND accrued interest, in other words the DP.

Thus the equation will present as follows:

$$\frac{100(1 + i/p)^{-4} + 3.875a_{\overline{4}|} + 3.875}{1 + (i/p \times .877778)} = 100.735474 \text{ DP.}$$

The i/p will be found as .038116754 which, when multiplied by 200 to find the YTM, will present as 7.623351% and it hardly needs much imagination to realise that, as it would be almost unheard of for the market to require a yield return of such unrealistic precision, it would more probably be 7.625%, namely 7-5/8ths.

CHAPTER 29

Floating Rate Certificates of Deposit

FRCDs are not traded on the London market.

This money instrument, a variation of the semi-annual dollar CD, has become increasingly popular since its inception in 1977. In that year, because of a dollar surplus in Japan, the Japanese government instructed the Japanese banks to suspend short-term dollar funding and only permitted medium-term dollar loans (3–5 years). These instructions aroused little enthusiasm for, with a weak dollar and a volatile prime rate, the Japanese investor was reluctant to commit funds medium-term, "locked in" to coupons which would almost certainly in the short term become both unrealistic and uncommercial.

As a result the Japanese banks merely changed the rules — and restructured their short-term borrowing from short-term CDs to medium-term CDs, a medium-term CD, however, with a difference. The concept of the then new CD was a "floating" coupon which could be changed every six months in line with current world interest rates.

This floating coupon is changed, if required, 2 days prior to the next interest payment date, anticipating the rate for the next 6 months. The rate is usually "fixed" as being "LIBOR plus a Quarter" (London Inter-Bank Offered Rate + ¼ of 1%).

The problem

The problem which must immediately focus the attention is how can a price for a CD on the secondary market be calculated and offered when the coupon is not constant, changing as it does every six months?

The bank method

Banks, when determining a price suitable to be client-quoted, first assume a required yield and, by a series of time-consuming calculations, proceed to work out a "notional price" which they will then convert to what, in the words of a bank hand-out "How to calculate FRCDs", they are pleased to call an "equilibrium price". An equilibrium price is merely a price rounded up or down to a suitable, sensible, price structure.

233

The calculation

I do not propose to set out the Japanese banking method which is sufficiently tedious to require computer facilities, for I evolved my own method which provides a resulting notional price so close to the "long method" that any required "mental adjustment" to the "equilibrium price" must be precisely the same — and this short method can be calculated on the back of an envelope with the simplest of calculators.

Short method formula

$$\left(100 \times \frac{36000 + (\text{coupon} \times \text{coupon days})}{36000 + \quad (\text{yield} \times \text{odd days})}\right) - \frac{\text{coupon} \times \text{a/i days}}{360} = NP$$

The NP (notional price) is then adjusted to a sensible quotation price, which when divided by 100 and multiplied by the face value of the FRCD equals the total cost or proceeds.

Having established the quoted price, the yield for the next six months ONLY can be established. For until realisation, with constantly changing coupon values since settlement, the true YTM can obviously never be found.

EXAMPLE: FRCD $500,000

Settlement: 6 March 1981
Maturity: 5 May   1983
Investment rate: 17% (coupon)
Assumed yield: 10% (coupon)
Terms: LIBOR + ¼

The only relevance the maturity date has, in this type of calculation, is to establish the payment dates, before and after settlement; in this example 5 November 1980 and 5 May 1981.

There are 60 days between settlement and the NEXT payment date.
There are 121 days between settlement and the PREVIOUS payment date.
The number of days in the coupon period therefore must be 181.

$$100 \times \frac{36000 + (17 \times 181)}{36000 + (10 \times 60)} - \frac{17 \times 121}{360} = 101.053871.$$

Now mentally adjust to a "sensible" price, such as 101.0625 (101-1/16th), or more probably 101.00, and

$500,000 \times 101/100 = \$505,000.00$ total cost.

The banker's computer-based calculation method finds 101.051991 which I suggest would be adjusted precisely as above.

The spread factor

Occasionally banks wish to provide some "concessions" to selected clients or for a particularly substantial loan and in order to scale down the cost they apply a "points spread". A "40 point spread" is .4% of the face value of the dollar certificate loan. If this ratio was applied to the total cost in the previous example: $500,000 × .4/100 = $2000.00 concession value, which when subtracted from the total cost $505,000 − 2,000 = $503,000 provides a modest saving on a ½ million dollar loan.

EXAMPLE
Those readers who are familiar with the bank "hand-out" mentioned above will recognise the example below.

FRCD	$1,000,000
Settlement	21 July 1980
Maturity	17 September 1982
Investment rate	$18\frac{7}{8}\%$ (18.875)
Assumed funding	9½%
Last coupon date	17 March 1980
Next coupon date	17 September 1980
Terms	LIBOR + ¼
SD to next payment date	58 days
SD to previous payment date	126 days
Coupon period	184 days

The "banking method" finds the notional price as 101.39.

The shortened method

$$100 \times \frac{36000 + (18.875 \times 184)}{36000 + (9.50 \times 58)} - \frac{18.875 \times 126}{360} = 101.39$$

Adjust to a sensible quotation such as 101.375 = $101\frac{3}{8}$.

101.375/100 × 1,000,000.00 = $1,013,750.00 total cost.

With a 37.5 points spread the total cost will be reduced to:

101/100 × 1,000,000.00 = $1,010,000.00.

Note
It will be seen that for the purpose of finding the "notional price", the yield is "assumed": for with a non-constant coupon the true YTM can never be established until maturity when, by that time, all the various coupon values will be known.

A CD postscript

As readers will be aware, having read the last few chapters, certificates of deposit are normal, uncomplicated, straightforward lending (to a bank) with instant liquidity if sold on the secondary market and as such no abnormalities are encountered — save perhaps one slightly unusual structure recently brought to my attention and one which, I have to admit, I had not previously met.

Apparently a local bank in Illinois, so I was told, some years ago advertised a 6 year $1500 certificate of deposit with no annual interest paid, but in lieu, an "instant gift" of two pistols — in a walnut case. The value of the said pistols, at the time of the issue, was advertised as $725 — having, so the bank pointed out, doubled in price over the previous 6 years. The bank averred that the value of the "gift" was equivalent to a yield of 15.50%.

Unless my mathematics are at fault it would appear that for the advertised yield to be valid not only would a willing buyer need to be found to purchase the pistols at the end of six years but one who was prepared to pay three times the present valuation. For to yield 15.50% over 6 years, with semi-annual interest payments, the total interest (yield value) must be:

$$(1500 \times 1.0775^{12}) - 1500 = \$2173.66$$

and $2173.66/725$ = 2.998 times.

Undoubtedly this is an interesting variation on some of the minor league banks' inducements to account-opening but should this type of money instrument become fashionable the mind boggles at the possible "gifts" for more substantial CDs. A summer cruise perhaps — or a missile?

CHAPTER 30

Maturity Discounting with Rolled-Up Interest

Another type of interest-bearing obligation, with no annual or semi-annual coupon rate, will be found in such units as US Tax Exempt Notes, the interest due being "rolled up" and paid at maturity, together with the return of the capital value.

As there is no "coupon", and no periodic interest (as in the case of certificates of deposit and other suchlike commercial paper), the calculations differ somewhat from previous examples in that they must relate to the "quoted interest rate" required, instead of the "coupon rate".

The formulae and examples are set out below:

$$\frac{\left(1 + \left(\dfrac{\text{ID–RD days}}{360} \times \dfrac{\text{rate}}{100}\right)\right) - \left(\dfrac{\text{price}}{100} + \left(\dfrac{\text{ID–SD days}}{360} \times \dfrac{\text{rate}}{100}\right)\right)}{\left(\dfrac{\text{price}}{100} + \left(\dfrac{\text{ID–SD days}}{360} \times \dfrac{\text{rate}}{100}\right)\right)}$$

And $\qquad$ above $\times \dfrac{360}{\text{SD–RD days}} \times 100 = \text{YTM\%}.$

$$100 \left(\frac{1 + \left(\dfrac{\text{ID–RD days} \times \text{rate}}{360 \times 100}\right)}{1 + \left(\dfrac{\text{SD–RD days} \times \text{YTM}}{360 \times 100}\right)} - \frac{\text{ID–SD days} \times \text{rate}}{360 \times 100} \right) = \text{Price}$$

Where: ID $\qquad$ = Issue date
  SD $\qquad$ = Settlement date
  RD $\qquad$ = Redemption date
  (ID–SD days) = Days between issue and settlement
  Rate $\qquad$ = The annual quoted interest rate %
  Price $\qquad$ = The quoted price.

EXAMPLE

Issue: 1 October   1984 ⎫
Settlement: 17 March   1985 ⎬ 166 (ID–SD) ⎫ 390 (ID–SD)
Maturity: 1 November 1985 ⎭ 224 (SD–RD) ⎭

Quoted interest rate 9.50%

Price 100.0625 $(100\frac{1}{16})$

Find the yield to maturity

$$\frac{\left(1 + \dfrac{390 \times 9.50}{360 \times 100}\right) - \left(\dfrac{100.0625}{100} + \dfrac{166 \times 9.50}{360 \times 100}\right)}{\left(\dfrac{100.0625}{100} + \dfrac{166 \times 9.50}{360 \times 100}\right)} \times \frac{360}{224} \times 100$$

$$= 9.000\%$$

$$8.999692223\% \text{ YTM}$$

Find the price

Employing the YTM and the above parameters:

$$100 \times \left(\frac{1 + \left(\dfrac{390}{360} \times \dfrac{9.50}{100}\right)}{1 + \left(\dfrac{224}{360} \times \dfrac{8.999}{100}\right)} - \left(\dfrac{166}{360} \times \dfrac{9.50}{100}\right)\right) = 100.0625 \text{ price.}$$

CHAPTER 31

Eurodollar Floating Rate Notes

General

In the previous chapter floating rate CDs (FRCDs) were examined. It was seen that this type of interest-bearing obligation served a useful and particular purpose. While short-term money market instruments are well catered for in the USA, Canada and the UK, this does not necessarily obtain in other countries. With Eurodollar floating rate notes (FRNs) this lack can be overcome — indeed many hold the view that the characteristics of such obligations produce a better return than bank deposits or CDs, providing excellent liquidity, if required, through the secondary market.

Floating rate notes are normally issued for a life of between 5–20 years, the shorter term being more usual. The coupon rate is, at Issue, stated as a minimum value — there being no maximum.

Every six months, (occasionally quarterly and very occasionally monthly), a few days prior to the commencement of the next coupon interest period, the coupon is "fixed", based on (usually) 1/4% or 1/8% over LIBOR (London Interbank Offered Rate) in the same manner as FRCDs.

The calculations

The calculations are always "Actual/360", in that the actual number of days are taken for the half coupon period but all subsequent calculations are based on 30/360 financial calendar.

EXAMPLE

Assume that on 28 September 1983 the new coupon rate of a Eurodollar FRN is "fixed" at 10% for the interest period 1 October 1983 to 1 April 1984, a matter of some 183 "days between". If a Deutschmark investor purchases one million Eurodollars worth of the issue, on 1 October 1983, priced at 99.80, what will his half annual yield be?

In these circumstances, the wise investor would hedge, over the next 6 months period, the same amount of dollars purchased and would also doubtless cover himself in regard to the dollar interest payments. The cost of such hedging will, of course, be reflected in his return (yield).

For calculation purposes assume that the DM exchange rate (spot rate) is 2.5000 and the 6 month forward premium (for the interest payments) is 0.0500.

239

Working first in Eurodollars:

The capital cost is 99.80/100 × $1M = $998,000.00

1/2 annual interest (10/2 × 183/180)/100 × $1M = $ 50,833.33

The future value, at the end of the half-annual coupon period:

$998,000.00 + 50,833.33 = $1,048,833.33

$$\left(\frac{1,048,833.33}{998,000.00} - 1\right) \times 100 = 5.093520\% \text{ Yield for first half year}$$

"Annualisation"

This yield, while true for a life of 183 days, if doubled would provide a nominal yield of 10.187041%; but this would incorrectly assume that the coupon for the following six months would be the same LIBOR rate as previously — which it almost certainly wouldn't be. The semi-annual rate is corrected for the precise number of days, 5.093520 × 180/183 = 5.010020% (half annual).

Because the usual convention and practice is always to deal in, and refer to, nominal rates the immediate inclination is to double the above semi-annual rate (5.010020 × 2) and treat 10.02% as the nominal rate. But because it is necessary to differentiate between a true nominal and a nominal semi-annual FRN rate (which only stands correct until the next half year's coupon has been fixed) the custom is to refer to the above 10.02%, the doubled half annual days-adjusted yield per cent, as the "annualised" rate %, which, however much the reader may dislike the term, is expressive!

$$\left(\frac{1,048,833.33}{998,000.00} - 1\right) \times \frac{180 \times 100}{183} = 5.010020\%$$
$$= 10.020040\% \text{ annualised.}$$

The premium

The premium is all-important to the calculations below and relates to the term of the FRN. If the FRN was quarterly or monthly based, then obviously 3 months or monthly premiums should be employed. (The .05 forward premium, quoted above, related to the six months FRN example, a comparable premium for 3 months forward would be probably around 0.05/2 or a monthly forward premium in the neighbourhood of 0.05 × 2/12).

Continuing in the domestic (DM) currency of the purchaser:

Capital DM cost = $998,000 × 2.500 = DM 2,495,000.00

DM Future value = $1,048,833.33 × (2.5000 − .0500) = DM2,569,641.67

$$\left(\frac{2,569,641.67}{2,495,000.00} - 1 \right) \times \frac{180 \times 100}{183} = 2.942606\%$$
$$= 5.885213\% \text{ annualised}$$

Formula to find FRN yields

$$\left(\left(\left(1 + \frac{\text{coupon} \times \text{days}}{360 \times \text{price}} \right) \times \frac{(\text{spot} - \text{premium})}{\text{spot}} \right) - 1 \right) \times \frac{36000}{\text{days}}$$

which equals the required yield, and applying the above example:

$$\left(\left(\left(1 + \frac{10 \times 183}{360 \times 99.80} \right) \times \frac{(2.5000 - .0500)}{2.5000} \right) - 1 \right) \times \frac{36000}{183} = 5.89\%$$

$$((1.050935 \times .980000) - 1 \times 200 \times 180/183 = 5.885212918\%$$

$$0.029916 \qquad \qquad \times 200 \times 180/183 = 5.885212918\%$$

To determine a price

Assuming that an annualised yield of 5.885212918% (admittedly unrealistic but for example purposes only – instead of a sensible 5.89%) was required for a semi-annual Eurodollar/DM FRN, find the price.

Formula to determine the FRN price

$$\frac{1}{\left(\left(\left(1 + \frac{\text{yield} \times \text{days}}{36000} \right) \times \frac{\text{spot}}{(\text{spot} - \text{premium})} \right) - 1 \right) \times \frac{360}{\text{cpn} \times \text{days}}}$$

which equals the required price, and applying the above example:

$$\frac{1}{\left(\left(\left(1 + \frac{5.885213 \times 183}{36000} \right) \times \frac{2.5000}{(2.5000 - .0500)} \right) - 1 \right) \times \frac{360}{10 \times 183}}$$

$$= \underline{99.80 \text{ Price}}$$

Mid-term purchase

Assume that the above Note was purchased 56 days prior to the next payment date. In that case the selling institution would quote a dirty price and a 56 day forward premium of (say) 99.80 + ((183 − 56)/180 × 10/2) = 103.33 DP and a forward premium of (say) .05 × 56/180 = .01560, thus producing an annualised yield of 5.605914%. The above price (99.80) and premium (.05), and indeed the spot rate (2.5000), are taken for example purposes only, for market conditions would probably have changed slightly since the beginning of the coupon period.

Classes of US Interest-Bearing Obligations

Money instrument	Base	Interest paid
Certificates of deposit (3)	Actual/360	Semi-annually
Certificates of deposit	Actual/360	At maturity
Certificates of deposit	Actual/360	Discounting
Corporate bonds	30/360	Semi-annually
Floating rate certificates of deposit	Actual/360	Semi-annually
Municipal bonds	30/360	Annually
Municipal bonds	30/360	Semi-annually
US Treasury bonds**	Actual/365	Semi-annually
US Treasury notes**	Actual/365	Semi-annually
Assessment supported bonds	30/360	Semi-annually
Assessment supported notes	30/360	At maturity
Assessment supported warrants	30/360	At maturity
Bankers acceptances	Actual/360	Discounting
Banks for Co-operatives debentures	30/360	At maturity
Certificates of indebtedness	Actual/360	At maturity
Commercial paper (2)	Actual/360	At maturity
Commercial paper	Actual/360	Discounting
Commodity Credit Corporation	30/360	Semi-annually
Export-Import Bank Particular Certificates	30/360	Semi-annually
Farmers' Home Admin. insured notes	Actual/365	Annually
Federal Home Loan Bank notes/bonds	30/360	Semi-annually
Federal Housing Admin. (FHA) debentures	Actual/365	Semi-annually
Federal Intermediate Credit Bank debentures (2)	30/360	Semi-annually
Federal Intermediate Credit Bank debentures	30/360	At maturity
Federal Land Bank bonds	30/360	Semi-annually
FNMA debentures	30/360	Semi-annually
FNMA short-term notes	Actual/360	Discounting
Foreign bonds (NOT Eurobonds)**	Actual/365	Semi-annually
GNMA bonds & Participating certificates	30/360	Semi-annually
Inter-American Development Bank bonds	30/360	Semi-annually
IBRD bonds	30/360	Semi-annually

**Employ quasi-coupon period method of calculation

Money instrument	Base	Interest paid
Merchant Marine bonds	30/360	Semi-annually
New Communities Act debentures	30/360	Semi-annually
Repurchase agreements	Actual/360	At maturity
Revenue supported bonds	30/360	Semi-annually
Revenue supported notes	30/360	At maturity
Revenue supported warrants	30/360	At maturity
Special supported bonds	30/360	Semi-annually
Special supported notes	30/360	At maturity
Special supported warrants	30/360	At maturity
Tax supported bonds	30/360	Semi-annually
Tax supported notes	30/360	At maturity
Tax supported warrants	30/360	At maturity
Tennessee Valley Authority bonds	30/360	Semi-annually
Tennessee Valley Authority notes	Actual/360	Discounting
U.S. Postal Service bonds	30/360	Semi-annually
U.S. Treasury bills	Actual/360	Discounting
U.S. Treasury Tax-Anticipation bills	Actual/360	Discounting

APPENDIX B

Solve for "i"

The concept — the iterative process and tolerance factor

The concept is that the computer first calculates a suitable "guess" rate and then works through the equation to find an answer to one or other of the given parameters.

There are, of course, many ways in which a programmer can instruct the computer to narrow the gap between the "first guess" and the final, correct, solution by interpolation, etc. The method outlined below is just ONE method — but one which is particularly suited to computer programs. It is quick, accurate and in terms of program "steps" short; it also has the advantage that it has a universal application. In other words it is not a program or method solely designed for one particular type of formula.

Given a £1000 loan, over 25 years, and the repayments being £118.74, in order to determine the correct interest rate the method would be to guess a rate and after calculating the annuities ordinary formula to check whether the repayments of capital equalled the required £1000.00 loan amount. Or taking the loan as £1000, that the payments were £118.74. Assuming that the method employed was to "find the loan amount", unless the first guess was precisely accurate to 10 sig.fig. (which it obviously wouldn't be), the answer from the first rate guess would find a loan value of +/− £1000.00.

The "difference", therefore, is the "absolute" difference between the given data value and the value of the next interpolated "guessed" amount, which is then compared to a "tolerance factor" (T). For instance, if the "last guess" found a value of (say) 999.9950 then 1000 − 999.9950 (the difference) would be 0.0050. If accuracy was not of great importance (for instance if an IRR was required accurate to only one decimal place), then the (T) factor would be 0.01 — and as .005 is less than .01 the rate employed to find the 999.995 would be presented as the IRR (internal rate of return, i/p × 100).

But if far greater accuracy was required, then the computer would continue to guess and interpolate until the "difference" became less than (say) 0.000001; and in that case the periodic rate, which determined that minor difference, would be considered accurate to 10^{-6}(.000001), or to 6 places of decimals.

244

The iterative discipline

In the method set out below, based, in general terms, on the Newton-Raphson method of interpolation, the tolerance (T) factor becomes an integral part of the calculations and not, as in some other methods, a basis just for comparing the "difference". As a result this method is extremely rapid and the (T) factor can be substantially less than in less sophisticated disciplines.

Generalisations are usually dangerous, especially in mathematics, but it could be said that, by this method, a (T) factor of (say) 0.001 will provide a resulting interest rate accurate to at least 6 places of decimals.

The "function"

The function is the basic formula/equation calculation for which the IRR is required. If, for example, the "i" rate was required for a mortgage calculation, then the "function" would be the repayment loan formula, for example:

$$\frac{1000.00}{a_{\overline{25}|}} \text{ at } 11\% = 118.74 \text{ pmts}$$

and $\quad (118.74 \times (1 - 1.11^{-25})/.11) - 1000 = 0 = f(x)$

The function, $f(x)$, in other words the formula/equation calculation, would be made so as to meet 0 — or the tolerance factor nearest to 0 required. Put another way, given the present value (here) of 1000, the FNC (the function) is the equation (derived from term, payments and guess rate) to find a PV — and thus the "difference" between the given PV and FNC's PV.

It will be seen later that any FNC can be "tacked on" to the iterative discipline — which is set out as follows.

The first guess

For any type of calculation to "solve for i" most statisticians, working in their own particular field, have their own pet methods of providing a suitable approximation — and this value becomes a suitable first guess for the computer program. Alternatively some programs are written so that the user can supply his own first guess (see "Roots" below). Although the method below should provide a correct solution from any first guess — unless totally unrealistic — obviously the closer the first guess is to the truth, the quicker the calculation will provide the correct solution.

The method

Let: FNC = the function
      D   = the "difference"

PD = the "previous" difference
T   = the tolerance factor (say .001 in the calculation below)
F   = (Rate % × T)

Note
The "Rate %" is the IRR, the NOMINAL rate, and NOT the i or i/p.

The "loop"

An algorithm is provided at the end of this Appendix.
1. Calculate, or make, a "first guess".
2. Employing this first guess (as the first rate), calculate the function to provide the first "difference" (D).
3. PHASE A:
   Assume that D now becomes PD.
   Adjust previous rate to (Rate + T).
   With this new ("next") rate calculate the next "D".
4. PHASE B:
   Adjust this rate by:

$$(\text{RATE} - \text{F}) - \frac{\text{F}}{(\text{D/PD}) - 1} = \text{"next" RATE.}$$

Test

If $\text{ABS} - \dfrac{\text{F}}{(\text{D/PD}) - 1} < \text{T}$ then the "next rate" above = IRR.

BUT if the above test finds that the value is greater than the T factor (in the example below, taken as .001), recalculate the FNC by the new ("next") rate above: THEN GO TO PHASE A above. This is the "loop", and the whole process starts again with the new, adjusted, rate.

Note
It may be unlikely, but if at any time during the calculations, in between the "tests", the difference (D) = 0, the current rate is automatically the IRR and can be produced as such.

EXAMPLE
Assume that we have found the payments for a £1000 loan, over 25 years, at a nominal interest rate of 11% as £118.74.

$$\frac{1000}{a_{\overline{25}|}} \text{ at 11\% nominal}$$

$$= \text{£118.74 pmts per year.}$$

What would the nominal interest rate be if the annual payments were reduced to £118 precisely?

Normally in this type of calculation a suitable approximation can be found from:

PMTS/LOAN $\times$ 100 = IRR   For instance (118.00/1000 $\times$ 100 = 11.80).

But in this case, obviously, the first guess should be fractionally less than 11%, say 10.9%.

Working through the FNC (the function calculation) to find a loan value, from the new £118.00 annual payments:

$118 \times ((1 - 1.1090^{-25})/.1090 = 1001.067072$

(assumed value $-$ given value) = DIFFERENCE (D)

$1001.067072 - 1000.00$ = 1.067072 (D)

Now we must assume that D becomes the previous difference, (1.067072 now = PD) and assuming that the T factor is .001 the next part of the calculation is:

PHASE A

$10.90 + (10.90 \times .001) = 10.9109\%$ new ("next") rate.

Recalculating, as above, with this rate will find a loan value of £1000.2666813 and so the *next* difference, which becomes "D" = 0.2668130 (D).

PHASE B

$$[10.9109 - (10.9 \times .001)] - \frac{.0109}{(0.266813/1.067072) - 1}$$

10.9 $- (-0.014534151) = \underline{10.91453415\%}$

(This rate 10.9145% is the "next rate" or a possible IRR.)

Now test. Is ABS 0.014534151 less than the T factor of .001?

As the test proves negative, go back to Phase A, and employing the new rate of 10.91453415% recalculate as before.

Continuing to calculate the FNC, it will be found that the next difference is 0.000242000 — BUT don't immediately jump to the conclusion that IRR is the current rate just because 0.000242000 is less than the T factor of 0.001. For remember that you are still in Phase A and that you MUST complete this phase correctly before any "test" is made.

The last difference 0.00024200 now becomes the previous difference (PD) and the current rate 10.91453415 becomes 10.91453415 $\times$ (1.001) = 10.92544868% (next rate).

Employing this rate we find a loan value of 999.2003692 which when 1000 is subtracted finds − 0.77996308 (D) = Difference.

We are now in Phase B again and to find the next rate:

$$10.91453415 \; - \; \frac{10.9145345 \times .001}{(-0.7996308/.0002420) - 1} \; = \; \text{Next Rate \%}$$

$$10.91453415 \; - \; (-0.00003302) \qquad\qquad = \; 10.91453745$$

Test Is ABS   (− .00003302) < .001?   YES

IRR = 10.91453745%

Again, it must be stressed that the "test" must be made in its correct order, namely AFTER the "next rate" calculation has been made.

The tolerance factor limit

In the FNC calculations the rate will almost always require to be converted to an i/p. It is therefore essential not to have the T factor less than

$10^{-6} = 0.000001$ (sometimes shown as $10 \wedge -6$)

For in this example the first guess rate was 10.90% which when converted to an $(1 + i/p)$, becomes:

$(1 + 10.90/100)$ = 1.109000000.

The calculated second rate will therefore be:

10.9×10^{-3} = 0.01090000 = F.

And this when added to the rate (10.90) becomes:

$10.90 + .01090$ = 10.9109,

which, when converted to an $(1 + i/p)$

= 1.109109000.

So far no problem.

BUT consider if the T value was chosen as 10^{-9}; if working to 10 decimal places, the first and second $(1 + i/p)$ values would inevitably be the SAME:

First $(1 + i)$ = 1.109000000

Second $(1 + i)$ $1 + \dfrac{10.90 \times (1 + 10^{-9})}{100}$ = 1.109000000

And without a different SECOND rate to provide the first "difference" the calculation becomes invalid. In any event, employing this discipline, a T factor of less than $10 \wedge -6$ (.000001) is not necessary.

EXAMPLE: from a fixed interest bond
For example purposes, assume the requirement is to find a YTM.

Data required	*Example values*
(n + k) factors	3.643835616
Dirty Price (DP)	97.16695205 (96.1875 CP)
½ Coupon	2.75
Redemption Value (RV)	100.00

In this case the suitable FNC will be:

$$\frac{100(1 + i/p)^{-3} + 2.75 \dfrac{1 - (1 + i/p)^{-3}}{i/p} + 2.75}{(1 + i/p)^{.643835616}} = 97.16695205 \text{ DP.}$$

First Guess Approximation. In the context of this particular function example, namely a YTM, the "first guess" could usefully be found from the approximation formula outlined in Chapter 17:

$$\frac{Cpn \times RV}{CP} = \frac{RV - CP}{n + k} = \text{Approx. YTM.}$$

Employing the example values above:

$$\frac{2.75 \times 100}{96.1875} + \frac{100 - 96.1875}{3.643835616} = 3.905286944 \text{ approx. ½ YTM}$$

$$(\text{say}) = 3.90\% \text{ as a "first guess".}$$

The method of calculation is the same as in the previous example with the function FNC being the bond yield formula.

1. For simplicity a tolerance factor of only 10^{-2} is employed below. Take the data values given in the example above and the approximate half YTM of 3.90% as the "first guess". With this rate (converted to an i/p) calculate the function (FNC). The difference (D) between the calculated DP (97.13032289) and the given DP (97.16695205) will be found as $97.13032289 - 97.16695205 = -.036629160$ (D).

2. Phase A
   3.900000000 + (3.900000000 × .01) =
   3.900000000 +   .039000000   = 3.939000000% next rate.

   Calculate the FNC.
   Difference   = −.163477380 (D)
   Previous difference = −.036629160 (PD).

3. Phase B

  3.939000000 − .039000000   = 3.900000000

$$3.900000000 - \frac{.03900000000}{(-.163477380/-.036629160) - 1}$$

  3.900000000 − .011261784   = 3.888738216% next rate.

Test: Is (ABS) .011261784 < .01? NO. Continue.

Calculate the FNC.
Difference   =   .000040630
Previous difference = −.163477380 (PD).

4. Phase A

  3.888738216 + (3.888738216 × .01) =

  3.888738216 +   .038887382   = 3.927625598% next rate.

Calculate the FNC.
Difference   = −.126504470 (D)
Previous difference =   .000040630 (PD).

5. Phase B

  3.927625598 − .038887382   = 3.888738216

$$3.888738216 - \frac{.038887382}{(-.126504470/.000040630) - 1}$$

  3.888738216 − (−.000012486)   = 3.888750702% next rate.

Test: Is (ABS) .000012486 < .01? YES. Conclude.

  The requirement rate is   3.888750702%
  which converts (× 2) to a YTM of   7.777501404%

Note
The above YTM would be presented as rounded to 7.778% or 7.777501%.

If the above calculation had been made with a tolerance factor of 10^{-6}

  the YTM would become 7.777501386%
  presented as   7.777501% rounded.

"Roots"

All "solve for i" calculations are in reality solving the root form of the equation. But, perhaps, we tend to think "solving i" relates more to calculations such as seen above, mortgages, interest rates etc, and that "root finding" relates to equations such as the one outlined below.

$$x^4 - 26x^2 + 49x \qquad = 25. \quad \text{Find x.}$$
$$x^4 - 26x^2 + 49x - 25 = 0 = f(x).$$

Above it was stated that when employing this discipline the IRR can be solved from any first guess "unless totally unrealistic". With a specific market in mind (mortgages, bond yields, savings etc) the statistician will immediately appreciate (from his approximation formulae) what is unrealistic or not. But the example above provides no clue as to what the root is likely to be and no clue, therefore, as to a realistic first guess.

Calculating with a totally unsuitable guess-rate can be time consuming; so the tip is to guess a rate and, providing the first difference is reasonably near 0, continue with it unaltered. If, however, the first difference is absurdly greater than zero, then adjust the first guess and try again. Don't worry if the first difference is a negative — unless the THIRD difference appears ridiculous. If it is, adjust the first guess and start again.

If we tried 3 as the first guess, in the example above, the first difference would be −31 which would not seem, at first glance, unreasonable. The second difference would (naturally) vary only fractionally (depending on the T factor chosen) but the THIRD difference, with a (T) factor of 10^{-6}, will be found to be 1,306,636.37 — which borders on the absurd!

If we abandon 3 as a guess and try 2 it will be found that all the differences continue as negative values (instead of just the first two) and this gives rise to the view that the rate should be adjusted upwards.

Raising the first guess rate to 4 the precise root of 3.875775370 will present fairly rapidly.

As 2 or 3, above, are not "totally unrealistic" a computer program employing this discipline should in fact, find the correct solution — ultimately; but an early adjustment of an unsuitable first guess will always save time in the long run. Hence the reason why some programs are written so that the user can input the "first guess" himself.

Finally, it is hardly necessary to say, always cross-check the answer by using the found root to meet the given requirement.

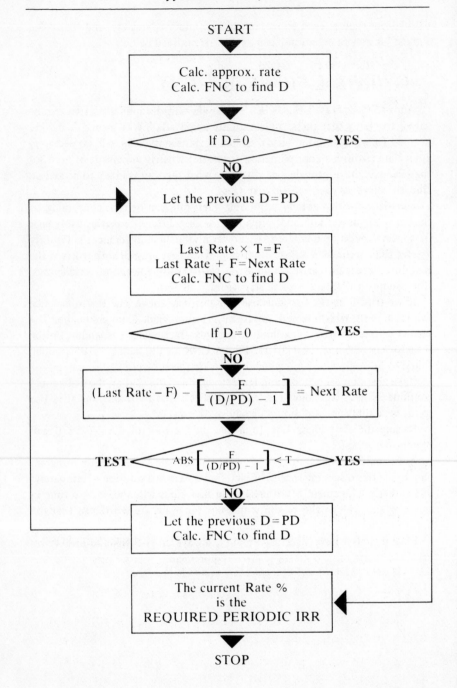

Methodology for Determining the Interest Payment Dates Before and After Settlement

General

To employ the quasi-coupon period method to evaluate bond yields and prices (Chapter 18), it is necessary not only to find the correct number of half-annual interest payment periods in the term of the loan but also the precise date on which interest payments are made before and after settlement date (SD), namely the payment date PRIOR to settlement (PPD), and the NEXT payment date after settlement (NPD), such dates being required in order to determine the number of odd and a/i days, and consequently the correct (n + k) factor for this type of calculation.

If settlement day was on April 1 1980 (4.261980) and redemption day on June 15 1995 (6.151995), and if interest payment dates are semi-annual, it hardly stretches our mental capability to realise that the payment date PRIOR to settlement is December 15 1979 and the next payment date AFTER settlement is June 15 1980 (6.151980). But a computer only has the mental capacity of its programmer and so it is necessary to have some method of finding the above answers mathematically. The method below is one way.

To simplify the calculations below, the American date format (mm.ddyyyy) has been used in the following examples.

To find payment date PRIOR to settlement (PPD)

(1) **If SD's [mmdd] is GREATER than RD's [mmdd]:**

(RD's [mmdd] + SD's [.yyyy])/100   = PPD

But if SD's [mmdd] − RD's [mmdd] is GREATER than 600 add 6.

(2) **If SD's [mmdd] is LESS than RD's [mmdd]:**

((RD's [mmdd] + SD's [.yyyy])/100) − 6 = PPD

But if RD's [mmdd] − SD's [mmdd] is GREATER than 600, re-add the 6 (previously subtracted) and subtract ONE year ($-10 \wedge -6$).

In any calculations, if the MONTHS (mm.) are LESS than ONE add 12 and deduct 1 year; or if the MONTHS (mm.) are ever GREATER than TWELVE subtract 12 and add 1 year.

To find the NEXT payment date after settlement (NPD)

PPD + 6 = NPD.

To find the correct number of HALF year periods

(RD's mm.ddyyyy − *NPD*'s mm.ddyyyy) $\times 2 \times 10^6$

= half annual interest payment periods.

But if the subtraction above provides an integer, *replace* by:

((RD's mm.ddyyyy − *PPD*'s mm.ddyyyy) $\times 2 \times 10^6$) − 1

= half annual interest payment periods.

EXAMPLE

Settlement Date (SD) is on April 26, 1980 (4.261980)
Redemption Date (RD) is on June 15, 1995 (6.151995)

As SD's [mmdd] is LESS than RD's [mmdd] use formula (2):
(426)   (615)

$$\frac{615 + .1980}{100} - 6 = 0.151980 \text{ PPD (provisional)}.$$

Test: (615 − 425) = 189 (less than 600) so above PPD stands, but as the integer (mm.) is 0, adjust

$(+12 - 10^{-6})$ = 12.151979 PPD

The NPD becomes

(12.151979 + 6) = 18.151979

but as the integer (mm.) is 18, adjust

$(-12 + 10^{-6})$ = 6.151980 NPD.

To find the correct number of (semi-annual) payment periods in the above example, 6.151995 − 6.151980 = 0.00001500 (no integer).

$0.000015 \times 2 \times 10^6$ = 30 half annual interest payment periods.

EXAMPLE

Settlement February 1 1984 (2.011984)
Maturity January 1 1988 (1.011988)

As SD's [mmdd] is greater than RD's [mmdd] the formula (1) obtains:
  (201)   (101)

$$\frac{101 + .1984}{100} = 1.011984 \text{ PPD}$$

As SD's [mmdd] − RD's [mmdd] is LESS than 600: 1.011984 stands,
  (201)   (101)   <   (100)

                              = 1.011984 PPD

and   1.011984 + 6   = 7.011984 NPD.

RD's mm.ddyyyy − NPD's mm.ddyyyy   =

  1.011988   −   7.011984   = 5.999996

As an integer results, in part, from the above subtraction, replace with the *alternative* method:

  RD's mm.ddyyyy − *PPD*'s mm.ddyyyy =

  1.011988   − 1.011984   = 0.000004

  (.000004 × 2 × 106) − 1 = <u>7 half annual interest payment periods.</u>

Note
Naturally care must be taken always to adjust any non-valid date. But a PPD of 6.311983 adjusted to 6.301983 will still find an NPD of 12.311983 (not 12.301983).

How to Construct a Computer "Calendar Program"

General

The term of nearly all rate interest calculations, practical market bargains rather than theoretical examples, is a matter of periods and odd days. Thus in nearly every case it becomes necessary to know how many days there are "between" two periods of time or, equally important, the ability to find a new date from a "date +/− days".

Chapters 1 and 20 provide sufficient guidance for all the various calculations outlined in this book − and Appendix E is available for all those without any computer/calculator "date" facilities and who require a one-off "days between" answer.

But recently, with the advent of the personal computer and the increase of home programming, many want some sort of date sub-routine applicable to their own financial programs − and, without wishing to incorporate off-the-shelf software, decide to write their own. Having often been asked to explain how date calculations are made or which is the best formula-method to adopt, I have added this appendix which, although it will not "write the program", will I hope be sufficient to help any programmer to overcome some of the difficulties often encountered.

The Julian calendar and the "Julian dating system"

The Julian calendar, named after Julius Caesar, measuring time in years and months (treating each fourth year as a leap year) was authorised for use in 42 BC. This calendar should not be confused with the astronomer's use of the Julian dating system, derived from a work published in 1582 by a Joseph (Julius) Scaliger (after whom it is called), measuring time from midday 4713 BC. Such esoteric items however, have little or no place in normal present-day calculations, related to dates and days between dates, for during the 16th century it was realised that the correct number of year/days was not, as had been thought, 365.25 days precisely but was, in fact, around 365.2425 days.

The Gregorian calendar (our everyday "actual" calendar)

As a result Pope Gregory XIII decided on a new style (NS) calendar aimed to correct such past errors and in order to effect such adjustments decided, inter alia, to treat all century years as NON-leap years — *unless* such years were precisely divisible by 400. Thus on 4 October 1582 the "Gregorian" calendar came into being, causing the removal, or the loss, of some 10 days from those using the old style (OS) calendar.

The British Empire, and consequently the then American Colonies, adopted the Gregorian calendar on 14 September 1752. So for UK/US date calculations, between the years 1582–1752, there is a difference of **eleven** days between the OS and NS calendars. For example, George Washington was born on 11 February 1732 (OS) and any celebrations nowadays to that end should therefore be related to 22 February (NS). (In practice, the United States annual holiday commemorating this event takes place always on the third Monday in February.)

From the above it will be realised that not all countries conformed immediately; Turkey, for one, was a little dilatory, waiting until 1927 to effect a change!

The date factor

To find the number of days between two dates, or a new date from a date + a number of days, the general idea is to find a "date factor"; this factor is then subtracted from another date factor to find the "days between". Or a date factor, with a number of days added (or subtracted), provides a new factor which must then be "unscrambled" to find a new date.

There are various formulae; those outlined below are, in my view, the easiest and the ones most suited to a simple computer program. Remember, stick to the one type of formula method — never mix them.

Formula: Date − Date = Days between

Where:

    DF = Date Factor
    Y   = Year
    m   = month

and

    Y′ = Year − 1   IF m = 1 or 2 (Jan–Feb)
        = Year   IF m > 2   (Mar–Dec)

    m′ = month + 13 IF m = 1 or 2
        = month + 1   IF m > 2

then

    $INT(365.25Y′) + INT(30.6001m′) + D = DF.$

EXAMPLE

Find the "days between" Christmas day 1976 and New Year's day 2000.

$$\text{INT}(1976 \times 365.25) + \text{INT}(30.6001 \times (12 + 1)) + 25 \qquad = \text{DF (Xmas)}$$

$$721734 \qquad\qquad + \text{INT}(397.80123) \qquad\qquad + 25 \quad =$$

$$721734 \qquad\qquad + 397 \qquad\qquad\qquad\qquad\quad + 25 \quad = 722156$$

$$\text{INT}((2000 - 1) \times 365.25) + \text{INT}(30.6001 \times (1 + 13)) + 1 = \text{DF}$$
$$\text{(New Yr)}$$

$$730134 + 428 + 1 \qquad\qquad\qquad\qquad\qquad\qquad = 730563$$

and $730563 - 722156 = \underline{8407 \text{ days between.}}$

"Less leap days"

If the requirement is to find the "days between" LESS leap days (as required for bond yield calculations), in the above formula, for 365.25 read 365 or employ the method outlined in Chapter 1.

Check:

$$(1976 \times 365) + 397 + 25 \qquad\quad = 721662$$

or $722156 - \text{INT}(1976 \times .25) \qquad = 721662$

$$(1999 \times 365) + 428 + 1 \qquad\quad = 730064$$

or $730563 - \text{INT}(1999 \times .25) \qquad = 730064$

and $730064 - 721662 \qquad\qquad\quad = 8402$ days less leap days

or $\text{INT}((2000 - 1)/4) - \text{INT}(1976/4) = 5$ leap days

and $8407 - 5 \qquad\qquad\qquad\qquad\quad = 8402$ days less leap days

(1980, 1984, 1988, 1992, 1996 are the relevant leap years.)

To find the days of the week

Let   1 = Monday through to 6 = Saturday; Sunday = 0 or 7:

$$\left(7 \times \left(\text{FRAC } \frac{DF - 2}{7}\right)\right) \qquad = \text{Day of week.}$$

$$\left(7 \times \text{ FRAC}\left(\frac{722156 - 2}{7}\right)\right) = 7 \times .857100$$

(always round up to integer) $= 5.99970 = 6 = \text{Saturday}$

and $7 \times \text{FRAC}((730563 - 2)/7 \quad = 5.99970 = 6 = \text{Saturday.}$

Formula: Date +/– Days = Date

Now to "unscramble" a "new date DF":

Where:

$$\text{month} = m' - 13 \quad \text{IF } m' = 14 \text{ or } 15$$
$$= m' - 1 \quad \text{IF } m' < 14$$
$$\text{year} \quad = Y' \qquad \text{IF } m > 2$$
$$= Y' + 1 \quad \text{IF } m = 1 \text{ or } 2$$

$$\text{Year} \quad = \text{INT} \frac{DF - 122.4}{365.25}$$

$$\text{Month} = \text{INT} \frac{DF - \text{INT}(365.25 \times Y)}{30.6001}$$

$$\text{Day} \quad = (DF - \text{INT}(365.25 \times Y)) - \text{INT}(30.6001 \times m)$$

EXAMPLE

Date 25 December 1976 + 8407 days: find the "new date".

If, of course, we did not know the DF of the above date we should have to find it in order to add the 8407. But from previous calculations we do and so the new date factor, now to be unscrambled, is 722156 + 8407 = 730563 DF.

Any "adjustments" (**) necessary, according to the above formula, must be made at the conclusion of the calculation when all the data are available. For example, the month below being 1 invites an addition of 1 to the year but before the adjustment is made the remainder of the calculation must be continued *at the pre-adjusted values.*

$$\text{INT}(730563 - 122.4)/365.25 \quad = 1999 = 1999 + 1 = 2000 \; \textit{year.}$$
$$\text{INT} \frac{(730563 - (1999 \times 365.25)}{30.6001} = 14 = 14 - 13 \quad = 1 \; \textit{month.}$$

$$[730563 - \text{INT}(365.25 \times 1999)] - \text{INT}(30.6001 \times 14) =$$
$$429 \qquad - \qquad 428 \qquad = 1 \; \textit{day.}$$

Alternatively, 1st January 2000 less 8407 days once again finds a DF which we have already calculated – which again will save time in explanations.
730563 – 8407 = 722156 is the DF which we have to "unscramble":

$$\text{INT}(722156 - 122.4)/365.25 \qquad\qquad = 1976 \; \textit{year.}$$
$$\text{INT} \frac{(722156 - (1976 \times 365.25)}{30.6001} = 13 = 13 - 1 \quad = 12 \; \textit{month.}$$

$$[722156 - \text{INT}(365.25 \times 1976)] - \text{INT}(30.6001 \times 13) =$$
$$422 \qquad - \qquad 397 \qquad = 25 \; \textit{day.}$$

The century zones

Before leaving the "actual" calendar, and examining the 30/360 calculations, we must consider one aspect of the above calculations which is important – particularly so to computer programmers.

Above it was stated that the "new" Gregorian calendar, the one in present-day use, dictates that the century years are NOT leap years – unless divisible precisely by 400. In this case the year 2000 is a leap year (2000/400 = 5.00) but some centuries are not, e.g. 1900/400 = 4.75.

In fact centuries 1600, 2000, 2400, 2800 et seq. are leap years whereas centuries 1700, 1900, 2100, 2300 et seq. are NOT. And because the year 2000 is precisely divisible by FOUR, as well as 400, certain difficulties present themselves in relation to the above formulae. So, when writing a program, remember that some arrangement must be made to "test" for century years by a 400 division, instead of the conventional division by 4 – *if dates exclusive of 28 February 1900 and 28 February 2100* are required.

Incidentally the problem of non-leap-year-centuries is the reason why the user instructions for many programmed calculators are valid "only between the years 1901–2099".

And if "crossing the century zones" is a requirement how can we achieve this mathematically, without "finger counting", in order to provide exactly the correct number of days and, equally important, the precise "day of the week", by a DF calculation?

Crossing the century zones

To overcome this difficulty, I suggest the employment of a neat little additional calculation as follows:

$$\text{INT } .75(\text{INT}(\text{Year}/100) - 7) = \text{Century zone factor (CZF)}$$

Where: Year = (Year − 1) if the date concerned is for the months January or February.

SUBTRACT the CZF from the DF to provide a true DF(CZF) which will always now correctly cross the Century Zones and require no further thought.

To find the "Day of the Week", when using this DF(CZF) method, do NOT subtract 2 from the DF (as outlined above),

e.g. $722156 - \text{INT } .75(\text{INT}(1976/100) - 7) = \text{DF(CZF)}$

$722156 - 9 \qquad\qquad\qquad = 722147 \text{ DF(CZF)}$

and thus the day of the week will show (as above) a Saturday (6):

$$(\text{FRAC } 722147/7) \times 7 = 5.99970 \qquad = 6.$$

Incidentally, between 1 March 1900 and 28 February 2099 (our present century zone) the CZF is always 9, the earlier century zone (1800) being 8, the next later (2100) being 10.

Common sense tells us that if 1 March 1900 is a Thursday (as it is) and the year 1900 is NOT a leap year then 28 February 1900 MUST be a Wednesday, with ONE day "in between".

Employing *conventional* DF calculations we find that while 1 March 1900 has a correct DF of 694098 (FRAC(694098 − 2)/7) × 7 = 4 = Thursday) by a similar calculation, 28 February 1900 presents as 694096, providing some TWO days "in between" and as a Tuesday (2). The reason for this discrepancy is that although the year 1900 is NOT a leap year the *conventional* calculation assumes it is − consequently providing for an erroneous 29 February an erroneous Wednesday, and the inevitable resulting muddle!

Now recalculate correctly, employing my DF(CZF) method:

$$(23\ \text{February})\quad 694096 - [\text{INT}\ .75(\text{INT}(1899/100) - 7)]\quad = \text{DF (CZF)}$$
$$694096 - 8\quad\quad\quad\quad\quad\quad = 694088$$

$$(1\ \text{March})\quad 694098 - 9\quad\quad\quad\quad\quad\quad = 694089$$

and
$$(694098 - 9) - (694096 - 8)\quad\quad = 1\ \text{day.}$$

And   28 February 1900 = (FRAC 694088/7) × 7 = 2.99990   = 3 = Wed.

A useful tip, worth remembering and "programming in" if any dates are likely to be required outside the 1901−2099 year period.

Naturally, for *intra-zone calculations*, if the century zone is *not* "crossed", for instance the number of days between (say) 25 March 1850 − 4 July 1884, the conventional DF calculation will find the correct "days between"; BUT the "days of the week" will be incorrect − unless the DF(CZF) method is employed.

Although the 200 year spread (1901−2100), with our present decade being almost central, is usually considered to be sufficient for financial calculations, if making a date program, the CZF additional calculation is so simple to program in that it would seem sensible to incorporate it − even if it might be thought quite unnecessary for purely financial calculations.

Even so, because it was known that I had this century zone program facility, some years ago I was approached by a leading City firm, in the UK, to discover if a certain day, well into the 22nd century, was a banking day or not. In fact it was, but I am still wondering what possible long-term loan stock they were contemplating!

A digression

About ten years ago, just about the time I was writing my first "date" computer program, in which I naturally included crossing the century zone calculation (CZF), the London *Times* made a small "offer" to its readers of half a dozen tea mugs, which I purchased and on which were reproductions of some of the newspaper's famous front pages, Coronations, the day the Great War concluded and other notable occasions. One of which was dated 1 January 1806 giving the day of the week as a Tuesday.

Checking the day of the week in question, imagine my horror to find that my new date program confidently stated it to be a Wednesday. Checking and rechecking and finding nothing wrong I was forced to the conclusion that, unhappily, it appeared that my CZF method had failed to measure up to practical requirements. However, rechecking yet again, both the program and the mathematics concerned, I became convinced that either I was crazy – or the *Times* had got it wrong! So I telephoned the *Times* Library and asked them to check the day of the week of their issue on the date in question – to be told that it was, indeed, a Wednesday. I advised the *Times* department concerned, who originally advertised and supplied the mugs, and they too were horrified. Some days later they telephoned the explanation. Apparently the mugs were not "printed-on" from the actual pages of old copies of the newspaper, as we had all presumed, but had been "free-painted" before the mugs were "fired" – and it was the suppliers who provided the incorrect day of the week.

Date formats and verification

There are many methods of formatting dates, the Americans putting the months first, then days, then the year; whereas most European countries prefer days/months/year.

As many computer and calculator programs emanate from the States or Japan, the American method is becoming prevalent in computer circles and many have become accustomed to this method. A really sophisticated program will, of course, give the user the option of either the American or European formats.

The possible "input" methods are many and varied, 25.121976 – 12.251997 – 12/25/1976 – 25/12/1976 – 25,12,1976 – 25 Dec 1976 – 12 December 1976 – December 12, 1976 and sometimes even 25,12,76.

For calculation purposes never curtail the year for input purposes, as '76 or '84, for this will nullify many of the required calculations in the conventional DF and century zone formulae methods.

The date formats employed in a computer program must obviously be according to the programmer's taste, in that some will find this or that format more suitable to their particular method of "breaking down" and "storing" the various portions of the date concerned. But whichever format is used, try and stick to it throughout all related programs.

Input date verification is all important: always make certain of having some sub-routine method for checking not only a "bad" input but also an invalid date such as 31 November – or, equally important, an input of 29 February in a non-leap year. And in your verification program if an invalid date produces "error" or "invalid date" on display, let the invalid input stand so that the user can see precisely the mistake made.

The financial (30/360) calendar

The basic method of calculating a date factor is the same as above but the 30 days month produces its own complications – and this affects both the first and second dates – as we shall see later.

Formula: Date – Date = Days between (30/360)

Where:
$$dd' \quad = \text{date 1}$$
$$dd'' \quad = \text{date 2 and} <> = \text{if not equal to.}$$

For DF1
$$\text{if } dd' = \quad 31 \text{ then } z = 30$$
$$\text{if } dd' <> 31 \text{ then } z = dd'$$

For DF2
$$\text{if } dd'' = 31 \text{ and } dd' = 30 \text{ or } 31 \text{ then } z = 30$$
$$\text{if } dd'' = 31 \text{ and } dd' < 30 \qquad \text{then } z = dd''$$
$$\text{if } dd'' < 31 \qquad\qquad\qquad \text{then } z = dd''$$

$$360(yyyy) + 30(mm) + z = DF.$$

Taking the example above, Christmas Day 1976 and New Year's Day 2000, find the days between by the 30/360 method.

$$(1976 \times 360) + (12 \times 30) + 25 \ = \ 711745 \text{ DF1}$$
$$(2000 \times 360) + (\ 1 \times 30) + \ 1 \ = \ 720031 \text{ DF2}$$
$$720031 - 711745 \qquad\qquad = 8286 \text{ days between (30/360).}$$

Find the days between (30/360) **31** August 1980 – 30 June 1985.

$$(1980 \times 360) + (8 \times 30) + \textbf{30} \ = 713070$$
$$(1985 \times 360) + (6 \times 30) + 30 \ = 714810$$
$$714810 - 713070 \qquad\qquad = 1740 \text{ days between (30/360).}$$

Date +/– Days = Date (30/360)

In the case of 30/360 calculations it is obvious that it will never be possible to determine whether the "next date" is on a 30th or 31st of a month, otherwise the calculation is simply one of "adjusting" as the calculation unfolds.

(a)   INT(DF/100)   = Year PROVISIONAL

(b)   FRAC(year) $\times$ 12   = Month PROVISIONAL

(c)   FRAC(month) $\times$ 30 = Day

Note

(c) must always be rounded up to integer value.

If month $<$ 1.00 then (provisional year $-$ 1) = Year

and   12 = Month

If day = 0.00 then (provisional month $-$ 1)   = Month

and   31 or 30 = Day.

EXAMPLES

Given a day of 30 June 1980, find the 30/360 date in 1965 (30/360) days' time.

(1980 $\times$ 360) + (6 $\times$ 30) + 30 + 1965 = 714975 DF.

INT(714975/360)   = 1986.041667 = 1985 *Year* **

0.041667 $\times$ 12   =   .500004 =   12 *Month* **

0.500004 $\times$ 30   =   15.000120 =   15 *Day*

** see note above.

Find the 30/360 date from a 30/360 DF of 720031:

720031/360   = 2000.086111 = 2000 *Year*

0.086111 $\times$ 12   = 1.033332   =   1 *Month*

0.033332 $\times$ 30 (rounded to integer)   =   1 *Day*

Find the 30/360 DF for May 31, 1984:

(1984 $\times$ 360) + (5 $\times$ 30) + for 31 read 30 (see formula) = 714420.

Unscramble:

714420/360 = 1984.50   = 1984 *year*

0.50 $\times$ 12   =   6.00 (provisional m = 6)

0.00 $\times$ 30   =   0.00 **

**

Resulting in Month (6 $-$ 1)   =   5 *month*

Day 30 or 31   =   31 *day*

Day of the week for 30/360 days

To find the correct day of the week an "actual" day of the week calculation *must* be made. This is not merely academic, for taking a 90 day loan, based on the 30/360 calendar, it is often necessary to check whether redemption is on a banking or non-banking day of the week. Employing the 30/360 DF, it will be seen, provides erroneous results.

$$7 \times (FRAC(720031 - 2)/7) = 2 \text{ (Tuesday)},$$

when, from above, we know that in fact New Year's Day 2000 is a Saturday. So correctly employing the "actual" DF(CZF) or DF (see previous pages):

$$7 \times FRAC((730563 - 9)/7) = 5.999700 = 6 = \text{Saturday DF(CZF)}$$
$$7 \times FRAC((730563 - 2)/7) = 5.999700 = 6 = \text{Saturday DF.}$$

Number of Days Table for the Two Years A to B

For anyone dealing continuously with accrued interest (a/i), "clean" and "dealing prices", gross yields, redemption yields, "k factor" etc, a "days table" (see overleaf) is a great convenience.

YEAR A

Days	1	2	3	4	5	6	7	8	9	10	11	12	13	14	15
Jan	1	2	3	4	5	6	7	8	9	10	11	12	13	14	15
Feb	32	33	34	35	36	37	38	39	40	41	42	43	44	45	46
Mar	60	61	62	63	64	65	66	67	68	69	70	71	72	73	74
Apr	91	92	93	94	95	96	97	98	99	100	101	102	103	104	105
May	121	122	123	124	125	126	127	128	129	130	131	132	133	134	135
Jun	152	153	154	155	156	157	158	159	160	161	162	163	164	165	166
Jul	182	183	184	185	186	187	188	189	190	191	192	193	194	195	196
Aug	213	214	215	216	217	218	219	220	221	222	223	224	225	226	227
Sep	244	245	246	247	248	249	250	251	252	253	254	255	256	257	258
Oct	274	275	276	277	278	279	280	281	282	283	284	285	286	287	288
Nov	305	306	307	308	309	310	311	312	313	314	315	316	317	318	319
Dec	335	336	337	338	339	340	341	342	343	344	345	346	347	348	349

(add one day, where applicable, for leap year)

YEAR B

Days	1	2	3	4	5	6	7	8	9	10	11	12	13	14	15
Jan	366	367	368	369	370	371	372	373	374	375	376	377	378	379	380
Feb	397	398	399	400	401	402	403	404	405	406	407	408	409	410	411
Mar	425	426	427	428	429	430	431	432	433	434	435	436	437	438	439
Apr	456	457	458	459	460	461	462	463	464	465	466	467	468	469	470
May	486	487	488	489	490	491	492	493	494	495	496	497	498	499	500
Jun	517	518	519	520	521	522	523	524	525	526	527	528	529	530	531
Jul	547	548	549	550	551	552	553	554	555	556	557	558	559	560	561
Aug	578	579	580	581	582	583	584	585	586	587	588	589	590	591	592
Sep	609	610	611	612	613	614	615	616	617	618	619	620	621	622	623
Oct	639	640	641	642	643	644	645	646	647	648	649	650	651	652	653
Nov	670	671	672	673	674	675	676	677	678	679	680	681	682	683	684
Dec	700	701	702	703	704	705	706	707	708	709	710	711	712	713	714

(add one day, where applicable, for leap year)

EXAMPLE
Find days between November 15 and October 21:

$$319 - 294 = 25 \text{ days}$$

YEAR A

16	17	18	19	20	21	22	23	24	25	26	27	28	29	30	31
16	17	18	19	20	21	22	23	24	25	26	27	28	29	30	31
47	48	49	50	51	52	53	54	55	56	57	58	59			
75	76	77	78	79	80	81	82	83	84	85	86	87	88	89	90
106	107	108	109	110	111	112	113	114	115	116	117	118	119	120	
136	137	138	139	140	141	142	143	144	145	146	147	148	149	150	151
167	168	169	170	171	172	173	174	175	176	177	178	179	180	181	
197	198	199	200	201	202	203	204	205	206	207	208	209	210	211	212
228	229	230	231	232	233	234	235	236	237	238	239	240	241	242	243
259	260	261	262	263	264	265	266	267	268	269	270	271	272	273	
289	290	291	292	293	294	295	296	297	298	299	300	301	302	303	304
320	321	322	323	324	325	326	327	328	329	330	331	332	333	334	
350	351	352	353	354	355	356	357	358	359	360	361	362	363	364	365

YEAR B

16	17	18	19	20	21	22	23	24	25	26	27	28	29	30	31
381	382	383	384	385	386	387	388	389	390	391	392	393	394	395	396
412	413	414	415	416	417	418	419	420	421	422	423	424			
440	441	442	443	444	445	446	447	448	449	450	451	452	453	454	455
471	472	473	474	475	476	477	478	479	480	481	482	483	484	485	
501	502	503	504	505	506	507	508	509	510	511	512	513	514	515	516
532	533	534	535	536	537	538	539	540	541	542	543	544	545	546	
562	563	564	565	566	567	568	569	570	571	572	573	574	575	576	577
593	594	595	596	597	598	599	600	601	602	603	604	605	606	607	608
624	625	626	627	628	629	630	631	632	633	634	635	636	637	638	
654	655	656	657	658	659	660	661	662	663	664	665	666	667	668	669
685	686	687	688	689	690	691	692	693	694	695	696	697	698	699	
715	716	717	718	719	720	721	722	723	724	725	726	727	728	729	730

EXAMPLE

Find the number of days between November 15 – April 5 (Year B leap year):

$460 + 1 - 319 = 142$ days.

List of Abbreviations

The first time any abbreviation appears in "Business Interest Calculations" full explanations are provided; nevertheless the list below may be found useful as a quick reference.

Part I

i	As the decimal of an interest rate
	For 10% $i = 10/100 = 0.10$
n	Number of years in the term of a loan
p	Number of payments (or compounding or discounting) in any one year
$(1 + i/p)$	If the rate was 10% and the compounding periods were monthly
	$(1 + i/p) = 1 + (10/1200) = 1.0083333$
$(1 + i/p)^{-np}$	May sometimes be shown as $(1 + i/p) \wedge -np$
a/i	Accrued interest
NOM	Nominal rate %
EFF	Effective rate %
APR (UK)	The *effective* rate truncated to one place of decimals, to include any extra charges
APR (US)	The *nominal* rate %
INT	Integer
FRAC	Fraction, e.g. 10.56 INT = 10, FRAC = .56
PV	Present value
FV	Future value
Pmt(s)	Payments
BAL	Balloon payment
LOS	Loan outstanding (the balance due)
SI	Simple interest
CI	Compound interest
e	Exponential factor (2.718281828)
LOG	Logarithm ("log natural")
ABS	"Absolute" (disregards negative: (ABS − 10) = 10)
DCF	Discounted cash flow
DEDCF	Decimal entry discounted cash flow
CF	Cash flow
IRR	Internal rate of return (the nominal rate %)
MIRR	Modified internal rate of return
FMRR	Financial management rate of return

OFT	Office of Fair Trading
BSA	Building Societies Association
BS	Building societies
LGA	Local government authorities
MIRAS	Mortgage interest relief at source

Actuarial	$a_{\overline{n}}$	Annuities ORDinary	$\ddot{a}_{\overline{n}}$	Annuities DUE
signs	$s_{\overline{n}}$	Savings ORDinary (sinking funds)	$\ddot{s}_{\overline{n}}$	Savings DUE (savings)

Part II (additional abbreviations related to this part only)

SD	Settlement date (day)
RD	Redemption date (day)
CP	Clean price (quoted price clean of a/i)
DP	Dirty price (quoted price including a/i)
RV	Redemption value
RV″	Notional redemption value
C	Coupon % (annual interest per year on £100)
D	Half annual coupon (C/2)
YTM	Yield to maturity
YTM(S)	Eurobond YTM adjusted to semi-annual interest payments
RY	Redemption yield (same YTM)
XD	Ex-dividend
CGT	Capital gains tax
NP	Notional price
FPP	Forward projected price
Per	Period (usually per $<$ or $>$ years)
(n + k)	Periods and odd-days fraction
(m + k)	A variation on (n + k)
AIBD	Association of International Bond Dealers
LABs	Local authority bonds
FIPD	Final interest payment date
NPD	Next payment date (after settlement)
PPD	Prior payment date (payment date prior to settlement)
CD	Bank certificates of deposit
FRN	Floating rate note
FRCD	Floating rate certificate of deposit
LIBOR	London inter-bank offered rate
PC	Personal computer
FNC	Function (Appendix B)
DF	Date factor (Appendix D)
CZF	Century zone factor (Appendix D)

Index